Windows® 8

Digital Classroom

D1299736

Windows® 8
Digital Classroom

Elaine Marmel

WILEY

Windows 8 Digital Classroom

Published by
John Wiley & Sons, Inc.
10475 Crosspoint Blvd.
Indianapolis, IN 46256

Copyright © 2013 by John Wiley & Sons, Inc., Indianapolis, Indiana
Published simultaneously in Canada
ISBN: 978-1-118-39285-0
Manufactured in the United States of America
10 9 8 7 6 5 4 3 2 1

For general information on our other products and services or to obtain technical support, please contact our Customer Care Department within the U.S. at (877) 762-2974, outside the U.S. at (317) 572-3993 or fax (317) 572-4002.

Wiley publishes in a variety of print and electronic formats and by print-on-demand. Some material included with standard print versions of this book may not be included in e-books or in print-on-demand. If this book refers to media such as a CD or DVD that is not included in the version you purchased, you may download this material after registering your book at www.digitalclassroombooks.com/Windows8. For more information about Wiley products, visit www. wiley.com.

Please report any errors at DigitalClassroomBooks.com

Library of Congress Control Number: 2013935782

About the Authors

Elaine Marmel has authored and co-authored over seventy books about Microsoft Excel, Microsoft Word for Windows, Microsoft Project, QuickBooks, Peachtree, Quicken for Windows, Quicken for DOS, Microsoft Word for the Mac, Microsoft Windows, 1-2-3 for Windows, and Lotus Notes. From 1994 to 2006, she also was the contributing editor to monthly publications *Inside Peachtree* and *Inside QuickBooks*.

Elaine left her native Chicago for the warmer climes of Arizona where she basks in the sun with her PC and her dog Jack.

Jennifer Smith created the video tutorials that accompany this book. She is a Microsoft MVP with an emphasis on application design for Windows 8 using the design tools within Blend for Visual Studio. She is the author of more than 20 books in the Digital Classroom series, and hundreds of training videos available at *DigitalClassroom.com*.

Acknowledgments

Elaine Marmel: Thank you to Rashell Smith, Graphics Supervisor, for your help with images of gestures. And thank you, Bill, who works for Dell Computers in Tennessee, not only for helping with my tablet but for searching for a providing background information regarding Windows 8. Finally, thanks very much, Gary, for letting us use your music as sample files in this book.

Credits

Video Contributor
Jennifer Smith

President, American Graphics Institute and Digital Classroom Series Publisher
Christopher Smith

Senior Acquisition Editor
Stephanie McComb

Technical Editor
Lauren Mickol

Editor
Karla E. Melendez

Editorial Director
Robyn Siesky

Business Manager
Amy Knies

Senior Marketing Manager
Sandy Smith

Vice President and Executive Group Publisher
Richard Swadley

Vice President and Executive Publisher
Barry Pruett

Senior Project Coordinator
Katherine Crocker

Project Manager
Cheri White

Graphics and Production Specialist
Jason Miranda, Spoke & Wheel

Media Development Project Supervisor
Chris Leavey

Proofreading
Jay Donahue, Barn Owl Publishing

Indexing
Michael Ferreira

Register your Digital Classroom book for exclusive benefits

Registered owners receive access to:

 The most current lesson files

 Technical resources and customer support

 Notifications of updates

 On-line access to video tutorials

 Downloadable lesson files

 Samples from other Digital Classroom books

Register at *DigitalClassroomBooks.com/Windows8*

DigitalClassroom

Register your book today at
DigitalClassroomBooks.com/Windows8

Contents

Starting Up

Lesson 1: Getting Started with Windows 8

Lesson 2: Using Touch-Sensitive Screens and Tablets

Lesson 3: Navigating and Customizing the Start Screen

Lesson 4: Working with Windows 8 Native Apps

Lesson 5: Working with Desktop Apps

Lesson 6: Using Files and Folders

Lesson 7: Surfing the Web

Lesson 8: E-mail and Contacts

Lesson 9: Networking with Windows 8

Lesson 10: Sharing Device Settings and Content

Lesson 11: Using Audio and Video in Windows 8

Lesson 12: Photos and Pictures in Windows 8

Lesson 13: Customizing and Maintaining Windows 8

Lesson 14: Keeping Your Computer Safe and Protecting Your Privacy

Lesson 15: Exploring Some Windows 8 Apps

Appendix A: Upgrading to Windows 8

Appendix B: Windows 8 Touch Gestures

Starting Up

About Windows 8 Digital Classroom

The *Windows 8 Digital Classroom* provides you with the skills you need to set up, use, and maintain Windows 8 on your computer, notebook, or tablet. With clear explanations and step-by-step instructions, *Windows 8 Digital Classroom* makes it easy for you to learn Windows 8 and quickly perform the tasks you need to accomplish. This book provides you with the essential skills you need to be productive using a wide range of Windows 8 capabilities. Whether you're upgrading to Windows 8 and need help working with programs that came from Windows 7 or Windows XP, or if you're working with a new touch-screen device using apps built specifically for Windows 8, this book is your perfect companion for getting started, organizing your files, connecting to a network, the Internet, and devices such as printers.

We refer to each chapter as a lesson, and each of them can be covered independent of the others. You can progress through all the chapters, or if you need to know about a specific topic, you can jump right to a specific section and get the information you need at that moment.

Upgrading or Starting With a New Computer

If you're completely new to Windows 8 and have purchased a computer that has Windows 8 installed on it, you should start right here, at the beginning of this book and work through it from the start. If you are upgrading an older computer to Windows 8, we've included information about upgrading in Appendix A which helps you find the right version of Windows 8 and how to transfer your files and settings as part of the upgrade process.

Windows 8 on Touchscreen Devices

We've written this book for users of traditional computers and for those using touchscreen devices. Because touchscreen devices are relatively new, we devoted an entire chapter to this topic in Lesson 2, "Using Touch-Sensitive Screens and Tablets," which helps you take advantage of the fantastic touch capabilities of Windows 8.

About operating systems

The operating system—or OS—serves as the cornerstone of your computer's applications, often referred to as apps. The OS provides the interface you use to interact with your computer. The operating system provides common features and consistent behavior from one program to the next, making it easier to work across different apps, and even allowing the apps to share information back and forth with each other. Understanding the operating system is the first step toward working effectively with any program on your computer.

The operating system provides the link between your computer's hardware—printer, hard drive, memory, mouse, keyboard, and so on—with the various software programs that you use. The OS makes certain that the hardware and software work well together, making it easy for you to browse the Internet, write a letter, work on a spreadsheet, send an e-mail, or perform many other tasks.

The operating system's primary function is managing the way apps work together with other hardware, such as a printer or wireless mouse, and the way you interact with the apps. The OS doesn't provide the functionality found in most apps. If you want to either write a letter, work on a spreadsheet, or create a presentation, you'll likely use Microsoft Office for these tasks. If you want to perform professional image editing, you'll use Adobe Photoshop, and to manage finances you might use Intuit's Quicken. These apps are purchased separately, and are separate from the operating system. The operating system will make sure they all work well together, and make it consistent so that the way you print a document or save a file in one app is similar to the way you perform these same functions in a different app.

While Windows is the most widely used operating system, there are other operating systems as well. These range from MacOS and Google Chrome to those used on operating systems and tablets. The apps built for one OS don't necessarily work on another OS.

Windows 8 versions

Windows 8 comes in four different versions, and this book covers how to use these different Windows 8 versions:

- Windows 8 RT
- Windows 8
- Windows 8 Professional (also called Windows 8 Pro), and
- Windows 8 Enterprise

Windows 8 and Windows 8 Pro are the most common versions for general users, while Windows 8 Enterprise is designed for larger corporations and enterprises with specific requirements. If you are evaluating the different versions of Windows 8, the following table will help you understand the differences. Keep in mind that Microsoft makes it easy to upgrade your version of Windows 8. If you start with Windows 8 and later need to upgrade to Windows 8 Pro, you simply purchase a product key from the Microsoft Store to unlock the additional features. Although you'll spend less money if you pick the right version initially, the upgrade prices are intended to be reasonable based upon the additional capabilities you'll be accessing.

Windows 8 RT is a version of Windows that you cannot purchase separately. If you have Windows 8 RT, it was preinstalled on a tablet PC at the time you purchased it. This version of the operating system is essentially baked-in to the computer, which is generally a tablet. Windows 8 RT was designed to run on devices that use less power and are not expected to perform as many complex tasks as a general computer. Its primary distinction from other editions is that you cannot run applications that worked on previous versions of Windows, such as Windows 7, or XP apps. For example, an older version of Adobe Photoshop or Intuit Quicken won't run on the Windows RT devices because they are optimized for use on tablets. To use both new and old apps, you'll want one of the other versions of Windows 8.

Many tablets running Windows RT also include versions of Microsoft Office 2013 that function under Windows RT; like Windows RT, these editions of Office are not available for purchase separately.

In addition, the Windows 8 Enterprise edition is available only to Microsoft Software Assurance program customers who buy software licenses in volume, such as large corporations. Because the distinction between the different versions only impacts some very specific capabilities, this book refers generally to Windows 8—and not to each individual version of Windows. Where there are differences or additional capabilities between the versions of Windows, they are noted.

The table provides a list of features and their availability in each version. The list is abbreviated to cover features typically important to most users.

FEATURE	WINDOWS 8 RT	WINDOWS 8	WINDOWS 8 PRO	WINDOWS 8 ENTERPRISE
Provides built-in apps native to Windows 8 like Mail, Calendar, Messaging, Photos, and SkyDrive, with many more available from the Windows Store.	✓	✓	✓	✓
Runs programs designed to use a keyboard and mouse such as the legacy programs that you used in the Desktop environment of previous versions of Windows		✓	✓	✓
Can play movie DVD's with appropriate add-on software.		✓	✓	✓
Offers enhanced data protection using the Encrypting File System (EFS) and BitLocker technology to help keep your information secure.	✓		✓	✓
Comes with a scaled-down version of Office Home & Student 2013 RT Preview preinstalled; the final version will be installed by Windows Update at no cost to you other than costs you incur to download software.	✓			
Includes Remote Desktop Connection so that your PC can serve as a host to which you can connect when you're sitting at a different computer.			✓	✓
Enables you to connect to your corporate or school network using Domain join.			✓	✓
On x64 versions, enables you to run virtual machines using Hyper-V, Microsoft's virtualization technology.			✓	✓
Supports Windows Media Center. Note that Windows Media Center is not included; you will have to buy it as an add-on.			✓	
Supports AppLocker, which enforces application whitelisting or blacklisting in a corporate environment to permit or prevent software execution based on name, version number or publisher.				✓
Supports booting from external hard drives or USB drives.				✓

What's New in Windows 8

One of the biggest changes in Windows 8 is the replacement of the Windows Start button, generally found in the lower-left corner of the display, and the corresponding Start menu. These have been replaced with the Windows 8 Start screen, which uses tiles to access programs instead of the icons used in earlier editions of Windows. The tiled interface is especially useful if you are using a touch device but it also responds to clicks from your mouse or touchpad. The left side of the Start screen contains tiles for apps that are new to Windows and work only in the Windows 8 environment—these are referred to as native apps because they have been designed specifically to take advantage of the capabilities of Windows 8. While older apps, from earlier versions of Windows, will still run on Windows 8, the Windows 8 native apps have been optimized to take advantage of everything from touch-sensitive screens to system-wide search capabilities, and other new features that Microsoft added to Windows 8.

The terms "program," "application," and app are interchangeable; all refer to software that you run to perform a function.

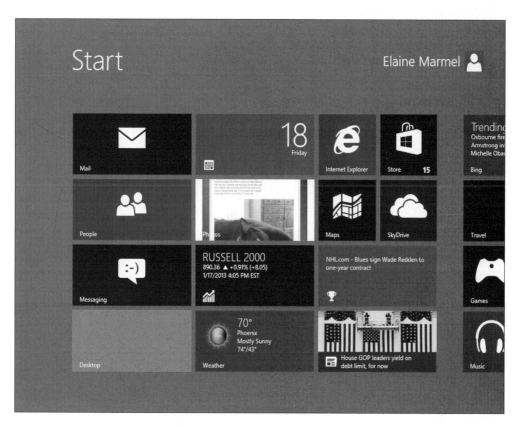

Windows 8 native apps appear on the left side of the Start screen.

Windows 8 also lets you access the Desktop. While it resembles the Windows 7 desktop, the Windows 8 Desktop contains no Start button. You can use the Desktop to access older apps, which are often referred to as legacy programs that were designed for older versions of Windows.

For users of earlier editions of Windows, the Desktop app will feel like familiar territory.

The Desktop's Task Manager has a completely new look, as well as new features. For example, using the Startup tab, you can identify and even prevent programs from loading when you start your computer.

A newly designed Desktop Task Manager window.

Common Windows 8 Functions

Following are some of the common questions you may have when working in Windows 8 and tasks you may want to perform, and where they are covered in this book:

- The Desktop's File Explorer, formerly called Windows Explorer, now uses the Ribbon interface common to Microsoft Office; for details, see Lesson 6, "Using Files and Folders."

- You can use two different commands to restore your operating system should it begin to misbehave: PC Reset and PC Refresh. See Lesson 13, "Customizing and Maintaining Windows 8" for details.

- Windows 8 presents two versions of Microsoft's web browser, Internet Explorer 10: the tiled version and the Desktop version. See Lesson 7, "Surfing the Web" for details.

- Windows 8 offers connectivity to the cloud. You can purchase Windows 8 native apps from the online Windows Store, and Windows 8 native apps get their updates online from the store. Separately, SkyDrive is integral to Windows 8. SkyDrive provides Internet-based storage for you to place your files online, whether you want to share the files between computers, with friends, or as a backup. The first 7 Gigabytes (GB) are included with your Windows 8 license, and, if you want more storage you can purchase it. You'll find a tile on the Start screen for SkyDrive, and you also can access it from Internet Explorer or any other Web browser. If you want, you also can download and install the Desktop app for SkyDrive, which offers some SkyDrive features you can't get any other way—such as automatically backing-up and synchronizing your files between your computer and SkyDrive. For details on using SkyDrive, see Lesson 10, "Sharing Device Settings and Content."

System Requirements

To run Windows 8 on your computer, it must meet the following basic requirements:

- Processor: 1 gigahertz (GHz) or faster with support for PAE, NX, and SSE2 (more info)
- RAM: 1 gigabyte (GB) (32-bit) or 2 GB (64-bit)
- Hard disk space: 16 GB (32-bit) or 20 GB (64-bit)
- Graphics card: Microsoft DirectX 9 graphics device with WDDM driver

In addition, certain features have additional requirements:

- To use touch, you need a tablet or a monitor that supports multi-touch; see Lesson 2 for more information.
- To access the Windows Store and to download and run apps, you need an active Internet connection, a screen resolution of at least 1024×768, and a Microsoft account.
- To snap apps to the side of the display, your monitor must support a screen resolution of at least 1366×768.
- To provide optimal performance, some games and programs might require a graphics card compatible with DirectX 10 or higher.
- Watching DVDs requires separate playback software; if your computer didn't come with movie playback software, you can buy an app such as Windows Media Center from the Microsoft store or you can try a free app like VLC Media Player.
- Windows Media Center licenses are sold separately, and your computer will need Windows 8 Pro as well as a TV tuner card to play and record live TV in Windows Media Center. In addition, free Internet TV content varies by geography, some content might require additional fees.
- Windows 8 Pro users who want to use BitLocker need either Trusted Platform Module (TPM) 1.2 or a USB flash drive, and BitLocker To Go requires a USB flash drive.
- Secure boot requires firmware that supports Unified Extensible Firmware Interface (UEFI) v2.3.1 Errata B and has the Microsoft Windows Certification Authority in the UEFI signature database.
- Running virtual machines using Client Hyper-V requires the 64-bit version of Windows 8 Pro or Enterprise with second level address translation capabilities and additional 2 GB of RAM.

Loading lesson files

The *Windows 8 Digital Classroom* uses files for the exercises in most lessons. These files are available for download at *www.DigitalClassroomBooks.com/Windows8*. You may download all the lessons at one time or you may choose to download and work with specific lessons.

For each lesson in the book, the files are referenced by the file name of each file. The exact location of each file on your computer is not used, as you may have placed the files in a unique location on your hard drive. We suggest placing the lesson files in the My Documents folder or the Desktop so you can easily access them.

Downloading and copying the lesson files to your hard drive:

1 Using your web browser, navigate to *www.DigitalClassroomBooks.com/Windows8*. Follow the instructions on the web page to download the lesson files to your computer.

2 On your computer, navigate to the location where you downloaded the .zip lesson folder and right-click, or click and hold on the .zip file until the contextual menu appears; choose Extract All.

3 In the Extract Compressed (Zipped) Folders window, specify the location where you want to save the files, and select Show Extracted Files When Complete.

Video tutorials

The *www.DigitalClassroomBooks.com/Windows8* site provides *Windows 8 Digital Classroom* book readers with video tutorials designed to help you understand the concepts explored in each of the book's lessons. Each tutorial is approximately five minutes long and demonstrates the concepts and features covered in the lesson.

The videos are designed to supplement your understanding of the material in the lesson and include exercises and examples that are some of the most useful parts of each lesson. You may want to view the entire video for each lesson before you begin that lesson. Please note that an Internet connection is necessary for viewing the supplemental video files.

Additional Video Training & Windows 8 Resources

The Windows 8 Digital Classroom book is one of several ways in which you can learn about Windows and related technologies. Here are some additional resources for learning Windows 8 and other technology topics:

Online Video Training

You can access comprehensive video training resources for Windows 8 and other topics at *www.DigitalClassroom.com*. The Digital Classroom site includes access to more than 2,500 videos, digital books, and lesson files. These include additional video tutorials from Microsoft MVP Jennifer Smith, who created the video tutorials that accompany this book. Find more online training at *www.DigitalClassroom.com*.

DigitalClassroomBooks.com

The *DigitalClassroomBooks.com* site includes updates, notes, and makes it easy for you to contact authors. You can also learn more about the other books in the series, including many books on popular creative software. You can also register your book here at *www.DigitalClassroomBooks.com/Windows8*.

Training classes, seminars, and workshops

The authors of the Digital Classroom series frequently conduct in-person seminars and speak at conferences, including the annual Digital Classroom Live Conference. Learn more about their upcoming speaking engagements and training classes at *agitraining.com*.

Resources for educators

If you are an educator, contact your Wiley education representative to access resources for this book designed just for you, including instructors' guides for incorporating the Windows 8 Digital Classroom into your curriculum. If you don't know who your educational representative is, you may contact the Digital Classroom books team using the form at *DigitalClassroomBooks.com*.

What you'll learn in this lesson:

- Understanding Windows 8 accounts
- Commonly used mouse and keyboard shortcuts
- Getting Windows 8 help
- Shutting down Windows 8

Getting Started with Windows 8

In this lesson, you have the opportunity to learn some basics about the Windows 8 environment, including starting up and shutting down Windows and navigating on non-touch-enabled devices.

Starting up

You will not need to work with any files for this lesson.

See Lesson 1 in action!

Use the accompanying video to gain a better understanding of how to use some of the features shown in this lesson. The video tutorial for this lesson can be found at www.DigitalClassroomBooks.com/Windows8.

Signing in to Windows

When you start Windows 8, the default appearance is for it to display a lock screen. You'll need to sign-in to Windows in order to perform any tasks such as checking email or writing a document.

The sign-in process involves moving past the lock screen, selecting an account to use, and entering the password for that account.

While it's possible to avoid the sign-in process and jump directly to the Start screen if you set up a local account, this option is not advisable for most users. The sign-in process requires you to enter your password, and keeps unauthorized users from accessing your account. For this reason, it's advisable to always use the sign-in process. You'll learn more about local accounts in the next section and also in Lesson 14, "Keeping Your Computer Safe and Protecting Your Privacy."

The Windows Lock screen appears when you first start your computer.

To sign-in to your computer and start using Windows 8, do any of the following from the Lock screen.

- Use your finger to swipe up the screen.
- Click your mouse anywhere on the screen.
- Press any key on your keyboard.

The Sign In screen appears; it will look like the one below and display an e-mail address below your name if you are signing in using a Microsoft account.

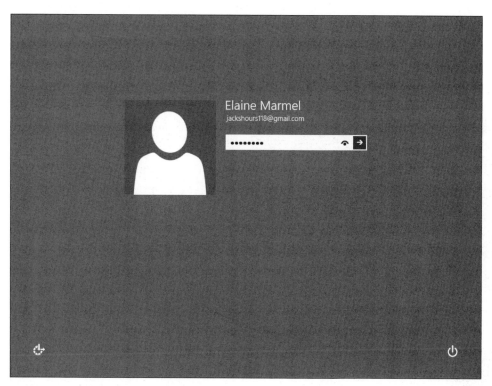

Elaine Marmel
jackshours118@gmail.com

········

The Windows 8 sign in screen.

Type your password and tap or click the arrow beside the password box to display the Windows 8 Start screen.

If you're using a touch device, the on-screen touch keypad automatically appears so that you can type your password.

Understanding Microsoft accounts and local accounts

Your account contains information about how you prefer your computer to operate, its appearance, along with the documents and applications you use. There are two types of accounts available with Windows 8. One option allows you to have your information shared between various computers you use with data backed-up over the Internet, the other is suitable if you only use computer and don't wish to have your data stored for you.

Microsoft accounts

Microsoft accounts are made up of an e-mail address registered with Microsoft and a required password. Microsoft accounts don't need to be from a Microsoft operated service. You can use your company email address or a personal email address from any provider. Yet all *hotmail.com*, *live.com*, and *outlook.com* e-mail addresses are automatically Microsoft accounts because Microsoft owns and manages these domains and e-mail addresses.

You don't need a hotmail.com, live.com, *or* outlook.com *e-mail address to have a Microsoft account. You can register any e-mail address as a Microsoft account.*

When you sign in to Windows 8 using a Microsoft account, you are connecting your computer to Microsoft's computers in *the cloud*. These computers are operated by Microsoft for the purpose of backing up your data and sharing your data between different computers you might own. If you sign into Windows 8 on your desktop PC, Windows automatically synchronizes some settings, such as your picture, backgrounds, Internet Explorer history and favorites to and from the cloud. If you sign in to Windows 8 on another device, such as a tablet PC, using the same Microsoft account, the synchronized settings from your desktop computer appear on your tablet PC. Many Windows 8 native apps require that you sign in to Windows using a Microsoft account.

Local accounts

Local accounts are made up of a name rather than an e-mail address and a password, which is optional. There are two types of local accounts: administrator and standard. You can read more about managing local accounts in Lesson 14, "Keeping Your Computer Safe and Protecting Your Privacy." As you start working with Windows 8, the key concept for you to understand is that when you sign in to Windows 8 using a local account, you are signing in to just your PC, not the cloud. No synchronization happens when you sign in using a local account. Windows 8 remembers your computer's settings just like previous versions of Windows did, and these settings are connected to one specific computer.

If you use multiple Windows 8 devices and want your settings to travel with you between devices and you also want to use the Windows 8 native apps, use a Microsoft account.

You can control the settings that Windows 8 synchronizes when you sign in using a Microsoft account. See Lesson 10, "Syncing Content and Devices Settings." for details.

Registering an existing e-mail address as a Microsoft account

If you have a *hotmail.com*, *live.com*, or *outlook.com* e-mail address, you already have a registered Microsoft account and can jump ahead to the next section. If you don't have one of these e-mail addresses and you will want to register an existing e-mail address as a Microsoft account using the following steps:

1   Open a web browser such as Internet Explorer. Right-click or swipe up or down the page to make the address bar visible.

2   Type **signup.live.com** in the address bar and press Enter to display the Microsoft account signup form.

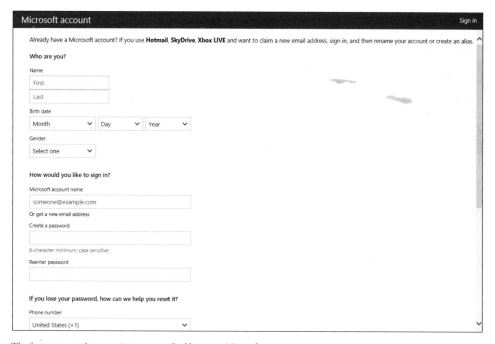

The form you complete to register an e-mail address as a Microsoft account.

3 Complete the form, supplying the e-mail address you want to use as your Microsoft account in the Microsoft account name text field.

Do not supply the password associated with the e-mail address; instead, make up a new password that you want to use to sign in to Windows 8 or any website where you will use your Microsoft account.

4 At the bottom of the form, tap or click the I accept button.

Using Windows 8 with a Mouse and Keyboard

Windows 8 works well, regardless of whether you are using a touchscreen device or traditional keyboard, mouse or trackpad. You will more about using Windows 8 on a touch devices in Lesson 2, "Using Touch-Sensitive Screens and Tablets."

If you are using Windows 8 with a traditional mouse and keyboard, there are hundreds of mouse and keyboard shortcuts that can help you work more efficiently; you can find a complete list at *http://windows.microsoft.com/en-US/windows-8/keyboard-shortcuts.*

In this section, you'll learn about the shortcuts you are likely to use most often.

Understanding Corner Navigation

Microsoft has built "hotspots" into each of the corners of the Windows 8 Start screen that aid both mouse and touch users. To take advantage of the corner "hotspots," you need to move the mouse to the corner of the screen, so the mouse pointer appears almost outside the screen edge. A portion of the pointer may disappear.

Getting back to the Start screen

To get back to the Start screen, open any app—from the Windows 8 Start screen. After you open an app, you can redisplay the Start screen by:

- Pressing the Windows logo key (), also known as the WinKey.

- Pointing the mouse at the lower-left corner of the screen until a small image of the Start screen appears, and then click it.

Click the image of the Start screen in the lower-left corner of your monitor to redisplay the Start screen.

You also can display the Start screen from the Charms bar which appears along the right side of your display. You can display the Charms bar along the right side of the screen by dragging your mouse down or swiping across the right edge of the screen then click Start to return to the Start screen.

If you are viewing the Start screen when you use any of these shortcuts, you can switch back to the last app you were viewing. Pressing the WinKey () switches you back and forth between the Start screen and the last app you viewed.

Your touch device may also have a Windows logo key () that you can press to redisplay the Start screen.

Displaying the Charms bar

You can use the Charms bar to perform a search on your computer, to share information between Windows 8 native apps, to display the Start screen, to connect hardware on your computer to Windows 8 native apps, or to display settings available for Windows 8 native apps or settings available for Desktop apps.

To display the Charms bar, shown in the figure, do one of the following:

The Charms bar appears on the right side of your screen.

- Press WinKey (⊞)+C
- Point the mouse in the lower-right or upper-right corner of the screen. Remember that you need to move the mouse to the corner of the screen, so the mouse pointer appears outside the screen edge.

You can then point the mouse at each charm on the Charms bar and click to select the appropriate charm.

You also can use the following keyboard shortcuts to directly open a Charm:

- WinKey (⊞)+I opens the Settings charm
- WinKey (⊞)+K opens the Devices charm
- WinKey (⊞)+H opens the Share charm
- WinKey (⊞)+Q opens the Search pane

Switching among open apps

The Desktop is an app

In earlier editions of Windows, the Desktop represented the operating system, and users did all their work from the Desktop. All programs (apps) required the Desktop to function.

Windows 8 introduces a new kind of app that doesn't need the Desktop to run. These Windows 8 native apps function in much the same way other computer programs function, each with their own set of commands you use to accomplish what you want. The Windows 8 native apps don't need the traditional Desktop you used in earlier editions of Windows. You can read more about using the Windows 8 native apps in Lessons 4, "Working with Windows 8 Native Apps" and 15, "Exploring Some Windows 8 Native Apps."

Once you understand that Windows 8 supports two kinds of apps (those that need the Desktop and those that don't), you'll find it easy to visualize the Desktop as an app, with its own set of commands that you use to control it. The Desktop has the distinction of being the only app that can run other apps. You can open multiple programs on the Desktop, just as users have done in earlier editions of Windows. But, because the Desktop is an app, you must use the Desktop techniques described in Lesson 5, "Working with Desktop Apps" to switch among open Desktop apps. You cannot use the techniques described in this section. When you switch among open apps as described in this section, the Desktop is a single app that you can display, even if multiple Desktop programs are running.

To switch among open Windows 8 apps, including the Desktop app , do one of the following from any running app:

- Press WinKey (⊞)+Tab
- Slide the mouse pointer to the upper-left corner of the screen; the last app you viewed appears. Slide the mouse down the left side of the screen to display the Running Apps bar.

No official name seems to exist for the bar that appears down the left side of your screen when you perform any of the actions listed above. Since it displays a list of apps currently running on your computer, in this lesson, we'll refer to it as the Running Apps bar.

Once the Running Apps bar appears, click the app you want to display.

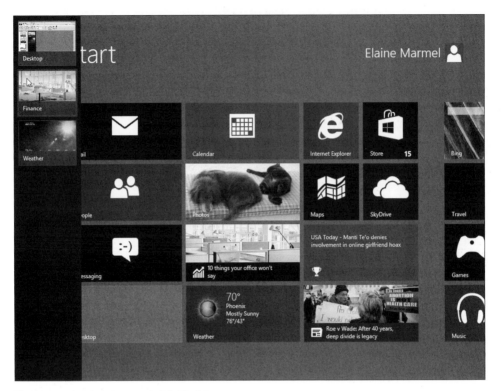

The Running Apps bar appears on the left side of the screen.

Alt+Tab works as it did in earlier editions of Windows. You can press and hold Alt as you press Tab to cycle through all the running apps. Release Alt when you see the app you want to switch to.

Displaying the Quick Link menu

The Quick Link menu displays a wide range of useful commands, especially for power users. With it, you can switch to the Desktop or open Desktop apps such as the Device Manager, Control Panel, Disk Manager, Computer Management Console, Task Manager, File Explorer, etc.

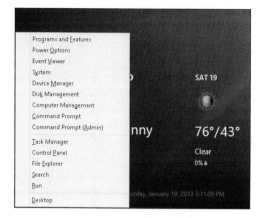

A useful context menu to help you quickly navigate to commonly used applications.

You can easily display the Quick Link menu by pressing WinKey (⊞)+X. To display it using your mouse, follow these steps:

1 From any app or on the Start screen, slide the mouse to the lower-left corner of your screen.

2 When the image of the last app you used appears, right-click it.

Closing an app

Closing a Windows 8 native app is not as obvious as closing a program that runs on the Desktop. You won't find a red X in the upper-right corner of Windows 8 native apps. While you don't have to close Windows 8 native apps most users, through force of habit, want to close them. These apps run in the background on your computer and don't take up as much memory as legacy programs do. You can do any of the following to close an app:

- On your keyboard, press Alt+F4.

- Using your mouse, do one of the following:

  a. Display the Running Apps bar on the Start screen as described in the section "Switching among open apps," then tap and hold, right-click a tile and tap, or click Close.

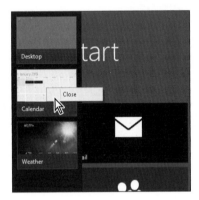

Display the Running Apps bar and tap and hold or right-click an app to close it.

b. While viewing the app, move the mouse pointer to the top of the screen until it changes to a hand. Then, click and drag down to the bottom of your screen. The app will minimize as you drag; when you drag it off the bottom of screen, the app closes.

Drag from the top of the app to the bottom to close it.

As mentioned previously, the Desktop app is in a category of its own. You can use either mouse technique to close the Desktop app, but the keyboard shortcut prompts you to shut down your computer. You will learn about shutting down your computer later in this lesson.

Displaying the Desktop

While the Windows 8 Desktop app is different from the desktop in earlier editions of Windows, the Windows 8 Desktop will be more familiar to Windows users than the Start Screen.

To display the Desktop app, you can:

- Press WinKey (⊞)+D.
- Click the Desktop tile on the Start screen.

Locking your computer

If you want to walk away from your computer, yet you don't want to shut it down, you can lock it. Locking the computer displays the lock screen shown at the beginning of this lesson and leads you to the sign in screen, where you must re-enter your password to sign in to your computer. You can lock your computer using either of the following methods:

- Press WinKey (⊞)+L.
- Click your name or picture on the Start screen and then click Lock.

Click your name or picture to view this menu, where you can lock your computer.

Zooming the Start screen

If you're not working on a wide-screen monitor, or if you are and you have lots of programs installed on your computer, you'll notice that you can't see all the tiles representing your programs on the Start screen, unless you swipe or use the scroll bar at the bottom of the Start screen to scroll to the right. Although you can reorganize the tiles on the Start screen as described in Lesson 3, "Navigating and Customizing the Start Screen," reorganizing might not solve the problem of viewing the tile you need. When you zoom out, the Start screen displays many small tiles. You can click an area of the screen to zoom in to that area so that you can click a tile and launch an app.

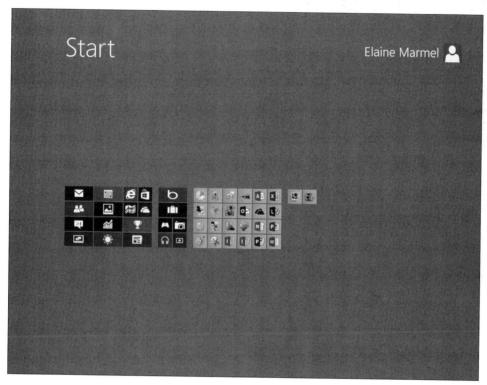

The Start screen when zoomed out.

You can zoom out or in the Start screen using any of the following techniques:

- Press Ctrl+minus (–) to zoom out and view a larger number of smaller tiles or Ctrl+plus (+) to view a smaller number of larger tiles.

- Press and hold Ctrl as you use the scroll wheel on your mouse.

- Click the Zoom button in the lower-right corner of the Start screen.

You can click the Zoom button to zoom out and view many small tiles on the Windows Start screen.

Getting Help

If you run into a problem using Windows 8, you can use web-based help or you can search the Desktop Windows Help and Support app using a search word or phrase to view a list of links to related Help articles.

To use web-based support:

1   Display the Charms bar.

2   Choose the Settings charm.

3   At the top of the pane, choose Help.

4 Select a topic, and the Windows 8 native app for Internet Explorer opens the Help page.

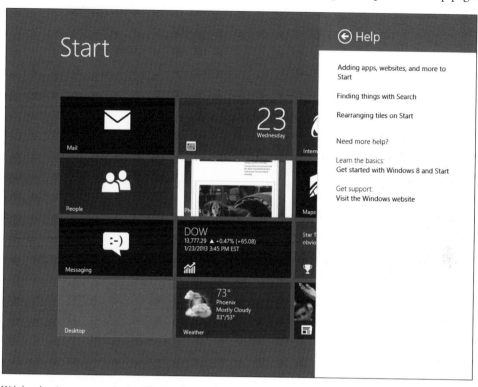

Web-based topics you can read using Windows 8 native help.

Using the Desktop Windows Help and Support app, you can control the search by supplying a search keyword or phrase. For example, you can search for help in using the built-in Windows word processing program, WordPad.

The fewer words you supply as your search criteria, the more results Help and Support will display.

The Windows Help and Support app runs as a Desktop program, but you launch it from the Start screen:

1   Display the Start screen.

2   Type Help to display a list of help sources.

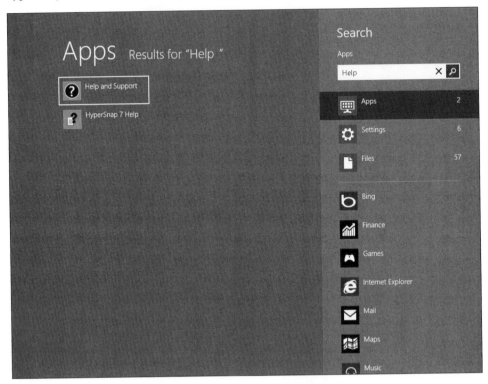

Any apps, settings, or file names containing the word "help" appear in a list.

3   Tap or click Help and Support.

4   Type **word processing**, in the text field at the top of the window and press Enter, or tap or click the magnifying glass button Windows Help and Support displays a list of links to articles that relate to the phrase you typed.

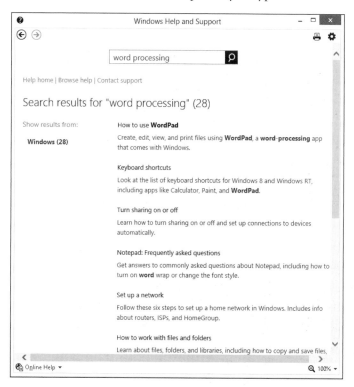

Type a keyword or phrase for which you want to search in the text field at the top of the Help and Support window.

5   Click or tap a link that seems relevant to display the article.

A typical article in the Windows Help and Support app.

You can also browse Help topics without searching. Tap or click the Browse Help link just below the Search text field to display the Help table of contents, which contains a series of topic links. Tap or click a link to see additional links related to that topic. As you click each link, your search narrows. Eventually, Windows Help and Support displays an article.

Shutting down Windows 8

Windows 8's default shut down and start up processes are different from those of all previous editions of Windows.

When you shut down a desktop computer, you'll see three choices:

- Sleep
- Shut Down
- Restart

Laptop and tablet computers may also display a "hibernate" option.

What's the difference between sleep, hibernate, restart, and shut down?

Sleep mode is a power-saving state. In Sleep mode, also called Standby mode, power is withheld from non-essential components. A computer can quickly resume operation, typically in seconds, when you wake it from Sleep mode, usually by moving your mouse or possibly by touching the power button on the computer. Once it awakens, you'll find everything exactly as it was when you put the computer to sleep—all open programs and running apps will be just where they were. You can think of a computer in Sleep mode in the same way you think of a DVD player that you have paused: both devices immediately stop what they are doing and start almost immediately when you tell them to start. The one danger you face from using Sleep mode on your computer comes from the potential for an external power failure. If power is cut off from your computer, the sleep state is lost. You won't be able to wake your computer; instead, you'll need to restart it. Because of the potential for power failure, you should save data in open programs before you put your computer to sleep. That way, you won't lose any information due to a power failure.

Hibernate mode is also a power-saving state, designed primarily for laptop computers. Sleep mode puts your computer's state (open programs, settings, etc.) in memory, while Hibernate mode saves your computer's state to a file on your hard disk, and then turns off your computer. Hibernate mode uses less power than sleep mode and restores your computer to an awake state fairly quickly, typically when you touch the Power button on the computer; when your computer wakes up, things will be just the way they were when you put the computer in Hibernate mode.

The Restart command does not attempt to save your computer's state; instead, it closes all open programs then temporarily powers off the machine and immediately powers it on again. The Restart process essentially clears everything out of your computer's memory and does not attempt to save your computer's state to your hard drive. Restarting your computer can be a useful problem-solving technique if your computer starts misbehaving

When you use the Shut Down command, you essentially turn off the computer so that it uses no electricity. Windows does not try to retain any record of open programs or files in memory or on your hard drive. Instead, Windows assumes that you will close all your programs and save all your work before you shut down the computer. If you don't, the Shut Down command closes your programs for you, without saving your work. Since shutting down a computer essentially eliminates the computer's use of power, a power failure has no effect on the computer, and you won't lose any work. At the same time, when you turn your computer back on, it will need to go through its startup process, which takes more time than awakening a computer from either Sleep or Hibernate mode.

Windows 8's Shut Down command performs the same function that hibernating performed in previous editions. Windows Help and Support refers to this behavior as "fast startup" and describes fast startup as follows:

"Fast startup is a setting that helps your PC start up faster after shutdown. Windows does this by saving system info to a file upon shutdown. When you start your PC again, Windows uses that system info to resume your PC instead of restarting it."

(continues)

What's the difference between sleep, hibernate, restart, and shut down? (continued)

Essentially, when you shut down a Windows 8 computer, the operating system performs a hybrid shutdown, closing all user sessions, then copying anything that is still running in RAM (primarily, the core of the operating system) onto the hard drive, and finally turning off the system hardware. When Windows 8 starts up after a hybrid shutdown, it performs an abbreviated startup. After starting the computer's hardware, Windows 8 reloads its core from the hard drive, picking up right from where it left off. Starting a powered-off computer that uses Windows 8 is typically much faster than starting a powered-off computer using earlier editions of Windows.

Since Windows 8 uses the Shut Down command differently than earlier editions of Windows, you might run into trouble trying to get into your computer's BIOS using traditional techniques such as tapping F2 while the computer starts up. You might need to contact your computer's manufacturer to find out how to bypass the Windows 8 startup process to get into the BIOS.

To shut down or restart your computer, or to put it to sleep, you can start the Desktop app and then press Alt+F4 to display this dialog box and choose an option from the list.

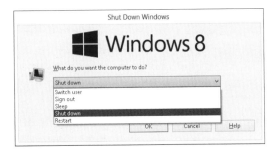

Select an option to shut down or restart your computer or put it to sleep.

Follow these step to shut down, restart, or put your computer to sleep:

1 Press WinKey ()+C to display the Charms bar.

2 Click or use the arrows keys on the keyboard to highlight and then select the Settings charm.

To directly display the Settings charm, press WinKey (■)+I.

3 Click the Power button.

4 Click a choice.

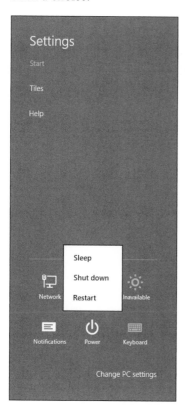

Select an option from the Power button, available on the Settings charm.

Self study

1   Practice corner navigation using the keyboard and the mouse. Display running apps, the Charms bar, and the useful context menu available in the lower-right corner of the screen.

2   Practice zooming on the Start screen using the keyboard and the mouse.

3   Using the keyboard and the mouse, practice displaying the Lock screen and then signing in to Windows 8.

Review

Questions

1   Can you switch to a specific open Desktop app from the Start screen?

2   How do you close a Windows 8 native app using the keyboard or the mouse?

3   What is a Microsoft account and what does it do for you?

4   How does a local account differ from a Microsoft account?

5   How do you launch Windows Help and Support?

6   How do you use the keyboard to redisplay the Start screen?

7   How do you shut down your computer using the keyboard or the mouse?

Answers

1   No. Since the Desktop is just one of many Windows 8 apps, you can switch to it from the Start screen. To switch to a specific open Desktop app, you must use switching techniques for Desktop programs as described in Lesson 4, "Working with Windows 8 Native Apps."

2   Using the keyboard, press Alt+F4. Using the mouse from the Start screen, display the Running Apps bar, right-click the app, and click Close. Using the mouse while viewing the app, drag from the top of the screen to the bottom of the screen.

3   A Microsoft account is a new method you can use to sign in to Windows 8; it connects your computer to the cloud so that you can synchronize settings across various Windows 8 devices. It also enables you to take advantage of the Windows 8 native apps. A Microsoft account consists of an e-mail address and a password, and you can register any e-mail address you want as a Microsoft account.

4   A local account functions the way user accounts functioned in earlier editions of Windows. A local account does not connect you to the cloud.

5   On the Start screen, type **Help** then tap or click Help and Support.

6   Press WinKey (⊞).

7   From the Desktop app, press Alt+F4 and choose Shut Down from the menu in the Shut Down Windows dialog box. From the Start screen, display the Charms bar, tap or click the Settings charm, tap or click the Power button, and tap or click Shut Down.

What you'll learn in this lesson:

- Discovering the number of touch points your mobile device supports

- Using gestures in Windows 8 native apps and in the Desktop app

- Working with the touch keyboard

- Protecting your mobile device while traveling

- Reviewing the most common mobile computing safety issues

- Choosing a power plan for your mobile device

Using Touch-Sensitive Screens and Tablets

Get familiar with using touch gestures to navigate the Windows 8 operating system and apps. This lesson is for those devices with touchscreens that can recognize at least two touch points.

Starting up

You will not need to work with any files for this lesson.

See Lesson 2 in action!

Use the accompanying video to gain a better understanding of how to use some of the features shown in this lesson. The video tutorial for this lesson can be found at www.DigitalClassroomBooks.com/Windows8.

Determining whether your device supports Windows 8 touch gestures

To use touch gestures while you work in Windows 8, your touch device must support at least two *touch points*; touch points are the number of simultaneous touches your device can understand and to which it can respond. You can find out the number of touch points your tablet or touchscreen device supports by looking at your computer's properties in the Desktop Control panel.

If you're using a laptop with a touchpad—also called a track pad—visit your laptop vendor's website and look for updated drivers for your touch device; you might be pleasantly surprised to find that many existing laptops can be upgraded to Windows 8 with full support for touch gestures using the built-in touchpad/track pad.

If you have a keyboard attached to your device, you can use the keyboard shortcut WinKey (🪟)+Pause to display the System window. Here you can determine whether your device supports touch. If you do not have a keyboard, follow these steps:

1   On the Windows 8 Start screen, type **Control**. The Search charm displays the apps that meet the search criterion.

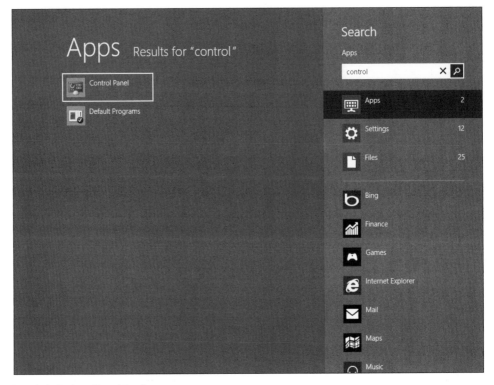

Launch the Desktop Control Panel.

2 Tap or click Control Panel. The Desktop Control Panel home page appears.

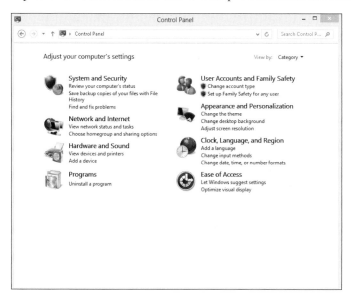

The home page of the Desktop Control Panel.

3 Tap or click System and Security.

4 Tap or click System. Information about your computer appears. At the bottom of the System section, you'll see information about the number of touch points your touch device supports. In this example, the device can understand and respond to five simultaneous touches, so up to five fingers could be used simultaneously on the tablet (or any five-number combination of fingers and styluses).

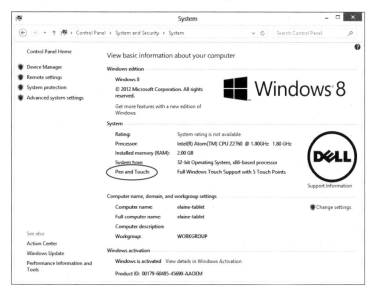

Display information about your computer.

5 Once you've determined whether you can use touch gestures, close the Control Panel by tapping or clicking the X in the upper-right corner of the window.

6 Close the Desktop app and redisplay the Start screen by dragging your finger or your mouse pointer down from the top of the screen to the bottom of the screen. Using your mouse, begin dragging when the pointer changes to a hand at the top of the screen.

Navigating Windows 8 native apps with gestures

Now that you've determined you can use touch gestures as you work, you should become familiar with the basic touch gestures. In this lesson, we'll assume you're using your fingers, but you can use a stylus to make a gesture.

Tapping

Tapping is the gesture equivalent of clicking your mouse. From the Start screen, tap a tile to open that app.

Displaying the App bar

The App bar displays options. On the Start screen, the App bar appears along the bottom of the screen and displays only one option; the opportunity to display all apps installed on your computer in a list format. If you display the App bar while viewing any Windows 8 native app, you'll see bars at both the top and the bottom of the screen that contain options specific to that app.

To display an App bar, slide up just slightly from the bottom edge of the screen. To hide the App bar, repeat the motion.

The Start screen's App bar.

The App bars in the Sports app.

Zooming

You can zoom out and see more information on the screen. To zoom out, make the opposite motion of pinching by sliding two fingers away from each other.

Zooming in on a web page can make the text easier to read.

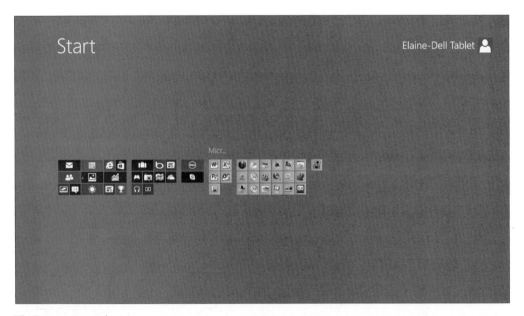

The Start screen zoomed out.

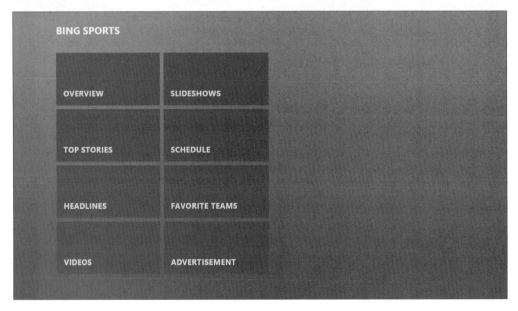

The Sports app zoomed in.

Scrolling

You can use one or two fingers to scroll either horizontally (also called *panning*) across your screen or vertically up and down your screen. Scroll horizontally by sliding one or two fingers to the left or to the right on the Start screen. Because of its design, you cannot scroll vertically on the Start screen.

You can scroll vertically while viewing web pages in web browsers: slide one or two fingers up to move a web page up or slide one or two fingers down to move toward the top of a web page.

Displaying the Charms bar

To display the Charms bar, start at the right edge of the screen and slide slightly in toward the center.

Switching apps

To see apps that are currently running and to switch apps, use the Running Apps bar that appears on the left side of the screen. To display the Running Apps bar, start on the left side of the screen and slide slightly to the center and then back again to the left side of the screen. With this gesture, your finger starts on the left and ends back on the left side of the screen, creating a small loop.

The Running Apps bar.

To switch to a selected open app, tap the app in the Running Apps bar. To cycle between open apps and switch to them, start at the left edge of the screen and slide your finger to the right. Don't slide your finger back to the left side of the screen as this will cause the Running App bar to appear again.

Closing an app

To close an app, slide your finger down from the top of the screen to the bottom. When your finger gets about halfway down the screen, the app minimizes. When your finger gets to the bottom of the screen, the app dims. At that point, you can lift your finger. Think of this gesture as dragging the app down and off the screen.

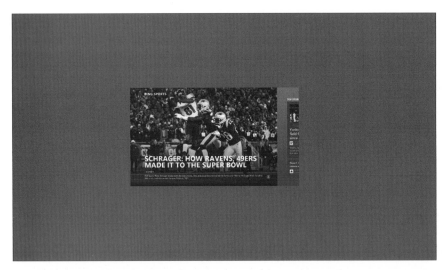

When you drag about halfway down the screen, the app minimizes.

When your finger gets to the bottom of the screen, the app dims, indicating you can lift your finger.

Using the Desktop app with gestures

While using the Desktop app, you can use all the gestures described in the previous section, but you won't be able to display the App bar. The App bar is only available on the Start screen and in Windows 8 native apps. In addition, you'll be able to zoom in and out and scroll vertically if the legacy app supports those actions. For example, most web browsers run on the Desktop and also support zooming in and out as well as scrolling vertically.

The Desktop and its legacy apps do respond to two gestures that don't work on the Start screen or in Windows 8 native apps: double-tap, and tap and hold.

Double-tap

Available in all legacy apps, the double-tap gesture is the gesture equivalent of double-clicking your mouse. With any action that occurs when you double-click your mouse, will also occur when you double-tap. For example, if you double-tap a WordPad document in File Explorer, both WordPad and the document open. If you have a shortcut on the Desktop and you double-tap it, the shortcut's program opens.

Tap and hold

The tap and hold gesture is equivalent to using your mouse to right-click. In most cases, you'll see a shortcut menu when you tap and hold. Just place your finger on the screen and hold it there.

Working with the touch keyboard

Even though you're using a touch device, you will need to type at times. For example, you'll need to type to supply a web address when you browse the Internet. For such cases, you can buy a keyboard that will connect with your touch device using a Bluetooth connection or a USB connection, or you can type using the touch keyboard.

Displaying and hiding the touch keyboard

Display the touch keyboard from the Settings charm in the Start screen.

1   From the right side of the screen, swipe in slightly to the left to display the Charms bar.

2   Tap the Settings charm.

3 Tap the Keyboard button.

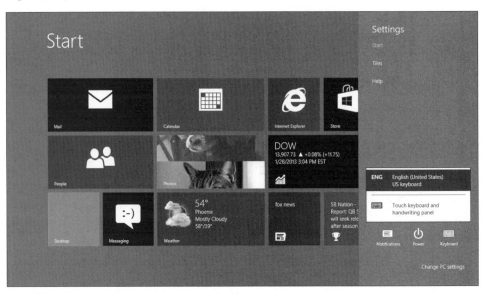

Tap the keyboard button to view keyboard choices.

4 From the menu that appears, tap Touch Keyboard and Handwriting Panel to display the on-screen keyboard.

The on-screen keyboard.

The default display of the Touch keyboard shows, primarily, alphabetic characters (letters). If you need numbers, you can tap the &123 key; tap it again to redisplay the letters.

If you need an emoticon, tap the "smiley face" character; tap it again to redisplay the letters.

From the Desktop, you can display the touch keyboard from the Desktop task bar. At the right edge, you'll see a button representing the keyboard. This button is visible as long as the Desktop task bar is visible.

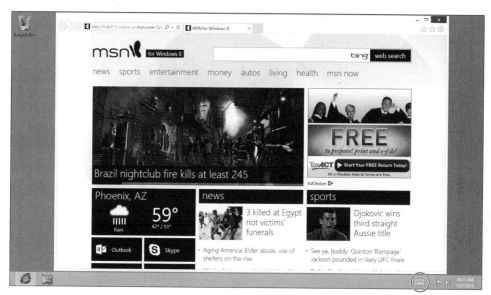

Use the keyboard button near the System tray to display the touch keyboard.

Tapping the button will cause the keyboard to appear and remain on-screen until closed.

To hide the keyboard from the Start screen or a Windows 8 native app, tap the keyboard button in the lower-right corner of the on-screen keyboard. From the choices that appear, tap the right-most button.

Tap the right-most button to hide the keyboard.

Hiding the Desktop touch keyboard is a little different than hiding the touch keyboard on the Start screen. You can close the Desktop touch keyboard by tapping the X in the upper-right corner.

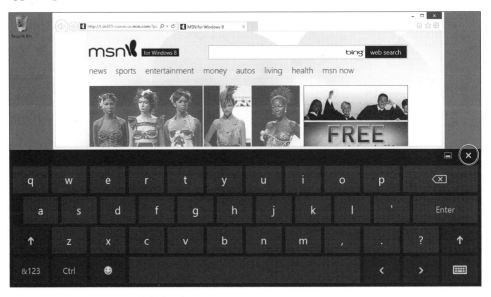

Tap the X to hide the Desktop touch keyboard.

Using the touch keyboard in split mode

If you prefer to display both letters and numbers on your keyboard, you don't need to use the &123 key to switch between letters and numbers. Instead, you can display the touch keyboard in split mode. In this mode, the numbers appear on a traditional number pad in the center of the keyboard. The placement of the letters will remind you of the arrangement on an ergonomically correct keyboard. On an ergonomically correct keyboard, half of the letter characters appear on the left, while the other half appear on the right.

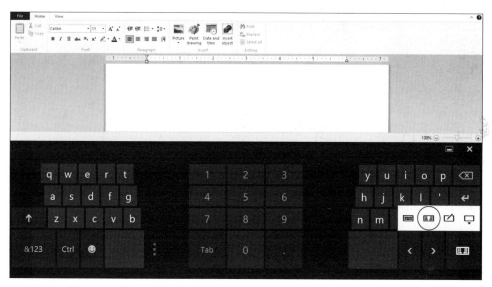

The touch keyboard in split mode.

To switch to split mode, follow these steps:

1   Display the touch keyboard.

2   Tap the keyboard button in the lower-right corner of the keyboard.

3   Tap the split mode button.

Writing vs. typing

Do you prefer writing to typing? If you prefer handwriting, you can use the touch keyboard to write rather than type. The touch keyboard will use character recognition to transcribe your writing into typing.

If your handwriting isn't particularly legible, the character recognition function might not work as expected. Try writing as clearly as possible for optimal results.

To write instead of type, follow these steps:

1. From the Start screen, search for the app, WordPad, and open the app.

2. Display the touch keyboard by tapping the keyboard button in the Taskbar at the bottom of the screen.

3. Tap the keyboard button in the lower-right corner of the keyboard.

4. Tap the handwriting button.

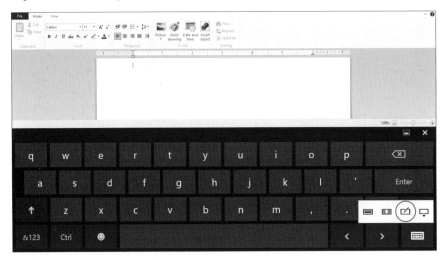

Display the touch keyboard in handwriting mode.

5. When two lines are displayed on the keyboard, start writing. As you write, character recognition attempts to translate what you write.

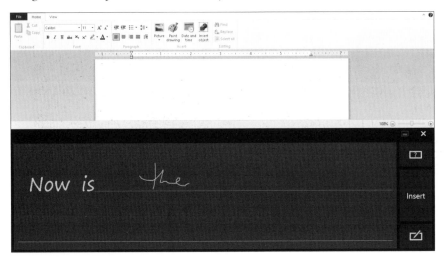

Character recognition at work.

6 When you finish writing, tap the Insert button. The touch keyboard moves the translated handwriting into the open app in typewritten form.

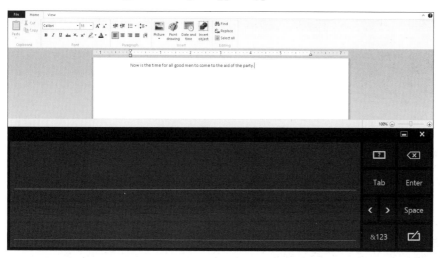

Handwriting translated into typing.

If you make a mistake as you're writing, you can correct it by immediately drawing a line through it. Then, just continue writing—don't tap and then write because tapping enters a period (.).

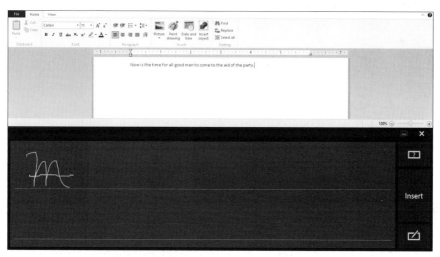

Correct a mistake as you write by "scratching it out."

You can correct mistakes before or after you've inserted the text into your document. To correct a mistake after you insert it, display the touch keyboard in handwriting mode. Then, drag your finger or stylus over the text in the document to select it, and it will appear in the touch keyboard so you can use the following correction techniques:

1 Tap the word containing the mistake. Small vertical lines appear, separating each letter.

2 Write over the incorrect letter. Again, don't tap and then write; just make the correction.

3 When the handwriting keyboard converts your handwriting to a typewritten letter, tap the small X just above the word to indicate you've finished correcting.

4 When you're ready to insert your handwritten text into your document, tap Insert.

Tap a word; small vertical lines appear to separate each letter, indicating that you can make a correction.

If two words run together, you can split them. Just draw a vertical line where you want the two words to split. When the words separate, tap Insert.

Draw a vertical line to split one word into two.

If one word appears as two words—with a space inserted incorrectly in the word—you can join them. Draw a small loop from the bottom of the first letter of the word on the right to the bottom of the last letter of the word on the left. To save the correction, tap Insert.

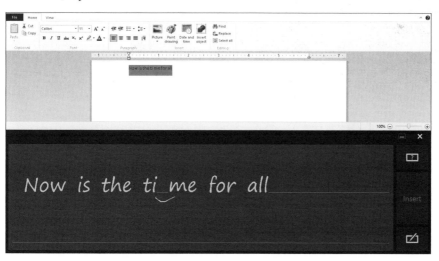

Connect two letters to join two words into one.

The Help button on the handwriting keyboard—the button containing the question mark—includes four small short videos that show you how to make corrections.

Traveling with your mobile device

The beauty of a mobile device is that it's mobile—but that's also its greatest disadvantage. With mobile devices, you need to consider factors that you don't need to consider when working on a stationary device. Your mobile device is vulnerable to thieves, or you could simply lose it.

Since entire books have been written on mobile computing and safety (i.e., *Mobile Device Security for Dummies* and *Laptops for Dummies Quick Reference*) consider this section and the next to be a broad overview of the topic.

Handling your device

When you travel with a mobile device such as a tablet or laptop, consider these common-sense actions:

- Avoid using computer bags. They announce that you're carrying a computing device. Instead, try using something more common, like a padded briefcase, suitcase, or backpack, to carry your device.

- Keep your device with you. Take it on the plane or train rather than check it with your luggage. When you go through airport security, hold your bag until the person in front of you has gone through the screening process. If you're traveling by car, keep your device out of sight. Lock it in the trunk when you're not using it. Try not to set your device down, and if you must, place it between your feet or lean it against your leg so you remain aware of it. Putting your device on the floor is an easy way to forget or lose track of it as you talk to a ticket agent or order coffee.

Use password protection and data encryption

To discourage unauthorized access to your device, use strong passwords that are difficult to break or guess. You can check the strength of your password by typing it into a password checker like this free one offered by Microsoft Security: *https://www.microsoft.com/security/pc-security/password-checker.aspx?WT.mc_id=MSCOM _EN_US_AW_A_laptopsecurity.*

In addition to protecting your device with a strong password, you can password-protect your files, and if you're using Windows 8 Pro or higher, you can encrypt important or sensitive data files. Password-protecting and encrypting files adds one more layer of protection; if somebody gets your device and manages to launch the operating system, that person won't be able to decrypt and see your information.

See Lesson 14, "Keeping Your Computer Safe and Protecting Your Privacy" for more information on the file encryption system in Windows 8 Pro.

Don't keep passwords in your device bag; that's a bit like leaving your house keys in the front door. Without your password or important access numbers, it will be more difficult for a thief to retrieve your personal and corporate information.

Consider a privacy screen

Consider using a privacy screen if you're working on sensitive information in a public area. Privacy screens help prevent someone from seeing your screen; if he or she peeks over your shoulder. You can search the Internet for "computer privacy screens."

Invest in a laptop security device or mobile security program

If you need to leave your device in a room or at your desk, use a laptop security cable to securely attach it to a heavy chair, table, or desk. The cable makes it more difficult for someone to take your device. Also consider a program or other devices that will report the location of a stolen computing device. Typically, when the protected device connects to the Internet, these security devices report the laptop's exact physical location, and some also offer additional abilities, such as remotely disabling a missing computer or remotely retrieving or deleting data. Search for computer tracking and recovery solutions.

If your device is stolen...

Despite all your precautions, your tablet or laptop can still be lost or stolen. Here are some additional precautionary security steps you can take if that occurs:

- Report the theft to local authorities and your company's IT department.

- Change your network password. This will help secure access to corporate servers.

- If customer data was on your device, contact your account representative, legal representative, or appropriate person at your company so they can take the necessary actions.

Safety and mobile computing

Even if you manage to keep your device under your control, connecting to a wireless network when you travel presents a security risk and can endanger your data.

Public Wi-Fi is not safe

Public wireless networks allow you to join without using a password and do not provide any safety for your data. Almost anything that appears on your screen can be seen by those around you, both by anyone who might be looking over your shoulder and by anyone who might be electronically monitoring (called *sniffing*) network traffic. Both types of snoops can obtain your user names and passwords as well as any data that you send over the Internet. Whenever possible, use a secure network that requires you to provide a unique password. If you must use a public network, do not work on sensitive material, shop online, or visit your bank's website. Wait until you can connect to a secure, private network to complete these activities.

Use a firewall

Before you connect wirelessly, make sure you are protected by a software or hardware-based firewall. A firewall uses a predetermined set of rules to analyze incoming and outgoing data and determine whether to allow the information in or out of your computer. A network's firewall typically connects an internal, secured and trusted network, to an external network, such as the Internet, that may not be secure and trusted.

Watch for secure sites

If you plan to enter information into forms or read sensitive material at a website, make sure that you are on a secure web page. Looking at the address bar in your browser, web address for an unsecured page starts with http, while the address for a secured page starts with https.

Plug in when you can

Plug into a wall Ethernet port when you can. Information that is transferred over wires is harder to intercept than information transmitted wirelessly.

Use the VPN

If possible, use your company's virtual private network (VPN). Most VPN connections use secure encryption technology that helps protect your information while allowing you to connect from any location and fully access all network resources, such as servers, printers, and network storage.

Mobile computing and battery life

Unlike their stationary counterparts, mobile devices are battery-powered; so you need to consider the best ways to manage your device's battery life.

Choosing a power plan

When you work on a mobile device, you need to balance battery use with device performance. If you want high performance from your mobile device, you will use more battery power. Alternatively, if you sacrifice performance, your battery power will last longer. Power plans, which are built into Windows 8, help you balance performance and battery life and establish an acceptable trade-off between performance and power consumption.

To view the available power plans, use the Desktop Control Panel:

1 While viewing the Start screen, type the first few letters of Control Panel. When you see the entry in the Search results, select it.

2 On the home page of the Desktop Control Panel, tap Hardware and Sound.

3 On the Hardware and Sound page, tap Power Options.

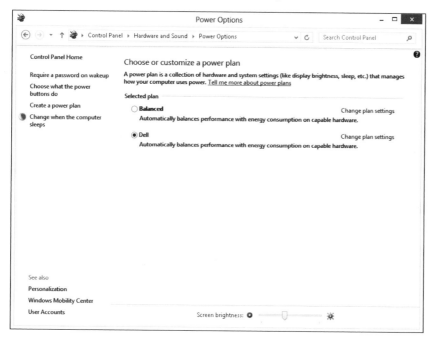

The available power plans appear on the Power Options page.

Customizing a power plan

You can make changes to both the basic plan settings and more advanced settings.

1 To view the basic settings for a plan, tap the Change Plan Settings link.

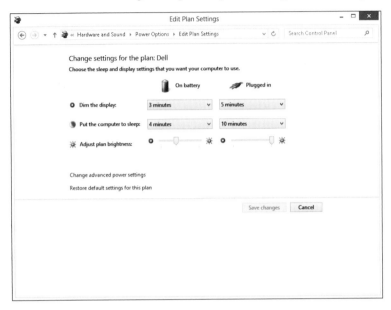

Basic power plan settings.

2 To control settings at a more detailed level, tap the Change Advanced Power Settings link to display the Power Options dialog box. In this dialog box, tap the plus sign (+) beside the setting you want to change to see the options available to you. When you finish setting options, tap OK.

Advanced power plan settings found in the Power Options dialog box.

3 To save any settings you made to a power plan, tap Save Changes.

Creating your own power plan

Suppose that you view the available power plans and none meet your needs; in this case, you can create your own power plan.

1   On the left side of the page, tap Create a Power Plan. Windows 8 will display a list of available plans that you can use as a model for your plan.

2   Select Balanced, then type **My Custom Plan 1** in the Plan name text field.

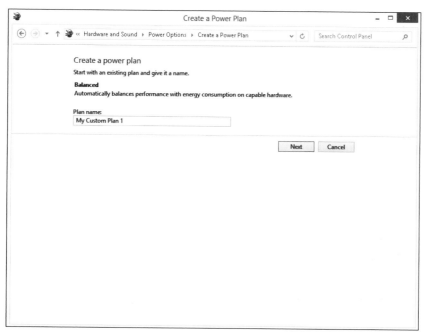

Name your custom power plan.

3   Tap Next. Windows 8 displays the settings for the plan you chose as a model.

4 Make changes to the time Windows 8 should wait before dimming the display and putting the computer to sleep when it's operating on battery and when it's plugged in.

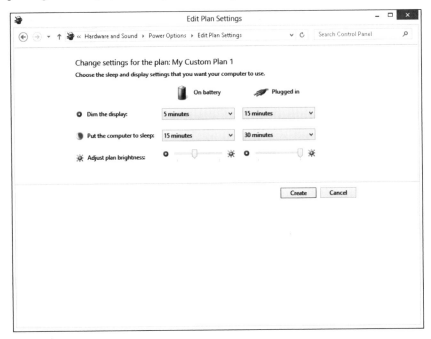

Establish basic settings for your custom power plan.

5 Tap Create. Windows 8 saves your plan and selects it as the current power plan for your device.

You can make more detailed changes to the plan using the steps in the section, "Customizing a Power Plan" earlier in this lesson.

Self study

1   Practice displaying the Charms bar on the Start screen and while using the Desktop app.

2   Practice displaying the Running Apps bar from the Start screen and while using the Desktop app.

3   Practice the zoom out and zoom in gestures.

Review

Questions

1   What effect does the Tap and Hold gesture have while using the Desktop app? While using a Windows 8 native app?

2   What gesture do you use to display options for a Windows 8 native app?

3   How would you describe the gesture you use to display the Running Apps bar?

4   What are some travel-related safety tips?

5   What are some measures you can take to compute safely while traveling?

6   What do power plans help you balance?

Answers

1   While using the Desktop app, it is the equivalent of right-clicking the mouse; a shortcut menu appears. The Tap and Hold gesture has no effect on the Start screen or on Windows 8 native apps.

2   Slide your finger up slightly from the bottom of the screen.

3   Starting on the left side of the screen, slide your finger slightly to the center then back to the left creating a small loop to display the Running Apps bar.

4   When you travel with your mobile device, make sure you are aware of its location at all times. Keep it hidden from site (i.e., don't use a computer bag or place your device in the trunk of your car). Consider a mobile security device or program and password protection and data encryption for sensitive data. Also, consider using a privacy screen in crowded locations.

5   Avoid public wireless networks. Whenever possible, use a firewall and secure sites. Use a wired connection instead of a wireless connection and use your company's virtual private network.

6   Power plans help balance performance and battery life.

What you'll learn in this lesson:

- Navigating on the Start screen
- Working with Tiles
- Searching
- Reorganizing the Start Screen
- Working with the Charms bar

Navigating and Customizing the Start Screen

The Windows 8 Start screen replaces the Start button in earlier editions of Windows. For long-time Windows users, the Start screen can look quite different. In this lesson, you learn how to take control of the Start screen and make it work for you.

Starting up

You will not need to work with any files for this lesson.

See Lesson 3 in action!

Use the accompanying video to gain a better understanding of how to use some of the features shown in this lesson. The video tutorial for this lesson can be found on www.DigitalClassroomBooks.com/Windows8.

Reviewing navigation

The Start screen was designed to accommodate users of touch devices, but those who are using a mouse and keyboard can still find their way around the Start screen. For common mouse and keyboard shortcuts you can use with Windows 8, refer to Lesson 1, "Getting Started with Windows 8." For details on navigating Windows 8 using a touch device, see Lesson 2, "Using Touch-Sensitive Screens and Tablets."

In this lesson, we'll begin with a short review of navigation techniques. The following table lists some common actions you'll take while using Windows 8, along with their mouse, keyboard, and touch equivalents.

 Blank boxes in the table below indicate that an equivalent action could not be found.

ACTION	MOUSE	KEYBOARD	TOUCH
Choosing	Click	Press Enter	Tap when using the Start screen or a Windows 8 native app; double-tap when using the Desktop app
Open any app (including the Desktop)	From the Windows Start screen, click the app		From the Windows Start screen, tap the app
Display the App bar, which contains commands and options for a Windows 8 native app	Right-click anywhere on the screen	Press WinKey (⊞)+Z	Drag up slightly from the bottom of the screen
Display the Start screen while working in an app (including the Desktop app)	Slide the mouse into the upper- or lower-right corner to display the Charms bar, and then click Start	Press WinKey (⊞)	From the right edge of the screen, swipe to the left slightly to display the Charms bar; then tap the Start button
Display a list of all apps installed on the computer	From the Start screen, right-click to display the Apps bar at the bottom of the screen; then click All Apps	From the Start screen, press WinKey (⊞)+Z and then press Enter	Drag up slightly from the bottom of the screen and then tap All Apps
Scroll horizontally (also called panning) from one side of the Start screen to the other	Use your mouse's scroll wheel	Click the arrow keys or drag the scroll box at the bottom of the screen	Slide your finger from left to right or from right to left
Scroll vertically in legacy apps	Use your mouse's scroll wheel	Use the arrow keys to scroll one line at a time or the Page Up or Page Down keys to scroll one screen at a time	Slide your finger up the page to scroll down and down the page to scroll up

ACTION	MOUSE	KEYBOARD	TOUCH
Display the Charms bar	Slide your mouse to the top- or bottom-right corner of your screen	Press WinKey (⊞)+C	Swipe in from the right edge of the screen
Switch apps	Slide the mouse pointer to the upper-left corner of the screen. When the last app you viewed appears, slide the mouse down the left side of the screen to display the Running Apps bar shown in the figure	Press WinKey (⊞)+Tab	From the left edge of the screen, swipe your finger to the right slightly and then back again to the edge to display the Running Apps bar, making a loop with your finger
Zoom the Start screen	Click the Zoom box in the lower-right corner of the Start screen	Press Ctrl+Plus sign to zoom in, or Ctrl+Minus sign to zoom out	Pinch your fingers together to zoom out; pinch them out to zoom in
Display the Quick Link menu	From any app or on the Start screen, slide the mouse to the lower left corner of your screen. When the image of the last app you used appears, right-click	Press WinKey (⊞)+X	
Using the Desktop app or a legacy program, display a shortcut menu	Right-click	Press Shift+F10	Tap and hold
Close a Windows 8 native app	Drag the mouse pointer down from the top of the screen to the bottom	Press Alt+F4*	Drag your finger down from the top of the screen to the bottom
Shut down your computer	Place the mouse pointer in the upper- or lower-right corner of the screen to display the Charms bar. Click the Settings charm, click the Power button, and then click an option	Display the Desktop App Using Alt+D. Then, Press Alt+F4 while viewing the Desktop App. From the Start Screen, press the Windows Logo Key (Windows Key Image)+I to display the Settings Charm; then press tab and the Arrow Keys until you highlight power. Then, press Enter to choose an option	Swipe in from the right edge of the screen to display the Charms bar. Tap the Settings charm, tap the Power button, and then tap an option

* The keyboard shortcut works for all apps, except the Desktop app; if you use the keyboard shortcut Alt+F4 while viewing the Desktop app, Windows 8 will prompt you to shut down your computer.

Microsoft has encouraged hardware manufacturers to introduce their own touch gestures; to find out whether your device supports additional gestures, go to your device manufacturer's website.

Corner navigation

The Windows 8 Start screen uses the corners of the display as "hot spots" for your finger or your mouse, with keyboard shortcuts available for each corner. Each corner has a function; remembering the function will help you immeasurably when navigating in Windows 8.

- The upper- or lower-right corner displays the Charms bar.
- The upper-left corner controls the display of the Running Apps bar.
- The lower-left corner controls the display of a handy context menu.

Be aware that the corner hot spots are very close to the edge of your screen. To access a hot spot with your mouse, you might need to move the pointer almost outside the screen.

Redisplaying the Start screen

Although we explained how to redisplay the Start screen in the table shown in the preceding section, it bears repeating, since you tend to start everything from the Start screen. If you're using a keyboard and mouse to navigate Windows 8, you can most quickly redisplay the Start screen by pressing the WinKey (⊞) on the keyboard. If you're using a touch device, swipe left from the right edge of the screen to display the Charms bar, then tap the Start button.

Repeatedly pressing WinKey (⊞) cycles between the Start screen and the last app you were viewing.

Searching

You can easily perform searches on your computer in Windows 8 in a couple of different ways. First, you can start typing while viewing the Start screen. For example, if you've installed Microsoft Office and you would like to run Microsoft Excel. While viewing the Start screen, start typing **Excel**. As you type, Windows displays the Search bar on the right side of the screen, and programs that match your search criteria on the left side of the screen. To run a program that appears in the search results list, tap, click it, or use the arrow keys on the keyboard to highlight it and press Enter.

To find a program you want to run, start typing its name while viewing the Start screen.

By default, when you type on the Start screen, Windows searches for apps. But the Search charm helps you narrow your search by enabling you to search for apps, settings, or files. These choices appear in the Search charm's Search bar on the right side of the screen. You can start typing, let Windows 8 search for an app, and when the Search bar appears, click Settings or Files to change the type of search.

Using the Search bar, you can narrow your search.

Using touch gestures or a mouse, you can select a search category if you display the Charms bar and select the Search charm, then select the search category from the Search bar. You can also use any of the following three keyboard shortcuts to specify a search category:

- WinKey (⊞)+Q searches for apps
- WinKey (⊞)+W searches for settings
- WinKey (⊞)+F searches for files

To use the Search charm and search for files

1 Display the Search bar for files by pressing WinKey (⊞)+F or by selecting the Search charm from the Charms bar and then tapping or clicking Files at the top of the Search bar.

2 In the Search box at the top of the Search bar, type the first few letters of the file for which you want to search. Possible files appear below the search box.

3 If the file you want to open doesn't appear in the list, type a few more letters.

4 When the file appears, tap or click it to open it.

Using the File search charm, search results appear below the Search box.

Do you have to specify the type of search you want if you are searching for something other than an app? Well, yes and no. Although Windows searches for apps by default, you can type on the Start screen and then change the type of search after Windows displays the Search bar.

1 While viewing the Start screen, type a couple letters of the file name (such as "Ge" of Gettysburg Address, in this example).

2 When the Search bar appears, select the type of search you really meant—Settings or Files. Windows 8 searches again, this time showing names that contain the letters you typed and match the type of search you selected.

3   If the file doesn't appear, type a few more letters.

4   Results appear on the left side of the screen. Tap or click one to open it.

You can type a search string on the Start screen and then specify the type of search without using the Charms bar.

Working with tiles

The Start screen contains tiles that represent the apps you run. You can think of tiles as the desktop icons you used in earlier editions of Windows to run programs. If you were concerned with icon organization in earlier editions of Windows, you could drag your icons around to place them where you wanted, pin them to the Windows task bar or the top of the Start menu, and even place them in folders on the Windows Start menu.

In Windows 8, you can also control and organize tiles. The tiles that represent Windows 8 native apps also display updated information on the Start screen—a phenomenon called *live tile*. Now, you have several ways that you can control tile behavior and the appearance of the Windows 8 Start screen to make it reflect the way you work.

Setting tile options

To set the options for a tile, display the options by right-clicking the tile or, on touch devices, you can display a tile's options by dragging the tile down slightly until a checkmark appears above the upper-right corner of the tile, then release the tile. The options appear at the bottom of the Start screen, and a checkmark appears in the tile you selected. In addition, the options you see depend on whether you select a Windows 8 native app tile or a legacy program tile.

You can hide tile options by right-clicking the tile or dragging the tile down slightly so that the checkmark disappears and then release the app.

For Windows 8 native apps, you can select any of the options shown in the following list.

OPTION	FUNCTION
Unpin from the Start screen	The app remains on your computer and you can still run it; you simply won't see a tile for it on the Start screen. For details on running an app that doesn't appear on the Start screen, see the next section.
Uninstall the app	This option removes the app from your computer and from the Start screen.
Control the size of the tile on the Start screen	This option allows you to resize your apps depending on organization or importance.
Tap or click the Turn Live Tile Off option	For tiles that can display updated information, this option makes the tile stop displaying that information.

The options you can set for a Windows 8 native app.

For legacy apps, the ones that run on the Desktop app, you can select any of the options listed in the following table.

OPTION	FUNCTION
Unpin from Start	The app remains on your computer and you can still run it; you simply won't see a tile for it on the Start screen. For details on running an app that doesn't appear on the Start screen, see the next section.
Pin to taskbar	Pin an icon for this app to the Desktop taskbar so that you can run the app directly from the Desktop.
Open a new window	This option enables you to run a second instance of a program that's already running.
Run as administrator	This option enables a user logged in using a standard local account to run a program using administrator level privileges.
Open file location	This option switches to the Desktop and launches File Explorer, displaying the folder containing the file used to run the program.

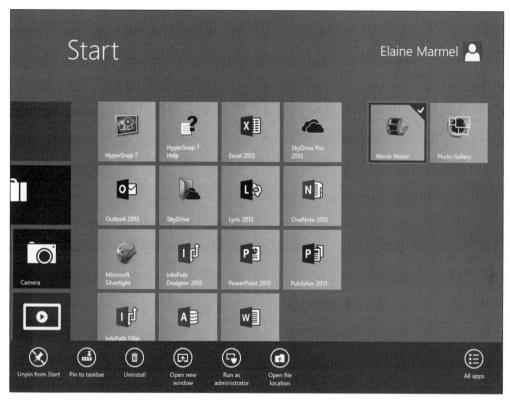

The tile options available for a legacy app.

If you change your mind and don't want to change an app's options, drag up slightly from the bottom of the screen or right-click the bar displaying the options.

Displaying tiles in list format

By default, when you first install Windows, the only apps that appear on the Windows 8 Start screen are the Windows 8 native apps. Windows legacy apps, such as WordPad, the Calculator, and Paint are installed, but are not pinned to the Start screen.

If you bought Windows 8 pre-installed on a computer, the manufacturer may have added apps to the Start screen, including some of the legacy apps.

You can quickly and easily display all the apps installed on your computer in list format by dragging your finger up slightly from the bottom of the screen or by right-clicking anywhere on the Start screen. When a bar appears at the bottom of the Start screen, tap or click All Apps at the right edge of the bar.

Display apps in list format on the Start screen.

The Windows 8 native apps appear, by default, at the beginning of the list, and as you scroll to the right, legacy apps appear. You can think of the groups in which the legacy apps appear as the folders that appeared on the Start menu in earlier editions of Windows.

Legacy apps are organized into groups.

 To redisplay apps in the default view, redisplay the Start screen.

Pinning and unpinning tiles

Most programs you install automatically create tiles for themselves on the Windows 8 Start screen. In addition, most of them place tiles into groups on the Start screen. But you can control the programs that appear on the Start screen.

For example, if you want tiles for certain Windows Accessories to appear on the Start screen, you can easily add tiles for these apps to the Start screen by *pinning*:

> *Pinning is the term used to describe adding a tile to the Start screen or the Desktop task bar; unpinning is the term used to describe removing a tile from either location. Note that unpinning is not the same as uninstalling, which completely removes the app from your computer.*

1 Drag your finger up slightly from the bottom of the screen or right-click anywhere on the Start screen to display the options bar at the bottom of the screen.

2 Choose All Apps.

3 Find the app for which you want to create a tile on the Start screen.

4 Right-click the app or drag the app down slightly. When a checkmark appears above the upper-right corner of the app, release it to display the bar at the bottom of the Start screen.

Display the options for the app.

5   Tap or click Pin to Start.

When you redisplay the Start screen in its default view and you scroll to the right, you'll find a tile for the app you selected at the end of the Start screen.

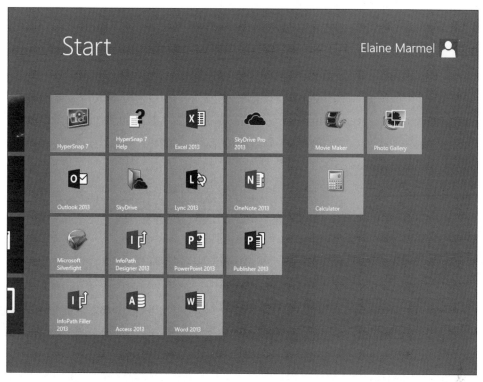

A tile for the app now appears on the Start screen.

To remove a tile from the Start screen, repeat the steps, choosing Unpin from Start in Step 4. Remember, unpinning is not the same as uninstalling. Even though no tile appears for the app on the Start screen, you can still run it by tapping or clicking it while viewing all apps.

You can also pin web pages to the Start screen; if you visit a site frequently, you might find pinning it to the Start screen useful. The following example uses the legacy Internet Explorer on the Desktop to find a website and then pin it to the Start screen. After the steps, you'll find a tip that tells you how to use the Windows 8 native Internet Explorer to pin a page to the Start screen.

1 Display the page in Internet Explorer.

2 Tap or click the Gear tool in the upper-right corner of the window.

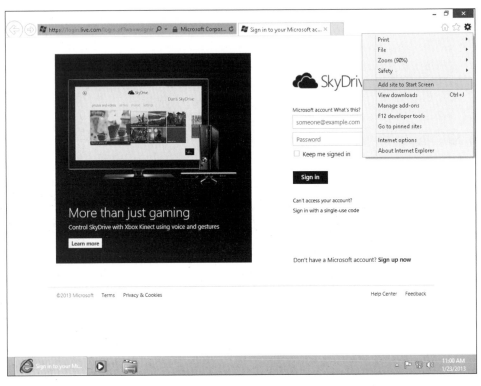

Adding a website to the Start screen.

3 Choose Add Site to Start Screen. Internet Explorer displays a dialog box showing the web site title and address.

4 Tap or click Add. Windows adds a tile for the website to the end of the Start screen.

The steps above work in both the legacy version and the Windows 8 native version of Internet Explorer. In the native version, for Step 2, tap or click the Pin icon at the bottom of the window and then tap or click Pin to Start. In the window that appears—the equivalent of Step 3 above—tap or click Pin to Start again.

Rearranging tiles

By now, you've noticed that you can easily launch programs that have tiles on the left side of the Start screen, but it's not quite as easy to launch a program that has a tile on the right side of the screen. You have to scroll to find it, or you need to type a few letters of its name.

The default order of the Start screen is not set in stone, you can move tiles around to suit your needs. For example, if you don't use a Windows native app, move it to the right or unpin it from the Start screen. If you use a legacy app regularly, move it to the left side of the screen.

How do you move a tile? Tap and hold the tile, then move it either up or down, and then drag it to a new position. Using a mouse, drag the tile in any direction to the new position.

To quickly move a tile a long distance, i.e., from one end of the Start screen to the other, drag the tile down to the bottom of the screen. Windows 8 zooms the Start screen to display all the tiles at once. You can then drag and drop the tile where you want it.

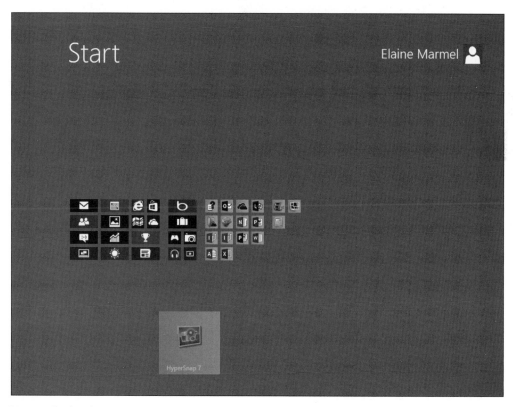

Moving a tile a long distance.

Before you dive into moving all your tiles around, consider creating groups for them and then move the entire group at once.

Creating and managing tile groups

For an even cleaner Start screen, you can organize tiles into groups. For example, if you added Movie Maker and Photo Gallery to your computer from the available Windows Essentials tools (formerly called Windows Live tools) along with some of the standard accessories that you use frequently, such as the Calculator, Notepad, and the Snipping tool. Storing these apps in a group and naming it "My Windows Tools" will enable you to use that screen space for other essential apps. You can begin by creating a new group.

1 Use the mouse to drag one of the tiles that should be part of the group to an open space until you see a vertical gray bar. Using a touch device, you can drag the tile down slightly until a checkmark appears above the upper-right corner of the tile, then drag the tile to an open space until the vertical gray bar appears.

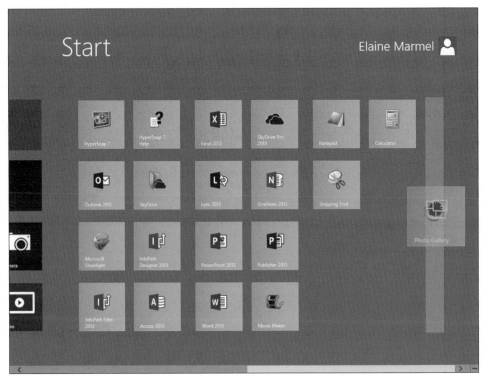

Creating a new group.

2   Release the tile. Windows 8 creates a new group and places the tile in that group.

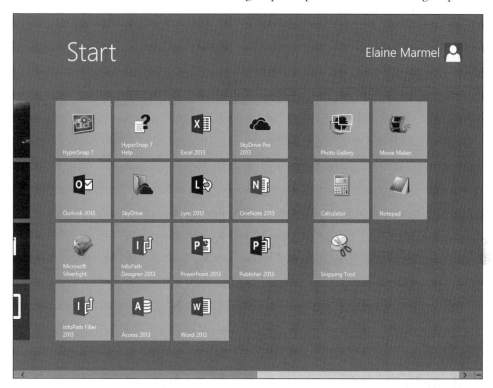

The tile appears in the new group.

3   Using the technique described in Step 1, drag more tiles next to the first tile.

4   Repeat Step 3 until all appropriate tiles appear in the group.

To name the group, follow these steps:

1　View all the tiles, or zoom out, by pinching your fingers together on the Start screen or clicking the Zoom button in the lower-right corner of the Start screen.

2　Select the group you want to name. Using a mouse, you can right-click the group to select it and display a bar at the bottom of the screen. To select a group on a touch device, drag the group down slightly until a checkmark appears. When you release the group, Windows displays the bar at the bottom of the screen.

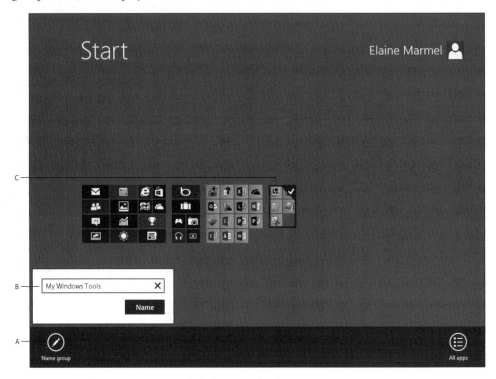

*A. Name group button. **B.** Name group dialog box. **C.** Selected group.*

3　Tap or click Name group from the bar at the bottom of the screen.

4　Enter **My Windows Tools**.

5 Tap or click Name. When you redisplay the Start screen in its default form, the group name you assigned appears above the group.

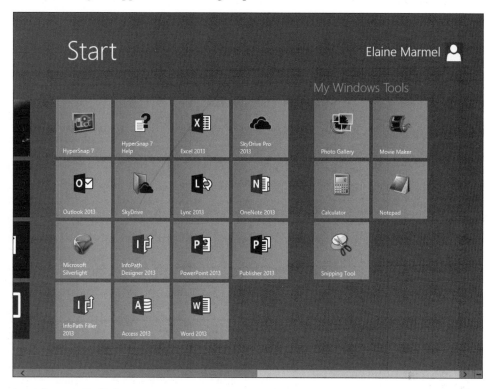

A named group on the Start screen.

You can move an entire group to a new position on the Start screen: complete Step 1 above; then select the group (if you select using touch techniques, don't release the group) and drag it to its new position on the Start screen.

Working with the Charms bar

The Charms bar is a multi-purpose bar that appears on the right side of the screen. If you display it from the Start screen, it can help you to:

• Perform searches on your computer

• Share information between Windows 8 native apps

• Display the Start screen or the last app you viewed

• Connect hardware on your computer to Windows 8 native apps

• Display settings available for Windows 8 native apps

The Charms bar appears on the right side of your screen.

Be aware that things look a little different if you display the Charms bar from the Desktop app. The Share and Devices charms function only for Windows 8 native apps; on the Desktop app, you won't see any available options for these two charms. You will, however, see options for the Settings charm that are specific to Desktop apps.

To display the Charms bar, do one of the following:

- Press WinKey (⊞)+C
- Point the mouse in the lower-right or upper-right corner of the screen
- Swipe in from the right side of the screen

Using keyboard shortcuts, you can open a Charm directly, as indicated in the following table.

SHORTCUT KEY COMBINATION	RESULT
WinKey (⊞)+Q	Opens the Search pane to search for apps
WinKey (⊞)+F	Opens the Search pane to search for files
WinKey (⊞)+W	Opens the Search pane to search for settings
WinKey (⊞)	Displays the Start screen or the last app you viewed
WinKey (⊞)+I	Opens the Settings charm
WinKey (⊞)+K	Opens the Devices charm
WinKey (⊞)+H	Opens the Share charm

We covered the Search charm and its associated pane earlier in this lesson. The Start charm simply displays the Start screen if you're viewing an app. If you're viewing the Start screen and select the Start charm, Windows 8 displays the last app you viewed. When using a keyboard and mouse, you can bypass the Start charm and press WinKey (⊞) to display the Start screen or toggle between the Start screen and the last app you viewed.

In this example, you will use the Devices charm while working in a Windows 8 native app to print a web page from the Windows 8 native version of Internet Explorer.

1   Open Internet Explorer from the Start screen and navigate to a web page.

2 Open the Charms bar and tap or click the Devices option. The Devices charm lists all devices—both wired and wireless—attached to your computer.

The Devices charm and the Windows 8 native app for Internet Explorer.

3 Choose a printer to use to print the page.

The Share charm is the Windows 8 native app equivalent to the Windows legacy app, Clipboard, that runs in the Desktop app. The Windows Clipboard is used to share information between legacy apps on the Desktop. The Share charm enables you to share information between Windows 8 native apps.

In this example, you will attach a picture to an e-mail.

1 From the Start screen, choose the Photos app. From the library options, tap or click one of the options: Pictures, SkyDrive, Flickr, Facebook, or an external device. You must have at least one photo in one of the libraries for this example.

2 Choose a photo from your chosen library. For more information about the Photo app and its libraries, see Lesson 12, "Photos and Pictures in Windows 8."

3   Open the Charms bar, and tap or click the Share option. Windows 8 displays a list of native apps with which you can share the picture.

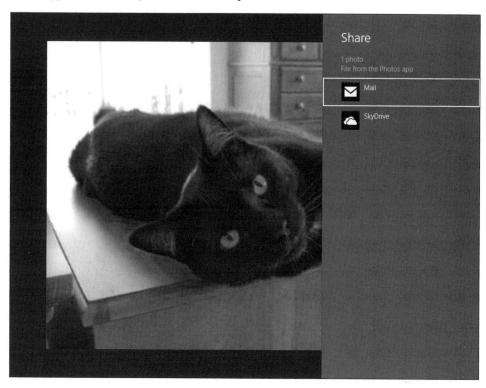

Display the Share charm while working in a Windows 8 native app, and you'll see other native apps with which you can share information.

4 From the list, select the Mail app. The Windows 8 native Mail app opens and an e-mail message is started for you with the photo embedded.

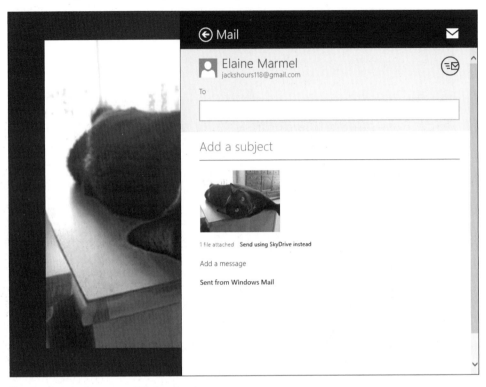

Sharing information between two Windows 8 native apps.

From the Start screen, you can control settings for tiles and also get Help. You can also access settings for your network, speaker volume, display brightness, display notifications, and change PC settings; shut down your computer, enable Sleep mode, or restart. From a touch device, you can display the on-screen keyboard.

You can read more about the settings you can control using the Settings charm in Lesson 13, "Customizing and Maintaining Windows 8."

The Settings charm as it appears from the Start screen.

If you open the Settings charm while working in a Windows 8 native app, options you can use to control the settings of that app are displayed.

There are different options available when you display the Settings charm from the Desktop. The options at the bottom of the Settings charm pane are the same as the ones you see when you display the Settings charm from the Start screen. But at the top of the Settings charm pane, you find options to display the Desktop Control Panel, the

Desktop Personalization window, your PC's information, and the Desktop Windows Help and Support app.

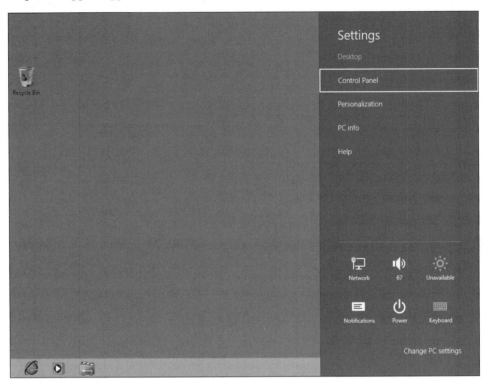

The Settings charm as it appears while using the Desktop app.

Self study

1 Practice changing a tile for a Windows 8 native app from a large tile to a small tile.

2 Practice moving a tile.

3 Create a new group on the Start screen, place tiles in it, and move the group to the left side of the Start screen.

Review

Questions

1 How do you display a list of all the apps installed on your computer?

2 How do you remove a tile from the Start screen?

3 How do you add a tile to the Start screen?

4 How do you move tiles on the Start screen?

5 How do you use the Devices charm to print an Internet Explorer page?

6 How do you share information between Windows 8 native apps?

Answers

1 Drag up slightly from the bottom of the Start screen, or right-click anywhere on the Start screen and tap or click All Apps.

2 Right-click the tile or drag the tile down slightly until a checkmark appears, then release it. From the bar at the bottom of the screen, tap or click Unpin from Start.

3 Display all the apps installed on your computer. Then, find the one you want to add to the Start screen and right-click it. On a touch device, drag it down slightly until a checkmark appears above the top right edge of the app and then release it. From the bar that appears at the bottom of the screen, choose Pin to Start.

4 Drag them. To move a tile a long distance, drag it to the bottom of the screen until Windows 8 zooms the screen. Then, drop the tile close to where you want it to appear.

5 Display the page you want to print using the native Internet Explorer app. Then, display the Devices charm and select a printer.

6 Open the Window 8 app that contains the information you want to share and select the information. Then, display the Share charm to select another Windows 8 app with which you can share the information.

What you'll learn in this lesson:

- Using the Windows Store
- Opening and closing apps
- Switching apps
- Viewing two apps simultaneously
- Printing and sharing Windows 8 native app information

Working with Windows 8 Native Apps

The apps are designed to take advantage of the new components available in Windows 8, such as the charms, app bars, and more. Windows 8 apps are very immersive, and distraction free, but are also different than the apps that run in the desktop mode. In this lesson you discover how to get the most out of your Windows 8 apps.

Starting up

You will not need to work with any files for this lesson.

See Lesson 4 in action!

Use the accompanying video to gain a better understanding of how to use some of the features shown in this lesson. The video tutorial for this lesson can be found at www.DigitalClassroomBooks.com/Windows8.

Working with the Windows Store

Microsoft has started referring to programs as "apps," and you can think of the new apps provided in Windows 8 as "Windows 8 native apps" to distinguish them from the legacy apps that run on the Desktop and have been available for 20 years or more. Windows 8 includes a fairly wide variety of the new Windows 8 native apps:

- Mail
- People
- Messaging
- Desktop
- Calendar
- Picture
- Finance
- Weather
- Internet Explorer 10, native version (you can use the legacy version on the Desktop)

- Maps
- SkyDrive
- Sports
- News
- Bing
- Travel
- Games
- Camera
- Music
- Video

But you aren't limited to using the apps that come with Windows 8. You can find more Windows 8 native apps at the Windows Store.

 Presently, only Windows 8 native apps are available at the Windows Store. In the future, the Windows Store may carry legacy apps as well as Windows 8 native apps.

Visiting the store

If you intend to download apps from the Windows Store, you will need a Microsoft account. If you didn't set one up as described in Lesson 1, "Getting Started with Windows 8," you can do it while you're in the Windows Store. See the sidebar, "If you need a Microsoft account..." in this section.

To visit the Windows Store—to browse, buy, or download a free app—tap or click the Store tile on the Windows Start screen.

Tap or click the Windows Store tile.

The home page of the Store app advertises some apps. Free apps are identified, and apps that users have rated show the average rating. You can use buttons on the right side of the screen to browse for the top paid apps, the top free apps, and newly released apps.

The home page of the Windows Store spotlights apps.

Scroll horizontally, and you'll find apps by category.

- Games
- Social
- Entertainment
- Photo
- Music & Video
- Sports
- Books & Reference
- News & Weather
- Health & Fitness
- Food & Dining

- Lifestyle
- Shopping
- Travel
- Finance
- Productivity
- Tools
- Security
- Business
- Education
- Government

In each category, you can browse top paid, top free, and newly released apps as well as the apps featured in the category. To display more details about an app, simply tap or click it.

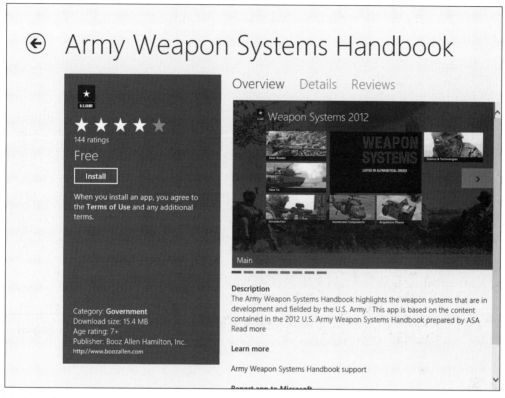

The details of an app appear when you tap or click it.

If you decide you want to download the app, tap or click the Install button. If you want to keep browsing, click the Back button in the upper-left corner of the screen.

If you are using a local account when you visit the Windows Store, tapping or clicking Install results in a prompt to add your Microsoft account. If you already established a Microsoft account as described in Lesson 1, "Getting Started with Windows 8." Fill in the e-mail address and password you selected at that time. If you haven't established a Microsoft account, see the sidebar, "If you need a Microsoft account…"

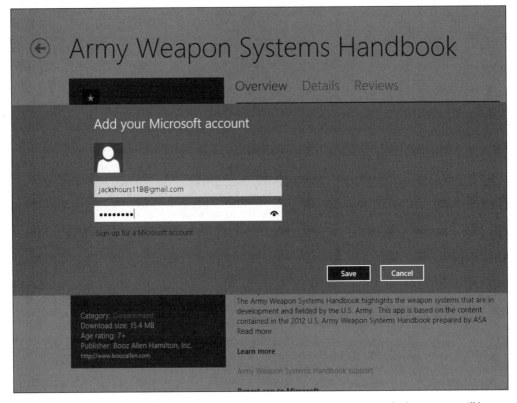

If you try to install an app from the Windows Store while you are logged into your computer using a local account, you will be prompted to add your Microsoft account.

After you supply your Microsoft account information, Windows 8 signs you into the Windows Store, and the app you selected is downloaded and installed. When the installation finishes, a message appears on-screen.

A message notifies you that your app was installed.

A tile for the app appears on the right side of the Start screen. Tap or click the tile to launch your app.

Tiles for newly installed apps appear on the right side of the Start screen.

If you need a Microsoft account...

If you have not established a Microsoft account when you opt to install a Windows Store app, a message appears, asking for a Microsoft account. Click the Sign up for a Microsoft account link to open Internet Explorer. Then follow these steps:

1   Fill in the form, supplying, in the Microsoft account name box, the e-mail address you want to use as your Microsoft account.

2   The form requests your phone number to help you reset your password if you lose it. If you don't want to provide your phone number, select and answer one of the security questions.

3   At the bottom of the form, tap or click the I accept button.

Once you've established your Microsoft account, go back to the Windows Store and click Install again. When prompted for your Microsoft account information, supply it and click Save. Your app will then be downloaded and installed.

You do not need to (and shouldn't) supply the password associated with the e-mail address. Instead make up a new password that you want to use to sign into Windows 8 or any website where you will use your Microsoft account.

Browsing through top apps

In any category, you can tap or click the Top Free button or Top Paid button to view the top-rated apps in that category.

1   Tap the Store tile on the Start screen to open the Windows Store app.

2   Scroll horizontally to the Books & Reference category.

3   Click Top Free (or Top Paid or New Releases, if you want to explore those types of apps).

4 Scroll through the top 100 apps. Tap or click on an app.

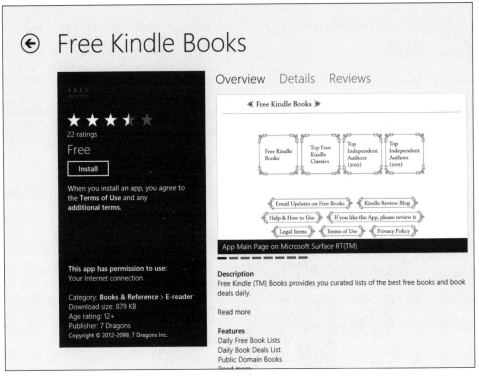

When you select an app, you see the overview information for it.

5   Tap or click Details to view release notes, recommended hardware, and more information.

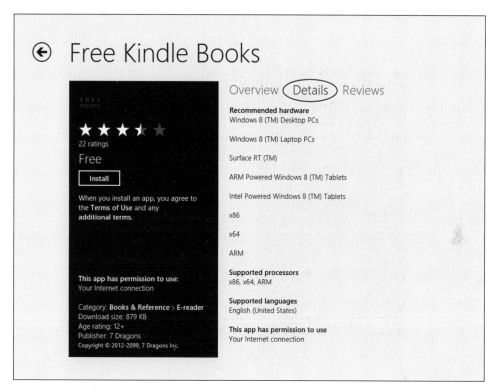

Viewing the details of an app.

6 Click Reviews to read reviews written by other users and to see the rating each user has assigned to the app.

You can read reviews and examine ratings for the app.

7 When you finish exploring the app, tap or click the Back button to redisplay the top 100 apps.

Rating an app

After you install an app, you can rate and review it so that others know what you think of the app. Follow these steps:

1 If you are not already in the app store, tap or click the Store tile on the Start screen to open the Windows Store app.

2 Right-click or swipe-up slightly from the bottom of the screen to display the App bar and Windows Store options.

3 Tap or click Your Apps.

4 From the dropdown menu on the Your apps screen, choose Apps Installed on.

5 Tap or click the app you want to review to display options for the app.

6 Tap or click View Details at the bottom of the screen.

Tap or click View details.

7 To write a review and rate the app, tap or click Write a Review.

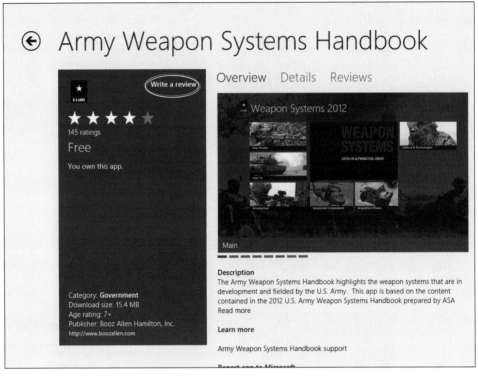

Tap here to prepare your review.

8 On the Write a Review screen, tap or click a rating of one to five stars (ratings are required) and then provide a title (this is optional) and a review (maximum allowed is 500 characters).

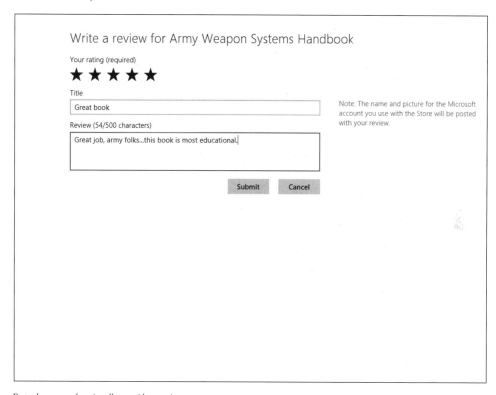

Rate the app and optionally provide a review.

The name and picture you use for your Windows Store Microsoft account will be posted along with your review.

9 Tap or click Submit.

Viewing the apps on your device

The Windows Store can show you apps installed on your computer, sorted by name or by the date you installed them.

1 If the Windows Store app is not already open, open it now.

2 Right-click or slide your finger up slightly from the bottom of the screen to display the available options for the Windows Store.

3 Tap or click Your apps.

4 Use the list boxes at the top of the screen to select All Apps and the method by which to sort them.

View a list of Windows 8 native apps installed on your computer, sorted by date installed or by name.

Updating Windows 8 native apps

In addition to serving as the place to find additional apps, the Windows Store also serves as the clearing house for app updates. Occasionally, you'll see a number in the Windows Store tile on the Windows 8 Start screen. This number indicates that apps on your computer have updates available.

When the tile for the Windows Store app contains a number, updates are available for some of your apps.

To update your apps, follow these steps:

1   If you are not already in the Windows Store, tap or click the Store tile on the Start screen to display the Windows Store.

2   Tap or click the Updates message in the upper-right corner to display the available updates.

Click Updates to view available updates.

3   When the available updates appear, all are selected; notice the checkmark in the upper-right corner of an update. To avoid updating a specific app, tap or click the app and the checkmark will disappear.

The Clear button in the App bar at the bottom of the screen deselects all apps.

4   To update your apps, tap or click Install.

To install updates for selected apps, tap or click Install.

The Installing apps screen appears; as apps update, the "Pending" bar below the app name changes to "Downloading" and then "Installing."

The screen as apps update.

When all updates finish, a message appears on-screen, telling you that updates are complete and your apps were installed. Tap or click the Back button to return to the Windows Store.

When updates finish, you can tap or click the Back button to return to the Windows Store.

Running a Windows 8 native app

Running any app—Windows 8 native or legacy—is easy: From the Start screen, tap the app's tile.

If you don't see the app's tile on the Start screen, there are two ways to find and run the app:

- Search for the app
- Use the list of all apps

Searching for an app

The Search charm searches for apps by default, so you don't need to display the charm. Instead, while viewing the Start screen, use your physical keyboard or the on-screen touch keyboard to type the first couple letters of the app's name. Windows 8 displays a list of apps that match the letters you typed.

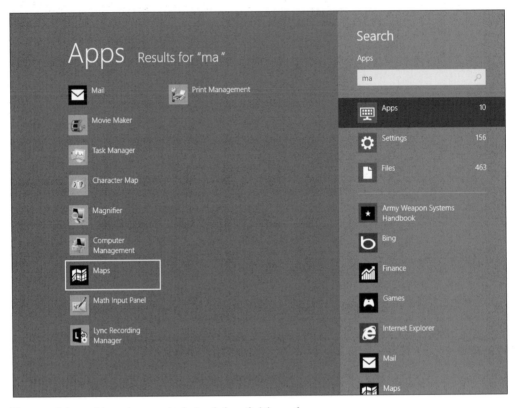

Type a couple letters of the app's name to let the Search charm find the app for you.

If you see the app in this list, tap or click it. If you don't see it, continue typing until it appears.

Selecting from the All Apps list

You can use the list of all apps installed on your computer to select and run an app.

1 While viewing the Start screen, right-click or drag your finger up slightly from the bottom of screen to display the Apps bar.

The Apps bar.

2 Tap or click All Apps to display a list of all apps installed on your computer.

Use the list of all apps installed on your computer to tap or click a tile and open an app.

3 If necessary, scroll horizontally to find the app you want to run.

4 Tap or click the app's tile.

Viewing the options for an app

Once you open an app, you can scroll horizontally to look for more information, and you can display the app's options to work in the app.

To display the available options for an app, right-click or drag your finger up slightly from the bottom of the screen. The options you see vary from app to app. In addition, options might appear along both the top and the bottom of the screen.

Closing an app

Windows 8 native apps use very little of your computer's resources, so you don't gain a great deal by closing them as you do when you close a legacy app. However, if you want to close a Windows 8 native app, you can press Alt+F4 on a physical keyboard, and the app closes.

If you don't have a physical keyboard attached to your computer, you can drag your finger or the mouse pointer (when it looks like a hand) down from the top to the bottom of the screen. As you drag, the app first minimizes.

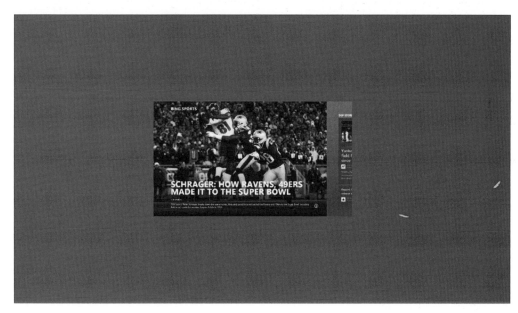

A minimized app.

As your motion approaches the bottom of the screen, the app dims. When the app dims, release the mouse button or lift your finger.

When the app dims, release the mouse button or lift your finger.

In the next section, learn another method to closing Windows 8 native apps.

Switching between Windows 8 apps

You don't have to close Windows 8 native apps. You can let them run in the background and you can easily switch between them as needed by using the Running Apps bar. Although the picture shows the Running Apps bar from the Start screen, you can display it from anywhere, including the Desktop.

Using gestures, you can display the Running Apps bar by sliding your finger from the left edge of the screen in toward the center and then back out, making a small loop.

If you're using a mouse, you can slide the mouse to the upper-left corner of the screen. When a small image of an open app appears, slide the mouse pointer down the left side of the screen. Images of the other open apps appear.

The Running Apps bar appears on the left side of the screen.

It's important to remember that the Running Apps bar displays one image for each Windows 8 native app. The Desktop app is considered an app. If you are running multiple legacy apps on the Desktop app, the Running Apps bar will not display individual images for each legacy app. Instead, you'll see one image in the Running Apps bar that represents the Desktop app.

To switch to any running app, display the Running Apps bar and then tap or click the app you want to use.

You also can use the Running Apps bar to close an app if you also have a mouse attached to your computer; display the Running Apps bar and right-click the image of the app you want to close. A shortcut menu appears that contains only one command, the Close command. Click Close to close the app.

Snapping apps

If you're using a screen that supports resolution set to 1366×768, you can snap two Windows 8 native apps so that you can view them simultaneously, with one taking up approximately three quarters of the screen while the other takes up the other quarter of the screen.

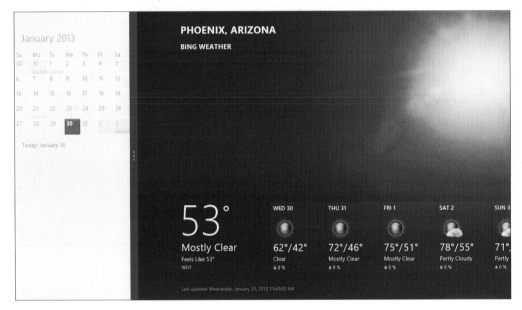

Two apps, snapped.

You can swap the size allotment by horizontally dragging (with your finger or your mouse) the vertical bar that separates the two apps, but you cannot change the ratio of each app. For example, you cannot allot half your screen to one app and half to the other.

It's also important to understand that, although you are displaying the apps simultaneously, they cannot share information; that is, there is no equivalent to the Desktop's Copy and Paste commands. Also, you can include the Desktop app as one of the two snapped apps, but you view only what is currently displayed on the Desktop. You cannot snap two legacy apps and view two Desktop apps along with a Windows 8 native app. You can, however, view two legacy apps simultaneously using Desktop commands as described in Lesson 5, "Working with Desktop Apps."

You can snap apps using the keyboard: display one of the apps; to snap it to the right side of the screen, press WinKey (⊞)+period (.); to snap it to the left side of the screen, press WinKey (⊞)+Shift+period (.).

To snap apps using the mouse or gestures, follow these steps:

1   Display the Running Apps bar.

2   Switch to one of the apps you want to snap.

3 Redisplay the Running Apps bar.

4 Slowly drag the image of the other app you want to snap from the Running Apps bar to the right. As you drag, a vertical bar appears on-screen.

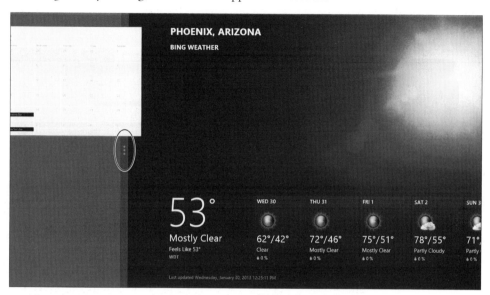

Snapping an app to the left side of the screen.

5 If you want the app you're dragging snapped on the left side of the screen, lift your finger or release the mouse button when the image appears on the left side of the bar. To snap the app to the right side of the screen, continue dragging to the right side of the screen. Eventually, the vertical bar will shift to the right side of the screen; when the app's image appears on the right side of the vertical bar, lift your finger or release the mouse button.

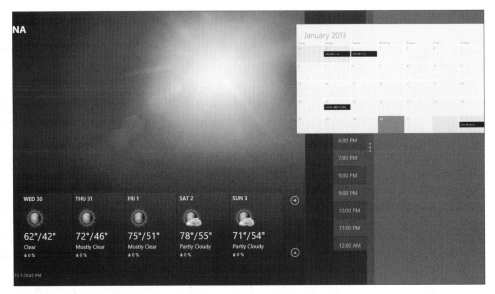

Snapping an app to the right side of the screen.

To eliminate the snapped effect, drag the vertical bar that separates the apps to either side of your screen. If you drag to the right, the app on the left remains on-screen after the apps are no longer snapped. If you drag to the left, the app on the right remains on-screen after the apps are no longer snapped.

Sharing information between Windows 8 native apps

Windows 8 native apps don't have a "Clipboard" like legacy apps do. You share information between Windows 8 native apps using the Share charm.

1   To e-mail a web page, display a web page using the Internet Explorer native app.

2   Display the Charms bar.

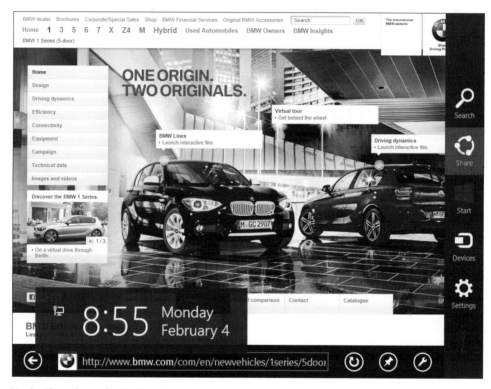

Use the Charms bar to select the Share charm.

3 Select the Share charm. Windows 8 displays a list of native apps with which you can share the web page.

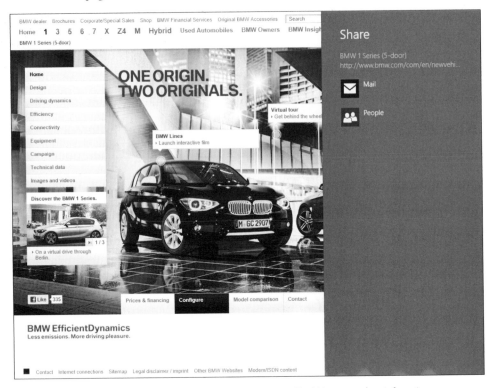

For Windows 8 native apps, the Share charm displays other native apps with which you can share information.

4   Select the Mail app. The Windows 8 native app Mail opens and starts an e-mail message with an image of the web page and its web address embedded in the message.

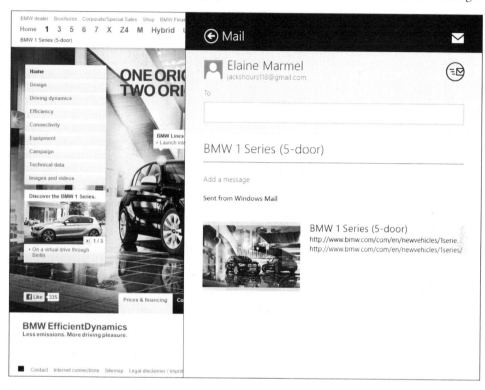

Sharing information between two Windows 8 native apps.

Printing from a Windows 8 native app

In the next steps, you'll learn how to print from within a Windows 8 native app. Specifically, you'll print a web page from the Internet Explorer app.

1   From the Start Screen, open the Internet Explorer app and navigate to a website. While viewing the page you want to print, display the Charms bar.

2   Tap or click the Devices charm. A list of available printers appears.

3   Tap or click the printer you want to use.

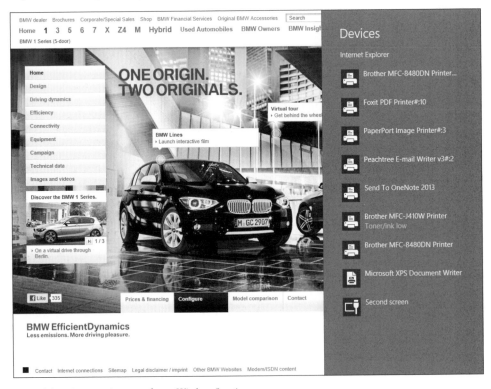

Tap or click a printer to print a page from a Windows 8 native app.

4   From the printer options screen, you can change how many copies, or the page orientation. If there are no changes, tap or click Print.

Self study

1 Practice browsing through the Windows Store and download a free app.

2 Open several Windows 8 native apps and practice switching between them using the Running Apps bar.

3 Practice snapping two apps.

4 Practice printing and sharing information between two Windows 8 native apps.

Review

Questions

1 How do you rate an app?

2 Describe how to close an app using a keyboard, a mouse, and a gesture.

3 To be able to snap apps, what screen resolution must you use?

4 Describe how to snap two apps using the keyboard, a mouse, and a gesture.

5 Describe how to print from a Windows 8 native app.

6 Describe how to share information between Windows 8 native apps.

Answers

1 In the Windows Store, view your installed apps. Then, tap or click the app you want to rate and tap or click the View Details button. When the details of the app appear, tap or click Write a Review.

2 **a.** Keyboard: Press Alt+F4.

b. Mouse: Drag the hand mouse pointer downward from the top to the bottom of the screen.

c. Gesture: Drag your finger from the top of the screen down to the bottom of the screen. Using a mouse or a gesture, the app minimizes about halfway down the screen and then dims when it approaches the bottom of the screen. When the app dims, release the mouse button or lift your finger.

3 1366×768.

4 **a.** Keyboard: Display one of the apps. Press WinKey (■)+period (.) to snap it to the right side of the screen or press WinKey (■)+Shift+period (.) to snap it to the left side of the screen.

b. Mouse or gesture: Display the Running Apps bar and select one of the apps you want to snap. Then, redisplay the Running Apps bar and slowly drag the image of the other app you want to snap from the Running Apps bar to the right. As you drag, a vertical bar appears on-screen. To snap the app on the left side of the screen, lift your finger or release the mouse button when the image appears on the left side of the bar. To snap the app to the right side of the screen, drag across to the right side of the screen; when the vertical bar shifts to the right side of the screen and the app's image appears on the right side of the vertical bar, lift your finger or release the mouse button.

5   Display the information you want to print and then use the Device charm to select a printer.

6   Display the information you want to share and then display the Share charm to identify the apps you can use to share the information.

What you'll learn in this lesson:

- Examining the Desktop

- Pinning and unpinning apps

- Working with the Recycle Bin

- Managing app windows

- Working with Desktop tools

Working with Desktop Apps

In this lesson, you will learn how to work with the Desktop app. You will also learn how to use and manage legacy apps within the Desktop.

Starting up

In this lesson, you will work with several files from the Windows05lessons folder. Make sure that you have loaded the files from the Win8Lessons folder onto your hard drive from *www.DigitalClassroomBooks.com/Windows8*. For more information, see "Loading lesson files" in the Starting Up section of this book.

See Lesson 5 in action!

Use the accompanying videos to gain a better understanding of how to use some of the features shown in this lesson. The video lesson for this tutorial can be found at www.DigitalClassroomBooks.com/Windows8.

Running Desktop apps

Although Windows 8 introduces a new type of app, you can still run most legacy apps—"legacy" refers to the type of application that has been around for 20 years or more. If your legacy app could run under Windows Vista or Windows 7, you can run it under Windows 8. You might even be able to run some apps dating back to Windows XP, but if those apps didn't work under Windows Vista and Windows 7, they won't work under Windows 8, either.

If you used "XP Mode" in Windows 7 to run programs that were written for Windows XP and didn't work properly in Windows 7, you'll need Windows 8 Pro. Using it and a licensed copy of Windows XP, you can set up and run a Hyper-V virtual computer that will let you run your old XP programs from inside Windows 8.

Run a Desktop app the same way you run Windows 8 native apps: from the Start screen, tap or click the tile of the app you want to run. The Desktop app opens, followed by your legacy app.

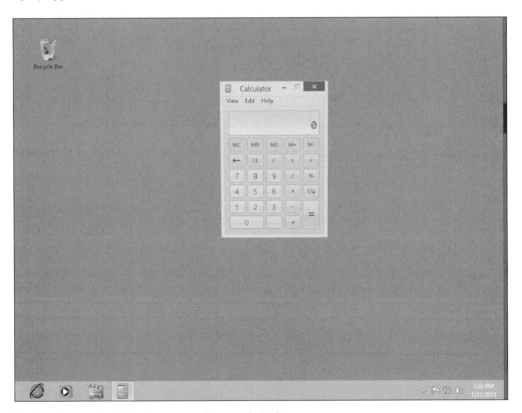

Opening a legacy app from the Start screen, opens the app on the Desktop.

You can open the Desktop app itself by tapping or clicking its tile on the Start screen or by pressing WinKey (■)+D.

Getting to know the Desktop app

From the Desktop app, you can run legacy programs that come with Windows, such as Internet Explorer, File Explorer, Windows Media Player, Paint, WordPad, and the Calculator, as well as legacy programs that you add to your computer, such as Microsoft Office and Intuit Quicken. As you will read in the "Pinning and Unpinning Desktop Apps" section later in this lesson, you can launch legacy apps from the Desktop and from the Start screen.

In Lesson 15, "Exploring Some Windows 8 Apps," you can explore some of the legacy programs that come with Windows.

Understanding the Desktop workspace will help you accomplish tasks quickly and easily.

A. Pinned apps: Internet Explorer, Windows Media Player, and File Explorer. B. Taskbar. C. Recycle Bin.
D. System Tray. E. Notification Area. F. Action Center. G. Network Access Indicator. H. Speaker Volume Control.
I. Date & Time.

You'll find the following elements available by default when you use the Desktop app:

- The Recycle Bin
- The Taskbar
- Pinned apps
- The System Tray

The Recycle Bin

When you delete a file from your computer, Windows doesn't delete it immediately. Instead, Windows typically moves it to the Recycle Bin, a temporary holding area for things you intend to delete. If you find you have mistakenly deleted a file, you can, in all likelihood, find it in the Recycle Bin and restore it. To permanently delete files, you empty the Recycle Bin. You can read more about the Recycle Bin later in this lesson.

The Taskbar

The taskbar displays buttons that represent apps you can open—pinned apps—and apps you have opened. You can tap or click a button on the taskbar to run an app pinned to the taskbar, and you can use the taskbar to switch between open apps, as described later in this lesson.

Pinned apps

By default, Windows pins two apps to the taskbar:

- Internet Explorer is the legacy version of the Microsoft web browser; you'll also find the Windows 8 native version of Internet Explorer on the Start screen. Both versions do the same thing: they let you visit websites of your choice.

- File Explorer is the program you use to work with files on your computer, viewing them, organizing them by creating folders for them, moving or copying them, renaming them, and deleting them.

You can learn more about using File Explorer in Lesson 6, "Using Files and Folders."

The System Tray

The System Tray consists, by default, of five elements that provide information about your computer.

The System Tray.

The Notification Area periodically displays messages pertinent at the time they appear. You can tap or click the arrow in the Notification Area to display icons for system and program features that have no presence on the desktop. In this example, the icon shown appears whenever an external hardware device, such as a USB thumb drive (also called a *flash drive*), is attached to the computer.

The Notification Area temporarily displays pertinent messages and icons for features that don't appear on the Desktop.

The flag in the System Tray represents the Action Center. When you need to take an action, a message will appear and the flag will contain a red X. If you tap or click the flag, the Action Center window opens, displaying a message about the action you need to take. You can tap or click the message in the middle of the window to address the problem. Once you resolve the problem, the red X disappears from the flag.

The Action Center window.

The appearance of the network access indicator depends on the type of connection your device uses. If your device uses a wired connection, the network access indicator resembles a monitor. If your device uses a wireless connection, the network access indicator displays bars that indicate the signal strength, with five bars being the strongest possible signal.

The network access indicator on a device using a wired connection.

The network access indicator on a device using a wireless connection.

You can tap the network access indicator to determine your current connection status and to find available networks to which a wireless device can connect; see Lesson 9, "Networking with Windows 8," for details.

You can tap or click the speaker volume control button to increase or decrease the volume of speakers connected to your device. If you use external speakers on a desktop computer, they typically have a volume control knob; you can control their volume using the volume control knob or using the button in the system tray. However, the speaker volume control button is most useful on portable devices that use internal speakers.

The speaker volume control button.

Besides displaying the current date and time in the System Tray, this area provides some additional functionality. If you point the mouse at the area, a tool tip displays the day as well as the date.

When you point the mouse at the date and time in the System Tray, the day and date appear.

If you click the date and time, the current month's calendar appears, with today highlighted. Today's date appears above the calendar, and the time appears on an analog clock. In Lesson 13, "Customizing and Maintaining Windows 8," you learn how to add two additional clocks to this display so that you can track time in up to three times zones from the System Tray.

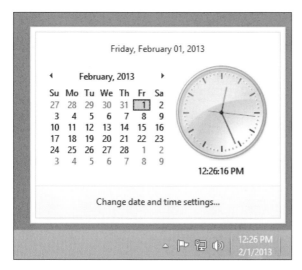

When you tap or click the date and time in the System tray, additional date and time information appears.

Pinning and unpinning Desktop apps

The tiles on the Start screen are the primary tools to use to start apps. But if you regularly use a legacy app that doesn't have a tile on the Start screen by default. You can pin the app to the Start screen.

If you work predominantly on the Desktop, you might find it more convenient to start legacy apps from the Desktop instead of from the Start screen. As you saw in the preceding section, Windows automatically pins Internet Explorer and File Explorer to the taskbar. You're not limited to just these apps appearing on the taskbar; you can pin any legacy app to the taskbar.

The Desktop app will also allow you to create shortcuts for legacy apps on the Desktop.

To the Start screen

By default, the Calculator doesn't have a tile on the Start screen; but you can always add a tile for the Calculator to the Start screen.

1 Display the Start screen.

To display the Start screen, slide the mouse into the upper- or lower-right corner to display the Charms bar and then click Start; press WinKey (⊞*); or, from the right edge of the screen, swipe to the left slightly to display the Charms bar, and then tap the Start button.*

2 Use a physical keyboard or the touch keyboard to type the first few letters of "Calculator" to locate the Calculator app.

3 Display the App bar by right-clicking the app tile or dragging the app tile down slightly until a checkmark appears above the tile, and then releasing the tile.

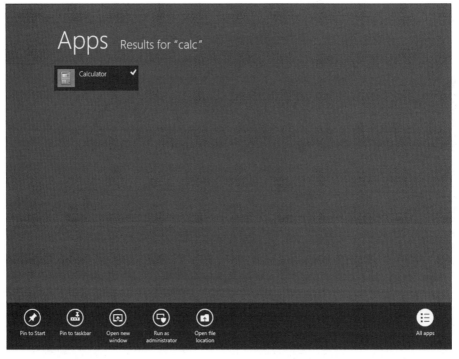

Display the App bar.

4 Tap or click Pin to Start.

Windows 8 adds a tile for the app to the right side of the Start screen.

If you change your mind and no longer want the tile on the Start screen, right-click or drag the app's tile down slightly until a checkmark appears above the tile and then release the tile. From the App bar, tap or click Unpin from Start.

To the taskbar

You can pin an app to the Desktop taskbar and then run the app by tapping or clicking the app's taskbar button. If you work on the Desktop a lot, you might find having a taskbar button for the app more convenient than having a tile for the app on the Start screen.

Start screen tiles and taskbar buttons are not mutually exclusive; you can have both for any app. Just follow the steps in the preceding section and in this section.

To pin an app to the Desktop taskbar, follow these steps:

1 Display the Start screen.

2 Use a physical keyboard or the touch keyboard to type the first few letters of "Calculator" to locate the Calculator app.

3 Display the App bar by right-clicking the app tile or dragging the app tile down slightly until a checkmark appears above the tile, and then releasing the tile.

4 Tap or click Pin to Taskbar.

Tap or click Pin to Taskbar in the App bar.

Nothing appears to happen on the screen, but if you launch the Desktop app, you'll find a button on the taskbar for the app.

You can run a legacy app from the Desktop taskbar if you pin the app to the taskbar.

To run an app that you've pinned to the Desktop taskbar, you can tap or click that button, or you can press WinKey (⊞)+a number that corresponds to the app's position on the taskbar. In the figure, Internet Explorer is in the first position, File Explorer is in the second position, and the Calculator is in the third position on the taskbar. You can open the Calculator if you press WinKey (⊞)+3. Similarly, you can open File Explorer if you press WinKey (⊞)+2, and Internet Explorer if you press WinKey (⊞)+1.

If you change your mind and no longer want a program pinned to the taskbar, you can remove it by doing one of the following:

- From the Start menu, follow the steps presented earlier in this section, but in Step 4, tap or click Unpin from Taskbar.

- From the Desktop app, right-click or tap and hold the shortcut on the Desktop taskbar; from the shortcut menu that appears, tap or click Unpin this Program from the Taskbar.

Unpinning the calculator from the Desktop taskbar.

To the Desktop

If you've used earlier editions of Windows, you should be familiar with shortcuts on the Desktop that run programs. You can still create shortcuts on the Desktop for any legacy program. Let's create a Desktop shortcut for the Calculator.

1   Display the Start screen.

2   Use a physical keyboard or the touch keyboard to type the first few letters of "Calculator" to locate the Calculator app.

3   Display the App bar by right-clicking the app tile or dragging the app tile down slightly until a checkmark appears above the tile, and then releasing the tile.

4   Tap or click Open File Location. File Explorer opens to the folder that stores the program.

5   Right-click or tap and hold the program to view a shortcut menu.

6   From the shortcut menu, tap or click Send To.

7   Tap or click Desktop (Create Shortcut).

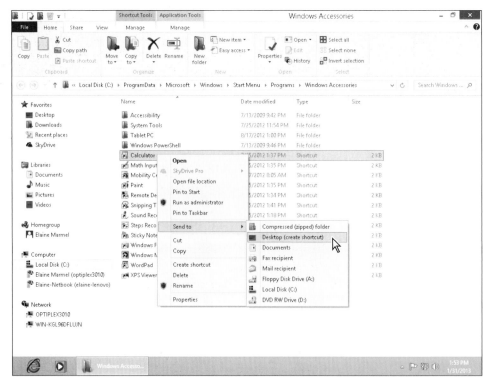

Creating a Desktop shortcut for the Calculator legacy app.

8 Tap or click the X in the upper-right corner of File Explorer to close it and view the Desktop, which now contains a shortcut to the Calculator app.

A shortcut for the Calculator app appears on the Desktop.

To run the Calculator using the shortcut, double-tap or double-click the shortcut.

If you change your mind and no longer want the Desktop shortcut, drag it into the Recycle Bin.

Viewing the contents of your computer

Information you create from various apps is stored in files. Windows helps you organize that information using folders in which you can place related files. *Related files* is a relative term—one that you define. By default, Windows creates four folders for you to use: Documents, Music, Pictures, and Videos. You can store all information inside any of these folders, but finding things later will be easier if you create folders inside folders. For example, you can separate pictures from various vacations into folders named for the vacation. You use File Explorer—called Windows Explorer in earlier editions of Windows—to help manage your files. You can read more about using File Explorer in Lesson 6, "Using Files and Folders."

The left side of the File Explorer screen is called the Navigation pane and displays common locations on your computer that you might need to review. The content of whatever you click on the left side of the screen appears on the right side of the screen. File Explorer opens by default to the Libraries folder (selected in the Navigation pane), and the right side of the screen shows that the Libraries folder contains four folders: Documents, Music, Pictures, and Videos.

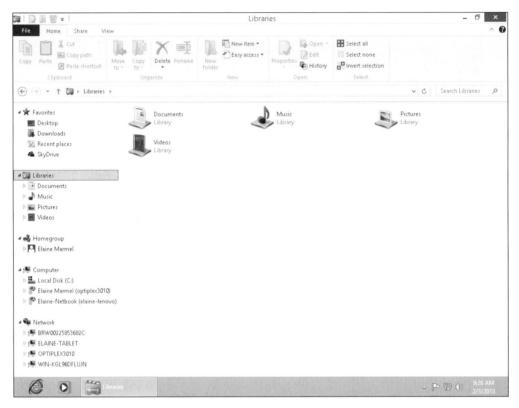

File Explorer as it appears when it opens.

At the top of the screen, you see File Explorer's toolbar and Ribbon interface; you can read more about using these tools in Lesson 6, "Using Files and Folders."

File Explorer can also show you information about storage media attached to your computer, including the computer's hard drive and any external hard drives, USB drives, and CD or DVD drives. To view the contents of your computer, follow these steps:

1   On the Desktop, tab or click the File Explorer button on the taskbar to display File Explorer.

2   In the Navigation pane, tap or click Computer. The right side of the screen displays devices connected to your computer; in the case of storage devices, such as your hard drive and external hard drives, you also see information about space usage.

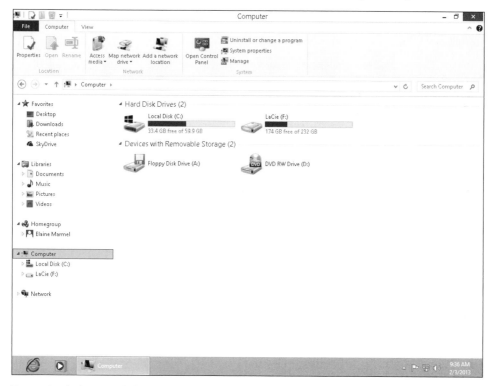

You can view the devices attached to your computer by tapping or clicking Computer in the Navigation pane.

3   Tap and hold or right-click Computer in the Navigation pane.

4   From the shortcut menu that appears, tap or click Properties to display your computer's information in the Desktop Control Panel.

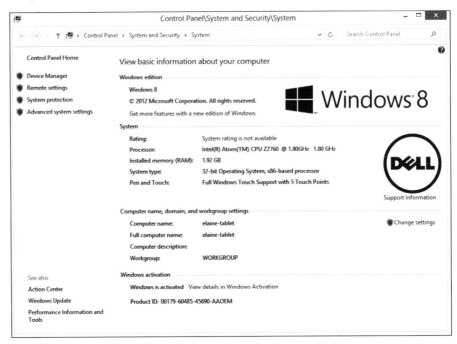

From the Desktop Control Panel, you can view information about your computer, including the version of Windows 8 you're using and the amount of memory contained in your computer.

5   Tap or click the X in the upper-right corner of the window to close the Control Panel and redisplay File Explorer.

6   To view more details about a storage device, such as your Local Disk C, tap and hold or right-click the device to display a shortcut menu.

7   Tap or click Properties to display the Properties box for that storage device.

*From a storage device's Properties box, you can
view a pie chart depicting used and free space.*

8   You'll find more information about the other tabs in the Properties box in Lesson 9, "Networking with Windows 8," and Lesson 13, "Customizing and Maintaining Windows 8," tap or click OK to close the Properties box.

Working with the Recycle Bin

The Recycle Bin's sole purpose is to serve as a holding tank for things you delete from your computer. That is, when you opt to delete something—a file you created, a shortcut to a program, etc.—Windows doesn't really delete the item. Instead, Windows places the item in the Recycle Bin. That way, if you accidentally delete something you meant to keep, you can open the Recycle Bin, find the item, and restore it.

As a general rule, don't delete files that you don't recognize just because you don't recognize them. For example, a file you don't recognize might be part of an app, and without that file, the app can't run. If you can't confirm a file's content, don't delete it.

Deleting a file

You can delete shortcuts on your Desktop or files you see in File Explorer. In fact, you can view items on the Desktop from File Explorer by tapping or clicking Desktop in File Explorer's Navigation pane. For this example, if you previously created a Desktop shortcut for the Calculator that you now feel you don't need. To delete it, do any of the following:

• Drag the shortcut on top of the Recycle Bin. When a tip appears, suggesting that you move the item to the Recycle Bin, lift your finger or release the mouse button.

Dragging an item to the Recycle Bin.

- Tap and hold or right-click the item to display a shortcut menu. Then, tap or click Delete. When confirmation message appears, tap or click Yes.

Tap or click Delete from the shortcut menu.

To move the item into the Recycle Bin, tap or click Yes.

- Select the item and press the Delete key on your keyboard. Once again, when the confirmation message appears, tap or click Yes.

Restoring a file from the Recycle Bin

If you accidentally deleted a file, follow these steps to open the Recycle Bin and restore the file.

1 On the Desktop, double-tap or double-click the Recycle Bin. File Explorer opens. Although you don't see the Recycle Bin in the Navigation pane, the address bar below the Ribbon and above the main part of the File Explorer window confirms that you're viewing the contents of the Recycle Bin.

If you prefer to use shortcut menus, you can tap and hold or right-click the Recycle Bin and choose Open from the shortcut menu that appears.

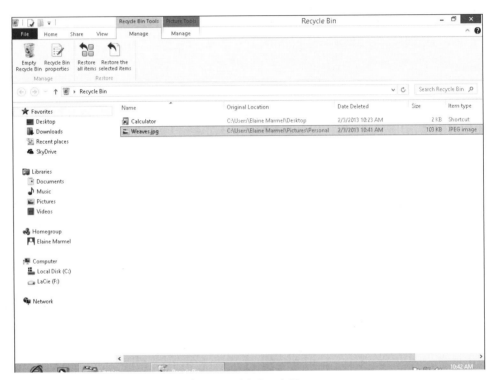

The address bar confirms that you are viewing the contents of the Recycle Bin.

2 Tap or click the item you accidentally deleted.

3 On the Ribbon, tap or click Restore the Selected Items. Windows removes the item from the Recycle Bin and replaces it in its original location.

Emptying the Recycle Bin

To truly delete a file from your computer, you must empty the Recycle Bin. You can tell when the Recycle Bin contains files waiting for deletion by its appearance on your Desktop. When the Recycle Bin is empty, it appears to contain no trash. When the Recycle Bin contains items, it appears to contain trash.

 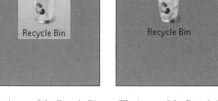

The image of the Recycle Bin when it's empty.   *The image of the Recycle Bin when it contains files waiting for deletion.*

The Recycle Bin is a special file on your computer that has a fixed size. If you never empty it, eventually Windows won't be able to store things you delete in the Recycle Bin because the Recycle Bin will be unable to hold additional items. In this case, when you delete, you delete permanently.

If you want, you can open and examine the contents of the Recycle Bin before you empty it, but that action is only necessary if it gives you peace of mind. To empty the Recycle Bin, do either of the following:

- Tap and hold or right-click the Recycle Bin on the Desktop and choose Empty Recycle Bin from the shortcut menu that appears.

- Double-tap or double-click the Recycle Bin to display it in File Explorer; then, on the File Explorer Ribbon, tap or click Empty Recycle Bin.

In either case, a confirmation message asks you to confirm that you want to empty the Recycle Bin (and permanently delete the items in it). Tap or click Yes.

Customizing the Recycle Bin

As mentioned in the previous section, the Recycle Bin is a special file and has a fixed size. However, you can change that size to suit your needs. For example, if you feel the Recycle Bin is taking up too much space, you can make it smaller. You also can control whether you must view and respond to the confirming message that appears when you move a file to the Recycle Bin, and if you're confident that you don't ever accidentally delete files, you can opt not to use the Recycle Bin at all.

Each drive attached to your computer has its own Recycle Bin used by Windows to manage files you delete on that particular drive.

To customize the Recycle Bin, first do one of the following to display the Recycle Bin Properties box:

- Tap and hold or right-click the Recycle Bin on the Desktop and tap or click Properties on the shortcut menu that appears.

- Double-tap or double-click the Recycle Bin to open it in File Explorer, and then tap or click the Recycle Bin Properties button on File Explorer's Ribbon.

Once the Recycle Bin Properties box appears, you can continue with the following steps:

Use this dialog box to customize the behavior of the Recycle Bin.

1   Select the drive containing the Recycle Bin you want to customize.

2   In the Settings section, tap or click an option. You can change the size of the Recycle Bin or opt not to use it.

3   To avoid viewing the confirmation message each time you place a file in the Recycle Bin, remove the check from the Display Delete Confirmation Dialog check box. Note that unchecking this box stops the confirmation message from appearing when you place a file in the Recycle Bin, but Windows continues to prompt you to confirm your action when you empty the recycle Bin.

4 Tap or click OK to save your settings.

Managing Desktop app windows

Every Desktop app appears in its own window. You can display multiple windows simultaneously, and in this section, you learn about managing open windows. To make your Desktop workspace more functional, you can:

• Resize a window,

• Move a window,

• Show windows side by side

• Switch between app windows

Exploring a Desktop app window

Although app windows may look different, each app shares some common elements with every other app. Learning to use these common elements can help you be more efficient while working on the Desktop.

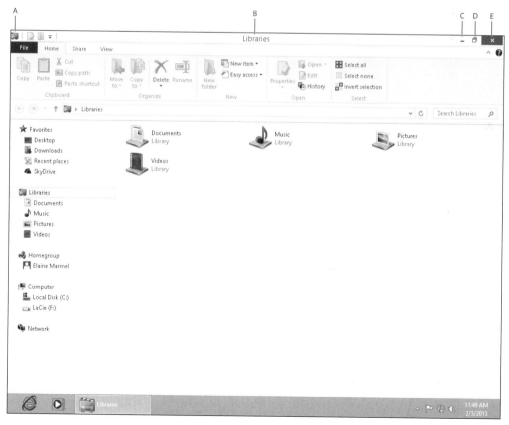

A. App control menu. **B.** *Title bar.* **C.** *Minimize.* **D.** *Restore.* **E.** *Close.*

Every app has a title bar, which typically—but not always—displays the app's name and the name of the document that is currently open. File Explorer doesn't display its app name, but instead displays the name of the folder currently selected in the Navigation pane.

The app control menu contains commands that help you control the size and appearance of the app window as well as close the window.

The three buttons in the upper-right corner provide you with shortcuts to the commands that appear on the app control menu. Tap or click the Minimize button to reduce the app window to a button on the taskbar. Tap or click the taskbar button to once again view the app.

When you minimize a running app on the Desktop, it appears as a highlighted button on the taskbar.

The Restore button appears only when an app window is maximized to fill the entire computer screen. If you tap or click the Restore button, Windows redisplays the window in a size somewhere between minimized and maximized. Displaying an app at a size between Minimize and Maximize is particularly useful when you want to view multiple windows simultaneously.

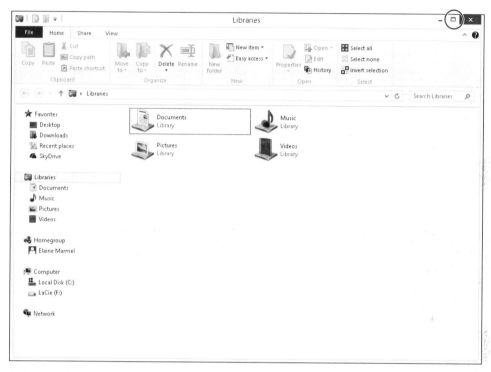

A window that is not maximized or minimized.

When you display a window in a size between Maximize and Minimize, the Maximize button becomes available; click it to make the window fill the screen.

Many legacy apps that work in the Desktop app use the Ribbon interface that Microsoft introduced with its Office 2007 apps. These apps contain a Ribbon and a Quick Access toolbar; both of these elements contain commands that pertain, for the most part, specifically to the app you're viewing, with a few exceptions. The exceptions apply in particular to commands that are common to all Desktop apps and are not really controlled by the legacy app, but rather by the Desktop. These exception commands are the Cut, Copy, Paste, and Print commands you'll read about later in this lesson.

A   B

A. Quick Access Toolbar. *B. A Ribbon.*

The Ribbon contains tabs of related commands. File Explorer's tabs are Home, Share, and View. Each tab further organizes commands into groups, and group names appear below each group; the Home tab contains the Clipboard, Organize, New, Open, and Select groups. You can tap or click a tab to view the commands available on it, and you can tap or click a command to use it.

In some apps, you might want to get the Ribbon out of the way while you work; you can minimize the Ribbon to display only the tab names by tapping or clicking the upward-pointing caret at the right edge of the Ribbon, just below the Close button. To use a command on the Ribbon, tap or click the tab containing the command, and the Ribbon appears until you select a command; then it minimizes again. To expand the Ribbon to its full size (so that it no longer minimizes), tap or click the downward pointing caret at the right edge of the Ribbon, just below the Close button.

The Quick Access Toolbar contains commands you might use frequently when working in the app so that you don't need to switch Ribbon tabs to find frequently-used commands: you tap or click a button on the Quick Access Toolbar to use that command. You can add buttons to the Quick Access Toolbar by tapping or click the right-most button—the arrow pointing downward—on the toolbar. A list of available commands appears; tap or click a command to add it to the Quick Access Toolbar.

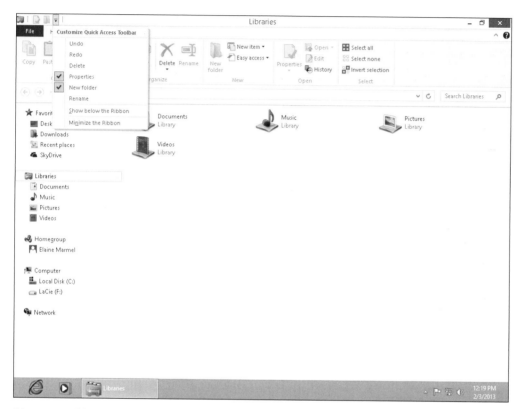

Select a command from this menu to add it to the Quick Access Toolbar.

Finally, most legacy apps that use the Ribbon interface have a special menu at the left edge of the Ribbon; typically, the File menu. When you tap or click that menu, you find commands common to most apps that enable you to, for example, open a document, close, or exit the program.

Resizing Desktop app windows

As long as an app's window is neither maximized nor minimized, you can control its size by dragging one of its edges. If you drag any corner of a window, you can maintain its proportionate size when you drag, increasing or decreasing its height and width simultaneously. If you drag an edge, you increase or decrease only the height or the width of a window.

You can resize a window by dragging either your finger or the mouse pointer. When you use a mouse while resizing, the mouse pointer changes to a pair of pointing arrows; if you resize using a corner, the arrows point diagonally.

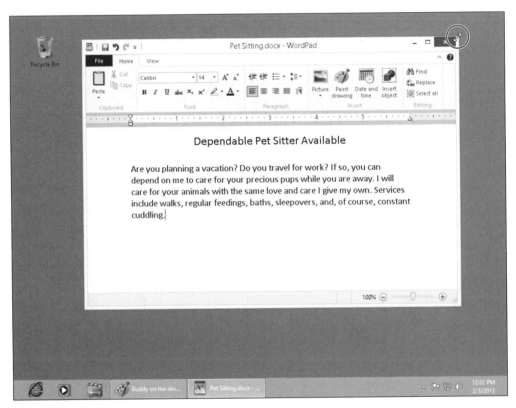

When you resize a window from a corner, the mouse pointer appears as a pair of diagonally pointing arrows.

Moving a Desktop app window

As you saw in the previous section, when a window is neither maximized nor minimized, you can resize the window. In addition, when a window is neither maximized nor minimized, you can move the window to a new position on the screen by dragging the app's title bar.

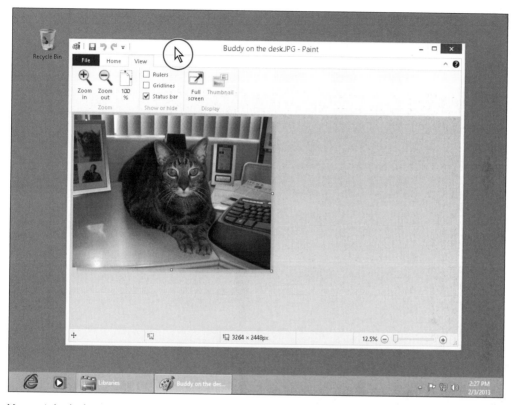

Move a window by dragging its title bar.

Showing windows side by side

Displaying windows side by side in the Desktop app is the equivalent of snapping Windows 8 native apps that you read about in Lesson 4, "Working with Windows 8 Native Apps." The most major distinction between the two techniques, however, is that legacy apps can share information across windows, as you'll see later in this lesson, but Windows 8 native apps cannot.

Many people copy files from one storage device to another, often to create a second copy—a backup—of an important document. It's easiest to copy a file from one drive to another if you open two File Explorer windows and place them side by side. Then, display the drive containing the file (the source drive) in one window and the drive where you will store the copy (the target drive) in the other window. You can then drag the file from the source drive to the target drive.

 You can display two File Explorer windows or the windows of two different legacy apps side by side; for example, you can display the legacy apps Paint and WordPad side by side.

For this example, you need to open two windows of File Explorer. To open the first File Explorer window, tap or click the File Explorer button on the Desktop taskbar or press WinKey (⊞)+E. To open another File Explorer window, do one of the following:

- Tap and hold or right-click the File Explorer button on the taskbar. When the menu appears, tap or click File Explorer.

- Press WinKey (⊞)+E again.

To display the two windows side by side, do any of the following:

- Click one window and press WinKey (⊞)+Right Arrow to place that window on the right side of the screen. Then, click the other window and press WinKey (⊞)+Left Arrow to place that window on the left side of the screen.

- Using your finger or your mouse, drag the title bar of one window toward one edge of the screen. When your finger or the mouse pointer reaches the edge of the screen, a window outline appears; lift your finger or release the mouse button. Repeat for the other window, dragging to the opposite side of the screen.

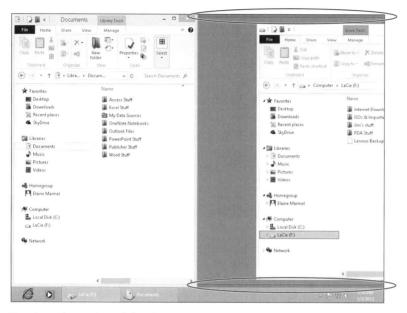

Dragging to place windows side by side.

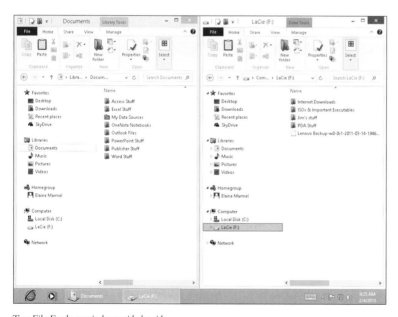

Two File Explorer windows, side by side.

The two windows operate independently; you can select one folder or device in the left window and a different one in the right window.

Switching between Desktop app windows

In this next section, you will use WordPad to create a flyer advertising a pet sitting service. You will also use the legacy app, Paint, to review all your available pictures to add to your flyer. Open both apps from the Windows Start screen.

In this example, you want to maximize the windows of both apps so that each app fills your screen. You can maximize both windows and then switch between the two apps using the Desktop taskbar.

Remember that an app's window is maximized when you see the Restore button in the upper-right corner. If you see the Maximize button in the upper-right corner, tap or click it to maximize the window.

To switch to the other open app, tap or click its button on the Desktop taskbar.

If you use a mouse, you can display a thumbnail of each running legacy app by pointing the mouse at the app's button on the taskbar.

Tap a button on the taskbar to switch to a different legacy app.

Using universal Desktop tools

Although you can run a myriad of legacy apps on the Desktop, some of the tools you use while working in those apps are actually controlled by the Desktop app itself. And those tools are quite powerful.

- You can share information between legacy apps using the Desktop Cut, Copy, and Paste tools.

- The Desktop app manages printing for all legacy apps, eliminating the need for you to describe your printer to each app.

Cut, copy, and paste

One of the most useful features available for Desktop apps is the ability to share information.

Copying information leaves the information you copy in the original document. If you want to move information, you "cut" it instead of copying it. Cutting information removes it from the original app.

To view the final product, follow these steps:

1　Open WordPad.

You might find the WordPad app most easily by typing its name on the Windows 8 Start screen.

2　Tap or click the File menu, and then tap or click Open.

3　Navigate to the Windows05lessons folder that you saved to your hard drive.

4　Tap or click the file called **Windows0501_done.rtf**.

5　Tap or click Open. The flyer appears in WordPad.

6　Now that you've seen the final product, tap or click the X in the upper-right corner of the WordPad window. If you are prompted to save, click Don't Save.

To copy information from one program to another, we'll use Paint and WordPad and two files stored in the Windows05lessons folder. Then, follow these steps:

1　Using the Search charm in the Charms bar, open both Paint and WordPad, and if necessary, maximize their screens.

2　In Paint, tap or click the File menu, and then tap or click Open.

3　Navigate to the Windows05lessons folder that you saved to your hard drive, tap or click the file called **Windows0501_Picture.jpg**, and then tap or click Open. The image appears in Paint.

4 Select the information you want to copy—in this example, the picture.

To select information in Paint, tap or click the Select tool on the Home tab and then drag over the information from the upper-left corner to the lower-right corner. Paint displays a dotted line around the selected area.

5 On the Ribbon, tap or click the Copy button.

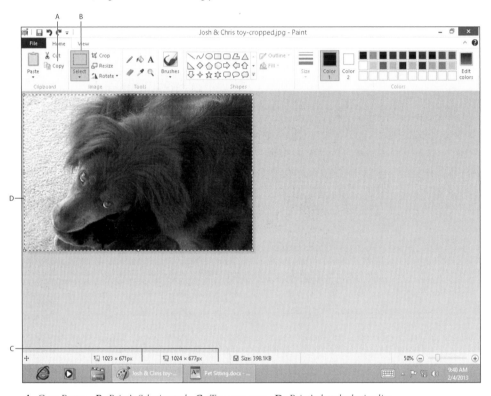

A. Copy Button. B. Paint's Selection tool. C. Two open apps. D. Paint's dotted selection line.

6 On the Desktop taskbar, tap or click WordPad to display it.

7 Tap or click the File menu, and then tap or click Open.

8 Navigate to the Windows05lessons folder that you saved to your hard drive, tap or click the file called **Windows0501_Text.rtf**, and then tap or click Open. The text for the flyer appears in WordPad.

9 Tap or click at the location where you want the information to appear—in this example, tap or click below all the text in the document.

10 Tap or click the Paste button. The information you copied (in this example, the picture from Paint) appears in the app you're currently viewing (in this example, WordPad). It also continues to appear in the original app you selected in Step 2.

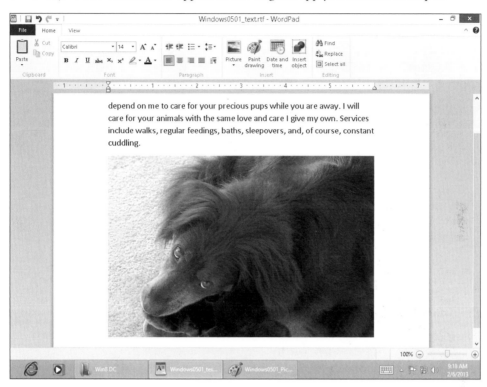

Paste the image, and the image appears in your WordPad document.

If you had tapped or clicked Cut in Step 5, the information you selected in Step 4 would no longer appear in the app you selected in Step 2 (in our example, the picture would disappear from Paint).

11 In WordPad, tap or click the File menu and then tap or click Save As. In the dialog box that appears, provide a new name for the flyer and tap or click Save.

12 Click the X in the upper-right corner of WordPad and then Paint to close the apps. If you are prompted to save, click Don't Save.

Printing

Windows has managed printing for all apps basically since its inception. Nothing has changed in that regard in Windows 8: essentially, whenever you work in an app and decide to print, you issue a print command to the app—typically by tapping or clicking the File menu and then tapping or clicking Print—and the app passes that command along to Windows. Using this approach, you only need to set up your printer once; it is then available to all apps on your computer.

The method used to set up a printer can vary, depending on the make and model of your printer. But one thing remains constant: once you set up the printer, you won't need to configure it again. You can work on any app as you normally would, and when you need to print, you use the app's Print command, which usually appears on the app's File menu (the left-most tab on the Ribbon for legacy apps that use a Ribbon). The app forwards your message to the operating system, which manages the rest of what needs to be done for you.

Use the Devices and Printers page of the Desktop's Control Panel to see images of installed printers.

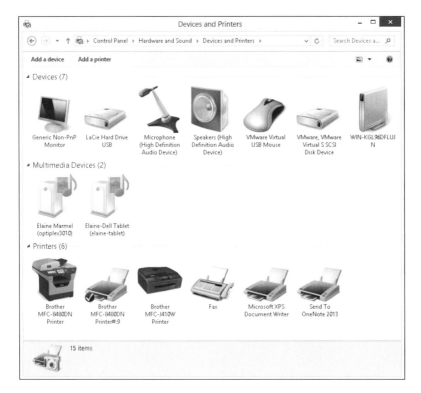

Printers available on your computer appear in the Printers section of the Devices and Printers page, which is part of the Desktop's Control Panel.

To display the Devices and Printers page, follow these steps:

1   Press WinKey (⊞)+X and then click Control Panel, or on the Start screen, type Control Panel and press Enter.

2   In the Control Panel window that appears, tap or click Hardware and Sound.

3   In the Hardware and Sound window, tap or click Devices and Printers.

4   After you've reviewed available printers, you can tap or click the X in the upper-right corner to close the Devices and Printers window.

The Default Printer

In the Devices and Printers window, the printer that contains the green checkmark is the default printer that Windows will use when you print from a legacy app. You can select a different default printer.

1   Tap and hold or right-click the printer that you want to set as the default printer.

2   Tap or click Set As Default Printer. The green checkmark moves to the printer you selected.

3   Tap or click the X in the upper-right corner to close the Devices and Printers window.

Self study

1 Identify the parts of the Desktop app, including the various parts of the System tray.

2 Describe the three places you can pin shortcuts to run Desktop apps.

3 Describe the parts of a Desktop app window and how to move or resize the window.

Review

Questions

1 How do you switch between Desktop app windows?

2 How do you maximize, minimize, and restore a window's size?

3 How do you show Desktop app windows side by side?

4 How do you copy information from one app to another?

5 How do you print from a legacy Desktop app?

6 How do you delete a file?

Answers

1 The easiest way is to use the Desktop taskbar: tap or click the button on the taskbar that represents the app you want to view.

2 Use the left and middle buttons in the upper-right corner of the window. The left-most button minimizes the window. If the middle button looks like a square, it maximizes the window. If the middle button looks like a pair of squares, the window is already maximized and tapping or clicking the button restores the window to a size between minimum and maximum.

3 Open the two windows you want to display side by side. Then, click one window and press WinKey (⊞)+an arrow key to place that window on the side of the screen to which the arrow pointed; repeat the process for the other window. You also can use your finger or your mouse to drag the title bar of one window toward one edge of the screen. When your finger or the mouse pointer reaches the edge of the screen and you see a window outline, lift your finger or release the mouse button. Then, repeat for the other window.

4 In the app containing the information, select that information and tap or click the Copy button. Switch to the app where you want to place the information, tap or click at the location where the information should appear, and tap or click the Paste button.

5 Typically, tap or click the File menu and then tap or click Print. You don't need to set up your printer for every app on your computer; set your printer up once and Windows will manage the printing process.

6 Drag the file to the Recycle Bin. You also can tap and hold or right-click the item to display a shortcut menu, and then tap or click Delete. Or, select the item and press the Delete key on your keyboard. In each case, a confirmation message appears; tap or click Yes to delete the file.

What you'll learn in this lesson:

- Navigating files and folders

- Managing files and folders with File Explorer

- Working with libraries

- Searching for files in File Explorer

Using Files and Folders

In this lesson, you'll examine the Desktop legacy app File Explorer, a powerful tool that helps you manage files on your computer.

Starting up

In this lesson, you will work with several files from the Windows06lessons folder. Make sure that you have loaded the files from the Win8Lessons folder onto your hard drive from *www.DigitalClassroomBooks.com/Windows8*. For more information, see "Loading lesson files" in the Starting Up section of this book.

See Lesson 6 in action!

Use the accompanying videos to gain a better understanding of how to use some of the features shown in this lesson. The video lesson for this tutorial can be found at www.DigitalClassroomBooks.com/Windows8.

Navigating in File Explorer

File Explorer, a legacy Desktop app that comes with Windows, is an organizational tool you can use to manage the files on your computer's hard drive. As you'll see in this lesson, you can create folders and place your files in them, delete files and folders, and copy and move files and folders. Before you begin the exercises in this lesson, you need to become familiar with File Explorer's interface.

To open File Explorer, follow these steps:

1   Open the Desktop app (tap or click it on the Start screen or press WinKey (■)+D).

2   Tap or click the File Explorer button on the Desktop taskbar.

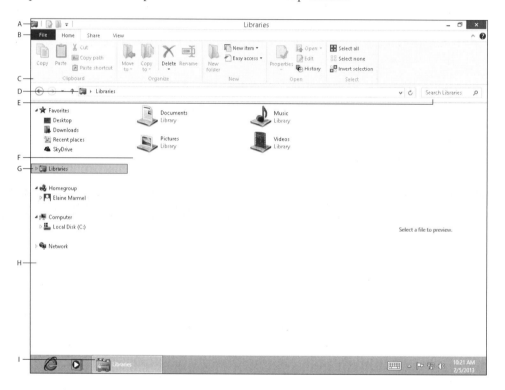

A. Quick Access Toolbar. B. Ribbon tabs. C. Ribbon. D. Address bar. E. Search box. F. Contents of the currently selected folder. G. Currently selected folder. H. Navigation page. I. Tap or click here to open File Explorer.

In the File Explorer window, you'll find:

• The Quick Access Toolbar: you can use this toolbar to quickly perform common activities in File Explorer, such as creating a new folder or viewing the properties of a file or folder.

• The Ribbon: the Ribbon contains commands you can use while you work in File Explorer. The commands are organized using tabs, and each tab contains groups; group names appear below the commands on the Ribbon. For example, the Home tab, shown in the figure, contains the Clipboard, Organize, New, Open, and Select groups.

- The Navigation pane: appearing along the left side of the File Explorer window, use this pane to navigate to folders and files you want to use.

- The currently selected folder: in the Navigation pane, the highlighted folder represents the currently selected folder. File Explorer opens, by default, to the Libraries folder.

Read more about the Libraries folder later in this lesson.

- The contents of the currently selected folder: once you select a folder in the Navigation pane, File Explorer displays the contents of that folder in the right pane. Folders can contain other folders as well as files. Since this pane has no official name, this lesson will refer to it as the "right-hand contents pane."

- The address bar: the address bar identifies the path name of the currently-selected folder and contains a Forward and Back button that you can use to navigate upward or downward through folders.

- The Search box: you can use this box to search for files or folders on your computer. Read more about the Search box later in this lesson.

Understanding Path and File names

All files typically are named using two parts that are separated by a period (.); although it is possible for a filename to contain several parts, all separated by periods. In all cases, the part to the right of the last period is called the extension and the part to the left—including any other periods—is called the filename. Filenames can be as long as you want, and typically consist of letters and numbers. Extensions are supplied by the program used to create the file and are typically either three or four characters long. By default, File Explorer doesn't display extensions, but displaying them can be most helpful when you work with files. (For more information, see the section, "Understanding and Viewing File Formats" later in this lesson.)

Folder names typically don't have an extension, but you can supply an extension when you name a folder.

A path name identifies the exact placement of a file or folder on your computer. For example, if your hard drive is drive C, the path name of any file or folder located on your hard drive begins with C. Traditionally, when you write out a path name, it includes the drive name, a colon, and a back slash (\), followed by folder names separated by back slashes, with the last entry in the path name being either a folder or a filename. A typical path name might be: C:\Users*username*\My Documents\Windows0601_01.jpg, where *username* is the name of the account being used on the computer—often your name.

When a folder contains additional folders, a small caret appears to the left of that folder in the Navigation pane. The direction of the caret visually indicates whether the folder is open or closed. A black, downward-pointing caret identifies an open folder, while a white, sideways-pointing caret identifies a closed folder. You can tap or click the caret to open or close the folder. Folders inside other folders appear indented in the Navigation pane.

Tapping or clicking a caret beside a folder opens the folder in the Navigation pane but does not display the folder's contents. You must tap or click the folder image or the folder name to view its contents in the right-hand contents pane.

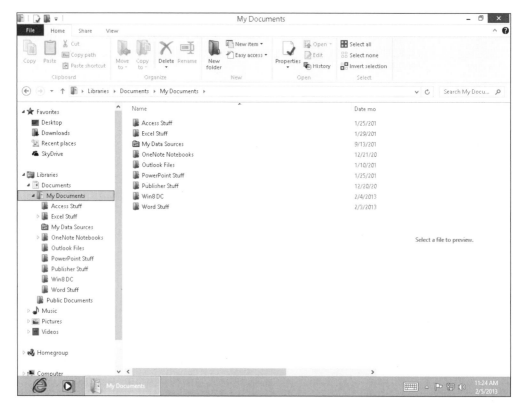

You can open folders to see their contents or close them to hide their contents.

Some folders have no caret beside them; these folders might contain files, but they don't contain any additional folders; the missing caret provides you with a visual indicator that a folder contains no additional folders.

Folders inside other folders are typically referred to as subfolders. *A folder that contains subfolders is typically referred to as a* parent *folder.*

Managing Files and Folders

Using File Explorer, you can manage the files on your computer's hard drive as if the hard drive were a digital filing cabinet. Windows creates some folders for you, and you can create additional folders as you need them. For example, you could drop all your vacation pictures into the Pictures folder, but you might prefer to organize them into folders that match the place you visited so you can find a picture more easily.

Understanding and viewing file formats

You can identify the format of a file by looking at its extension; after a while, you become familiar with the various extensions apps assign to their files. Here's a basic overview of common file formats:

- Program and system files—typically files you want to leave alone—usually have an extension of .EXE, .DLL, or .DRV. Files with .EXE extensions are program files; should you open one of them, you open a program.

- Document files typically have extensions of .TXT, .DOC, .DOCX, and .RTF. Windows legacy app Notepad uses the .TXT extension, while WordPad most often uses .RTF or .DOCX. .DOC is used by Microsoft Word 97 through Microsoft Word 2003. Typically, each vendor creates an extension for each product's document; for example, WordPerfect files use an extension of .WPD, Adobe Photoshop uses .PSD, Microsoft Excel uses .XLS or .XLSX, Microsoft PowerPoint uses .PPT and .PPTX, and a wide number of free apps can read .PDF files, making the .PDF file widely used to distribute reading material.

- Graphic files are visual in nature and contain images, such as photographs, pictures, drawings, and images of computer screens. While a graphic file can contain text, you typically cannot edit the text in a graphic file without using an app that creates and edits files that combine text and graphics, such as the legacy app Paint, Adobe Illustrator, and Corel Paint Shop Pro. Graphic files come in many different types; some common extensions you'll see for graphic files include .JPG, .BMP, .GIF, .PNG, and .TIF (or .TIFF).

- Audio and video file formats are called multimedia formats and include music, movies, and videos. Like graphic files, audio and video files come in many formats .MP3, .WMA, and .WAV are common music file formats. Video files often use extensions of .MP4, .MPEG, .AVI, .WMV, and .MOV.

File Explorer doesn't display file extensions by default, but you can change your settings to help you identify a file's type. Follow these steps:

1 Tap or click the View tab in File Explorer.

2 Tap or click the Options button to display the Folder Options dialog box.

Use the View tab of the Folder Options dialog box to control the way filenames appear on your computer.

3 Tap or click the View tab.

4 Remove the checkmark from the Hide Extensions for Known File Types checkbox.

5 Tap or click OK.

Changing views

You can control the way files appear in the right-hand contents pane using any of eight views; each view provides you with different information.

Switch views by tapping or clicking the View tab, and then selecting a view from the Layout group.

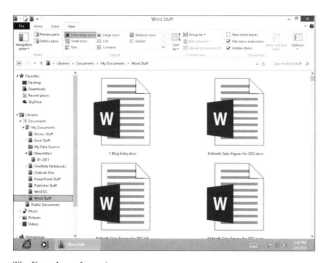

The Extra Large Icons view.

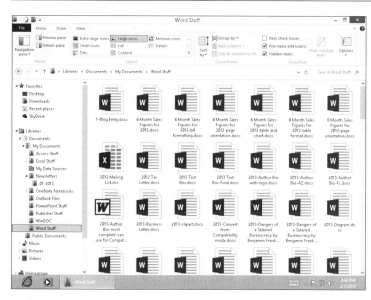

The Large Icons view.

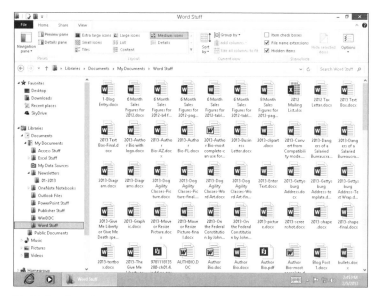

The Medium Icons view.

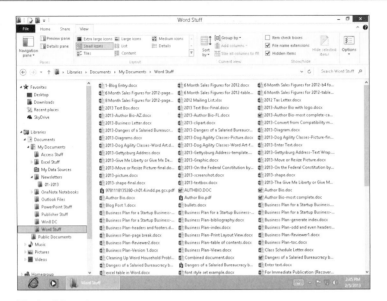

The Small Icons view.

The List view.

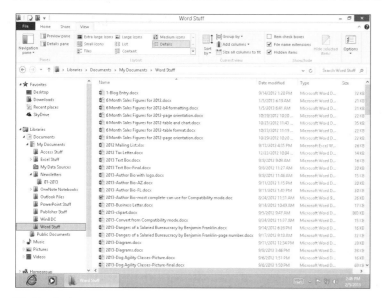

The Details view.

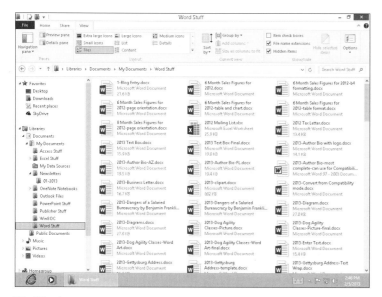

The Tiles view.

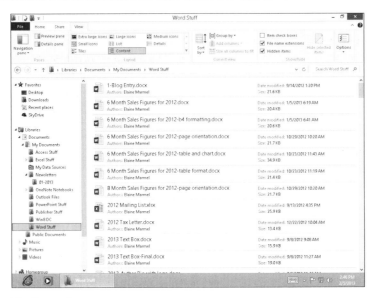

The Content view.

When you view pictures, you might find the Preview pane handy. For example, in the right-hand contents pane, you can view your pictures in List view, Details view, Small Icons, Medium Icons, or any other view; to see a larger view of one of your pictures in the Preview pane, tap or click the image file in the right-hand contents pane.

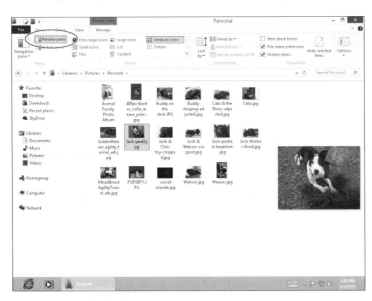

Viewing a picture in the Preview pane.

To display the Preview pane, tap or click the View tab, and in the Panes group, tap or click Preview Pane.

Creating a new folder

The most commonly used folder on a computer that uses Windows is the My Documents folder. You can store all documents in the My Documents folder, but that would be the equivalent of putting all the papers in your office in one file cabinet that had only one drawer. You'd have a better time finding things if you organized your papers into folders and established an organizational scheme for the folders within the file cabinet drawers—for example, many people organize file folders alphabetically.

You can think of your computer's hard drive as a digital file cabinet, but your digital file cabinet has one advantage over a physical file cabinet: it has, essentially, no limit on the number of folders it can hold.

Most files take up very little space, with graphic files taking up more space than document files. But the size of today's hard drives is so large that you'd have to work very hard to fill up your hard drive, even if you store many years' worth of pictures on it from annual vacations. For the most part, you have an almost limitless amount of space in which to store information.

When you create a new folder, you first select the parent folder in which you want to place the new folder. Follow these steps to create a set of folders for a newsletter project.

1   In the Navigation pane, tap or click the caret beside Libraries to open the Libraries folder.

2   Tap or click the caret beside Documents to open the Documents folder.

3   Tap or click the caret beside My Documents to open the My Documents folder. Any folders already in the My Documents folder appear in the Navigation pane.

All four default Library folders each contain two folders: one private and one public. For example, the Documents folder contains the My Documents and Public Documents folders. If you share your computer with other people, you can place files in the Public Documents folder and everyone who uses your computer will be able to see them and work with them.

4   Tap or click the words "My Documents" in the Navigation pane. Any folders already in the My Documents folder appear on the right side of the File Explorer screen.

5   Tap or click the Home tab on the Ribbon.

6 Tap or click the New Folder button. A new folder appears in the right-hand contents pane of File Explorer; the words "New folder" appear highlighted in blue, waiting for you to replace them with a folder name.

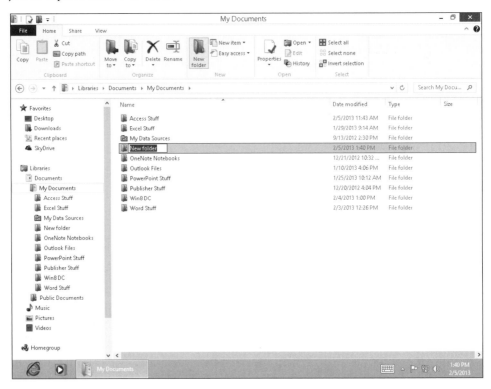

Creating a new folder in the My Documents folder.

7   Type **Newsletters** and press, tap, or click Enter.

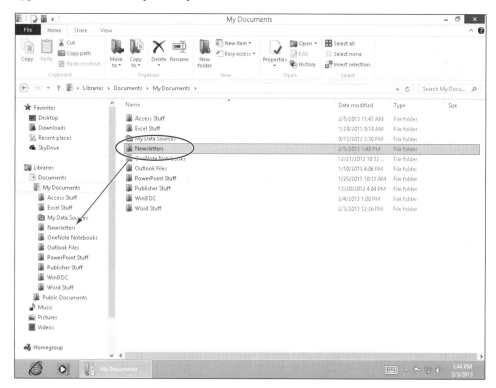

The newly created folder appears in the Navigation pane and in the right-hand contents pane.

To create a folder within the Newsletters folder follow these steps:

1   In the Navigation pane, tap or click the Newsletters folder.

2   Tap or click the Home tab on the Ribbon.

3   Tap or click the New Folder button. A new folder appears in the right-hand pane of File Explorer; the words "New folder" appear highlighted in blue, waiting for you to replace them with a folder name.

4 Type **01-2013** and press, tap, or click Enter. The new folder appears in the right-hand contents pane.

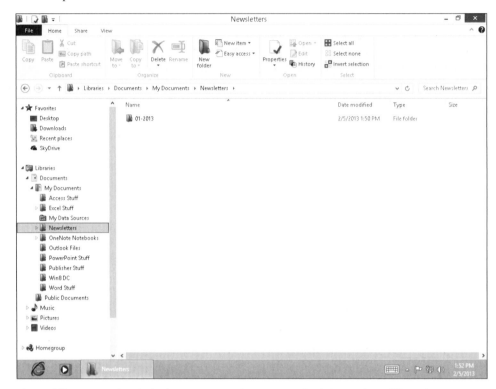

The new folder appears in the right-hand contents pane, and a caret appears beside the Newsletters folder in the Navigation pane.

In the Navigation pane, File Explorer organizes folders inside of other folders in alphabetical order by default, and digits, from 0–9, come before letters. In our example, the newsletter will have monthly issues; naming the folders using numbers for each month ensures that the monthly folders appear in order from January to December for the year.

Selecting and deselecting files

Whenever you want to rename, copy, move, or delete a file or folder, you must first select the file or folder. Although you can select folders in the Navigation pane, most people prefer to focus on selecting files or folders in the right-hand contents pane. Consequently, most people prefer to tap or click in the Navigation pane primarily to make the information they want to work on appear in the right-hand contents pane.

Typically, a user might choose to work in the Details view because this view provides the most information about a file on a single line.

To select a single file, tap or click that file in the right-hand contents pane. File Explorer highlights the selected file in blue.

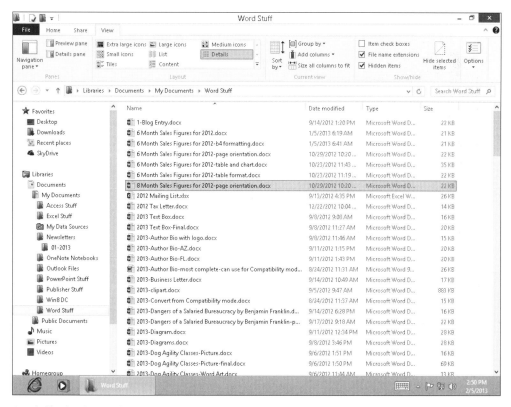

A single file selected in Details view.

To cancel a selection, tap or click anywhere outside the selection; for example, you could tap or click a different folder in the Navigation pane.

To select multiple files using a touch device, display item checkboxes beside each filename. On File Explorer's View tab, in the Show/Hide group, tap Item Check Boxes. A blank column appears to the left of the filename. To select any file, tap in the blank space beside that filename; a checkbox appears and the box beside the file you tapped contains a checkmark.

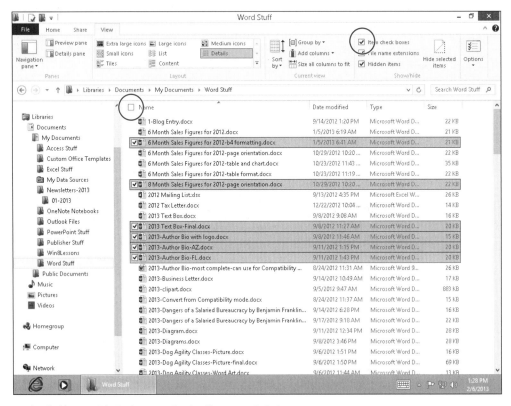

Display checkboxes in File Explorer to easily select files on a touch device.

You can quickly select all the files in a folder by tapping the checkbox that appears above the column and beside the Name column heading.

To use a keyboard to select multiple files simultaneously, use either of the following two techniques.

To select multiple contiguous files:

1   If necessary, switch to Details view.

2   Tap or click the first file.

3   Press and hold the Shift key.

4   Tap or click the last file you want to select. All selected files appear highlighted in blue.

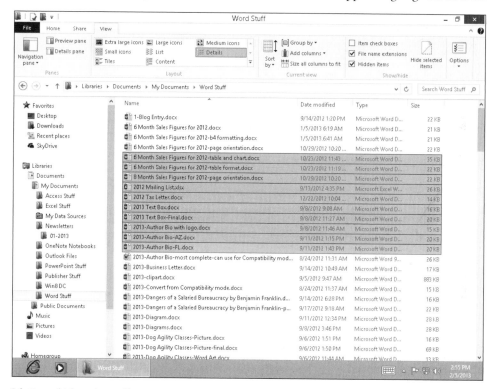

Selecting multiple contiguous files.

To select multiple files that do not appear contiguously in Details view:

1   Tap or click the first file you want to select.

2   Press and hold the Ctrl key.

3   Tap or click the next file you want to select.

4   Repeat Steps 2 and 3 for each file you want to select. All selected files appear highlighted in blue.

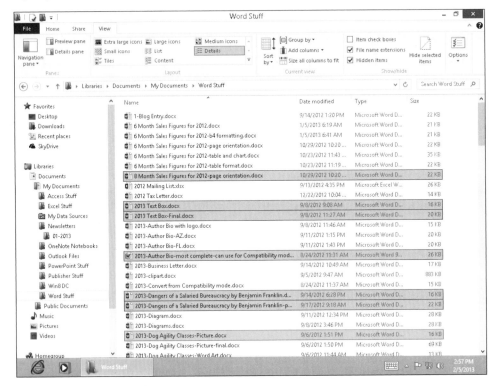

Selecting multiple non-contiguous files.

Renaming files and folders

You may find that you want to change the name of a file or folder to keep things organized or, perhaps, there was a mistake in the filename. In such cases, you can easily rename files or folders using File Explorer; the technique used is applicable to both files and folders.

If you rename a file, only rename the filename portion; don't change the extension, or the app that created the file won't be able to recognize and open it.

In the next exercise, you will rename the folders you created for your newsletter project. Follow these steps:

1 Tap or click My Documents in the Navigation pane.

Tap or click the caret beside the folder you select in Step 1 so that any folders inside the selected folder are visible in the Navigation pane. That way, you can more easily see the effects of renaming the folder.

2 In the right-hand contents pane, tap or click the Newsletter folder.

3 Press F2 on the keyboard or, on the Home tab, tap or click the Rename button in the Organize group. The folder name appears in the right-hand contents pane highlighted in bright blue.

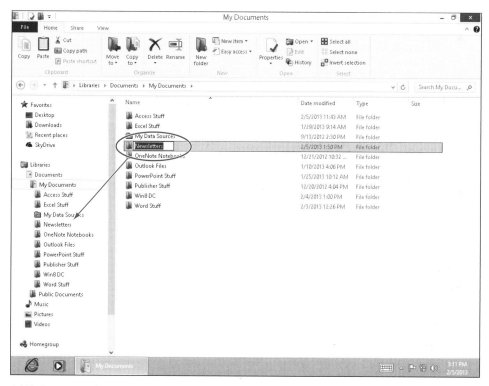

A folder being renamed.

4 Type **Newsletter-2013** for the new name of the folder and press, tap, or click Enter. The folder appears in both the Navigation pane and the right-hand contents pane with its new name.

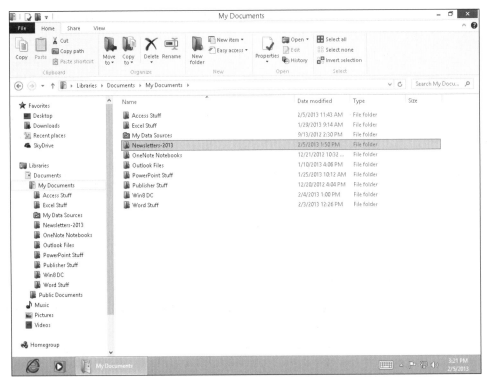

The folder after renaming.

Moving files and folders

Moving a file or folder is a two-part operation—you first select and cut the file or folder and then you paste it in the new location. The technique you use to move a file is the same as the technique you use to move a folder; this example demonstrates how to move a file from one folder to another.

Some users find moving and copying files easier if they can view two folders simultaneously: the source folder containing the file they want to move and the target folder where they want to move the file. For this example, we'll display two windows of File Explorer side-by-side, as described in Lesson 5, "Working with Desktop Apps."

To open the first File Explorer window, tap or click the File Explorer button on the Desktop taskbar or press WinKey (■)+E. To open another File Explorer window, do either of the following:

- Tap and hold or right-click the File Explorer button on the taskbar. When the menu appears, tap or click File Explorer.
- Press WinKey (■)+E again.

To display the two windows side by side, do either of the following:

- Click one window and press WinKey (■)+Right Arrow to place that window on the right side of the screen. Then, click the other window and press WinKey (■)+Left Arrow to place that window on the left side of the screen.
- Using your finger or your mouse, drag the title bar of one window toward one edge of the screen. When your finger or the mouse pointer reaches the edge of the screen, a window outline appears; lift your finger or release the mouse button. Repeat for the other window, dragging to the opposite side of the screen.

Now we'll move a file from the Win8Lessons folder for this chapter to the Newsletters-2013\01-2013 folder.

1   In File Explorer on the left side of your screen, use the Navigation pane to navigate to and select the Windows06lessons folder that you saved to your hard drive.

2   In File Explorer on the right side of your screen, use the Navigation pane to navigate and select to the folder in which you want to place the file.

You can identify which File Explorer window is active by the on-screen colors. By default, selected files appear light blue in the active window.

3   In File Explorer on the left, tap or click the file called **Windows0601_test.rtf**. File Explorer selects the file.

4   On the Home tab of the Ribbon, tap or click the Cut button.

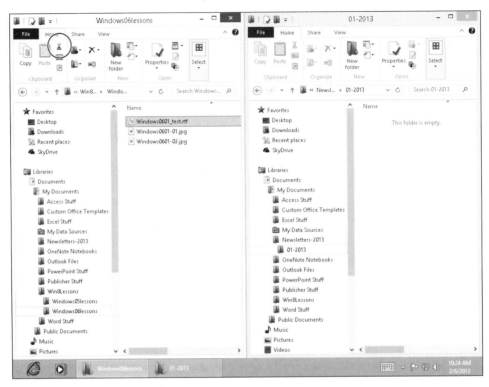

Moving a file from the selected folder on the left to the selected folder on the right.

5   Tap or click the title bar of File Explorer on the right side of your screen.

When windows are set side by side, File Explorer remembers the last folder you selected in both windows. You don't need to reselect the folder on the right; you can simply tap or click the title bar on the File Explorer window on the right.

6   On the Ribbon, tap or click the Paste button. The file you selected in Step 3 appears in the folder you selected in Step 2 and disappears from the folder you selected in Step 1.

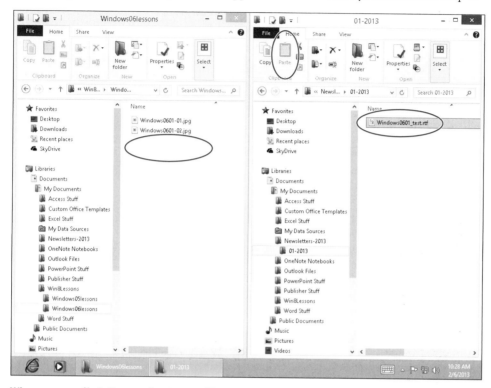

When you move a file, it disappears from its original location.

Move a folder using the same technique, but select a folder instead of a file in Step 3.

Copying files and folders

At some point you may have a document that would serve as a good starting point for a new document, but you don't want to lose the original form of the document. You can make a copy of the document. The technique you use to copy a file is the same as the technique you use to copy a folder; this example demonstrates how to copy a file from one folder to another.

In this example, we'll copy a file from the Windows06lessons folder to the Newsletters-2013\01-2013 folder. Copying files or folders is also a two-part operation: you first select and copy a file or folder, and then you paste it.

1 In File Explorer, use the Navigation pane to navigate to the Windows06lessons folder that you saved to your hard drive.

2 Tap or click the file called **Windows0601_test.rtf**. File Explorer selects the file.

3 On the Home tab of the Ribbon, tap or click the Copy button.

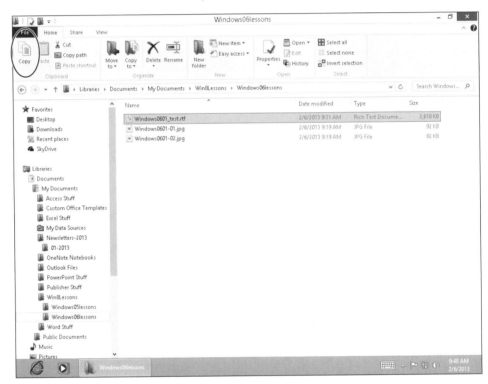

Select the file you want to copy and tap or click the Copy button on the Ribbon.

4 In the Navigation pane, tap or click the folder in which you want to place the file.

5   Tap or click the Paste button on the Ribbon. A copy of the file appears in the folder you selected in Step 4.

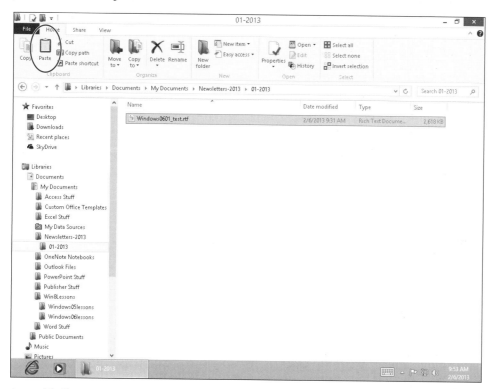

A copy of the file appears in the folder selected in the Navigation pane.

6   To verify that the original still appears in the folder you selected in Step 1, use the Navigation pane to redisplay that folder.

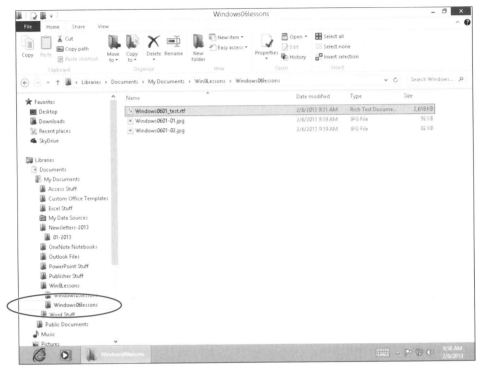

The original file still appears in the folder you selected in Step 1.

Copy a folder using the same technique, but select a folder instead of a file in Step 2.

Copying files and CDs

You can copy files to CDs using the steps presented in this section with a few modifications. Before you choose to store files on a CD, be aware that CDs can fail without warning.

To copy files to a CD, place a blank CD into the CD/DVD drive. In the Navigation pane, tap or click the CD/DVD drive, and File Explorer displays the Burn a Disc wizard. Optionally, supply a disc title, and then tap or click Like a USB Flash Drive to create a CD to which you can add files to the disc at a later date. Tap or click Next. File Explorer formats the disc in the CD/DVD drive and then displays a File Explorer window with the CD/DVD drive selected in the Navigation pane and a message in the right-hand pane that tells you to drag files to the folder to add them to the disc. You can drag and drop files on the disc, or you can copy and paste files using the buttons on Home tab of the Ribbon, the same way you'd copy and paste any file or folder. When you Paste, select the CD/DVD drive as the target location.

Zipping and unzipping compressed files

At times, you might receive an e-mail attachment or download a file from the Internet that arrives in *compressed* form; the compressed file actually contains one or more files that were compressed to save space, making the e-mail or download delivery time shorter. To use those files, you need to extract the files from the compressed file.

Because a compressed file actually contains multiple files, File Explorer treats the compressed file like a special type of folder. You'll hear these special files called *compressed folders*, *zipped folders*, *zipped files*, or *ZIP archive files*.

You also can create compressed folders to send large files, such as pictures, via e-mail.

In this example, we'll create a compressed folder using some of the files in the Windows06lessons folder.

1   In File Explorer, use the Navigation pane to navigate to the Windows06lessons folder

2   Select the two files named **Windows0601-01.jpg** and **Windows0601-02.jpg**.

Remember: to select both files using the keyboard and mouse, click the first file and then press and hold Ctrl as you click the second file. To select both files using a touch device, display Item Check Boxes using the View tab on the Ribbon; then, tap each file to check the boxes beside the filenames.

3   Tap and hold or right-click the selected files to display a shortcut menu.

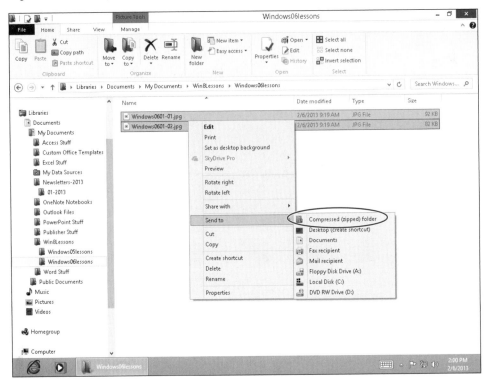

Creating a compressed folder.

4   From the shortcut menu, tap or click Send To.

5   Tap or click Compressed (zipped) folder. File Explorer zips your files into a new compressed file and suggests, for the file name, the name of the last file you selected to zip. File Explorer presents the name highlighted so you can change it.

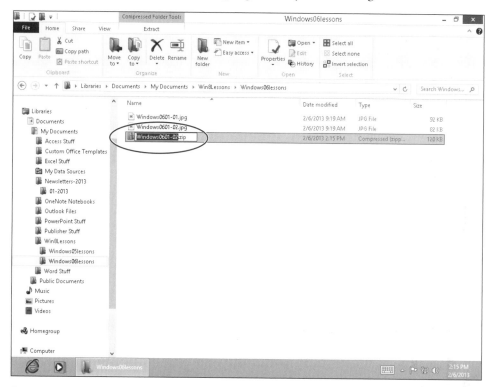

A new compressed file appears ready to be renamed.

6   Type **Lesson 6 Pictures** and press Enter or tap or click an empty spot in the window.

To use the files in a compressed folder—for example, to open them in an app—you should extract them from the compressed folder. Follow these steps:

1 In the Navigation pane, select the folder that contains the compressed folder. On its left, the compressed folder displays an icon that looks like a folder containing a zipper.

2 Tap or click the compressed folder to select it.

3 Tap or click the Extract tab on the Ribbon.

4 Tap or click the Extract All button. File Explorer displays the Extract Compressed (Zipped) Folders window and suggests a destination folder in which to place the file it extracts. By default, the folder name is the name of the compressed file and will appear inside the same folder that contains the compressed file. In this example, File Explorer will place the unzipped files in a folder call Lesson 6 Pictures, and that folder will appear inside the Windows06lessons folder.

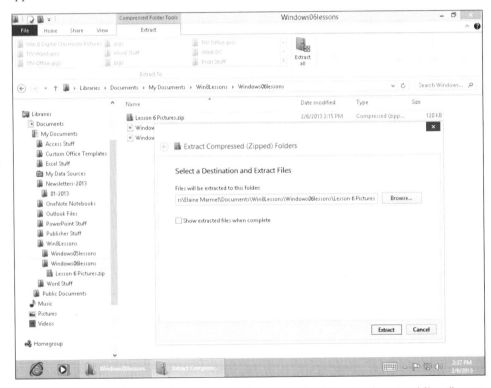

File Explorer suggests using the name of the compressed folder for the name of the folder where the unzipped files will appear.

5 Tap or click the Show Extracted Files When Complete checkbox to deselect it.

If you leave the box selected, File Explorer will not only extract the files, but also open another File Explorer window to display the files. To avoid this distraction, uncheck the box.

6   Tap or click the Extract button. File Explorer extracts the files to the new folder, which appears along with the original zip file.

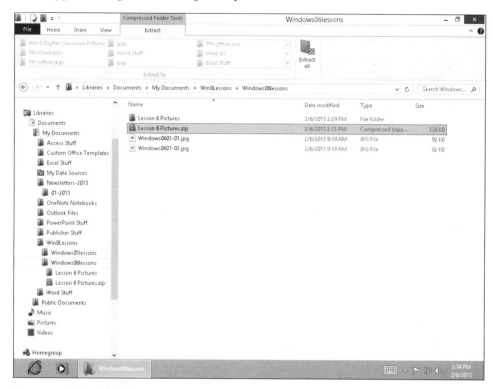

The compressed file and the folder containing the extracted files both appear in the same folder.

You can now select the new folder just as you would select any other folder and work with the files in the new folder.

Deleting files and folders

You might find that you don't need a particular file or folder anymore, so you can choose to delete it. For example, now that you've extracted the files in the Lesson 6 Pictures.zip compressed file, you can delete the file.

Only delete documents you have created or documents that someone else has given to you. Do not delete any files associated with Windows 8 or any of your programs; if you do, a program or your computer might no longer work. As a rule of thumb, don't delete anything unless you can confirm its content and know it is something you don't need.

To delete a file, select it by tapping or clicking it. You can select multiple files to delete at the same time. Then, press the Delete key on your keyboard or tap the Home tab on the Ribbon and tap the Delete button.

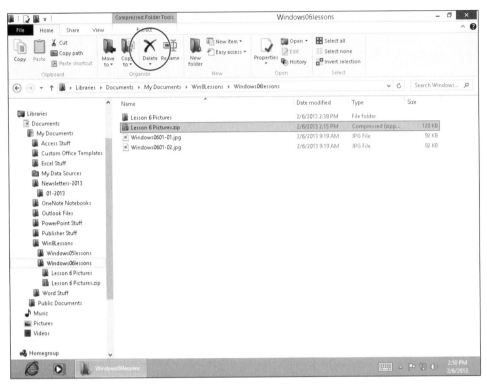

Tap or click the Delete button to delete the selected file(s) or folder(s).

When you delete a file or folder, it typically moves to the Recycle Bin. If you accidentally delete a file, you can restore it from the Recycle Bin. On the Desktop, double-tap or double-click the Recycle Bin; the contents of the Recycle Bin appears in a File Explorer window.

A file might not appear in the Recycle Bin if there is no room in the Recycle Bin for the file. File Explorer will warn you before you delete a file that won't fit in the Recycle Bin.

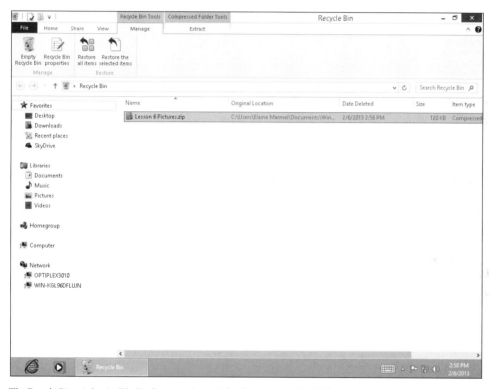

The Recycle Bin window in File Explorer contains special tools to manage deleted files.

Tap or click the file you want to restore; if you want to restore multiple files, select them all. Then, on the Manage tab of the Ribbon, tap or click Restore the Selected Items. File Explorer removes the file(s) from the Recycle Bin (they no longer appear in the window) and returns them to the folder that contained them when you deleted them.

Emptying the Recycle Bin

The Recycle Bin is a special file on your computer that has a fixed size. If you never empty it, eventually Windows won't be able to store things you delete in the Recycle Bin because the Recycle Bin will be unable to hold additional items. In this case, when you delete, you delete permanently. We strongly suggest that you periodically empty the Recycle Bin.

For your peace of mind, you can choose to open and examine the contents of the Recycle Bin, but it's not necessary. To empty the Recycle Bin, do either of the following:

• Tap and hold or right-click the Recycle Bin on the Desktop and choose Empty Recycle Bin from the shortcut menu that appears.

• Double-tap or double-click the Recycle Bin to display it in File Explorer; then, on the File Explorer Ribbon, tap or click Empty Recycle Bin.

In either case, a confirmation message asks you to confirm that you want to empty the Recycle Bin (and permanently delete the items in it); tap or click Yes.

Working with Libraries

Libraries are another type of special folder that you can use to help you organize your files. Windows comes with four libraries already created for you—Documents, Music, Pictures, and Videos, each of which contains a public and private folder—but you can create your own libraries to support the way you work.

For example, imagine you've transferred vacation pictures to your hard drive and to your external hard drive, with each vacation's pictures stored in its own folder. Now, you want to assemble an album using photos from many different folders stored on separate hard drives. Your first step would be to create a library.

Another example is if you create a monthly newsletter that contains pictures to go along with the text. Although you can keep everything in one folder, the large number of files in one folder might make things difficult when you start to work. On the other hand, if you use separate folders for text and pictures, your information is spread out and can be much more difficult to track and use. Your best solution is to keep your information organized in separate folders and use a library to collect the folders you need to use simultaneously.

Libraries are *virtual folders*. Libraries don't actually store your files; instead, they are shortcuts to the folders that store your files. Using a library enables you to gather and work with files that are stored in several folders in different places—even on separate hard drives. If you delete a file in the folder, the library updates to reflect the change. Similarly, if you delete a file in the library, the folder updates to reflect the deletion.

The default libraries display physical folders that you can find if you use File Explorer's Navigation pane to display C:\Users*username*\\, where *username* is the name of the account you're using when you sign in to your computer. If you examine the contents of the My Documents, My Music, My Pictures, and My Videos folders, you'll find it matches exactly to the content that appears when you display these folders under Libraries in the Navigation pane.

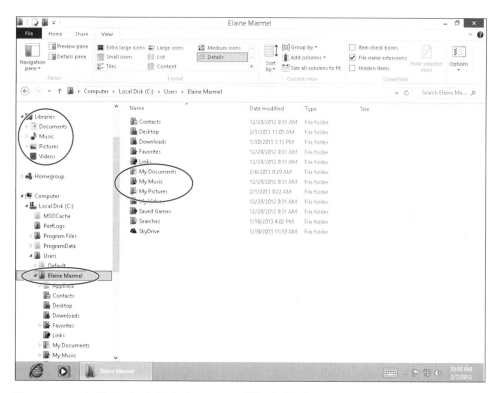

View your account in File Explorer's Navigation pane to see folders for My Documents, My Music, My Pictures, and My Videos, all of which appear in the default libraries.

Creating a library

You can easily create your own libraries; each library you create can include up to 50 folders.

To illustrate how to create libraries, follow this exercise to create a library for your monthly newsletters:

1   Tap or click Libraries in the Navigation pane.

2   On the Home tab, tap or click the New Item button in the New group.

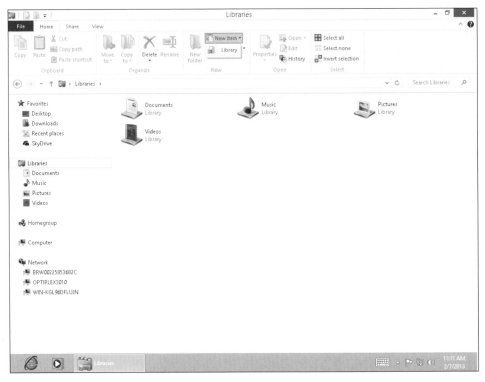

Creating a new library.

3   Tap or click Library. A new folder appears in the right-hand contents pane, with the name New Library highlighted in blue, waiting for you to provide a name.

4   Type **Newsletters**. The new library is empty; you need to include folders in it.

5   In the Navigation pane, tap or click the new library you just created. The right-hand contents pane indicates that your library contains no folders. Read on to learn how to include folders in your library.

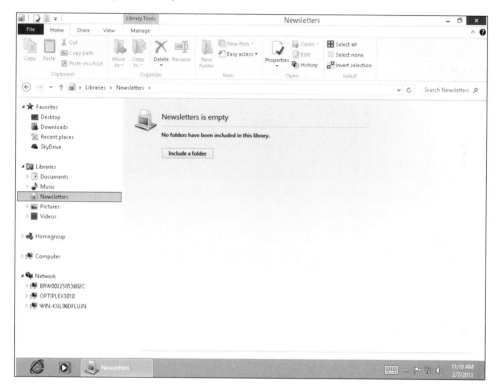

An empty library.

Adding the Downloads folder as a library

You might want to consider adding the Downloads folder, which appears in the Navigation pane as a favorite, to your libraries. That way, when you download information from the Internet, you can easily keep all your downloaded information organized in one place. Setting up the Downloads folder as a library makes the Download folder easy to find since you can navigate to Libraries easily. To add Downloads to your libraries, follow these steps:

1   In the Navigation pane, tap and hold or right-click Downloads.

2   From the shortcut menu that appears, tap or click include in library.

3   From the shortcut menu that appears, tap or click Create New Library to add the Downloads folder to the Libraries folder.

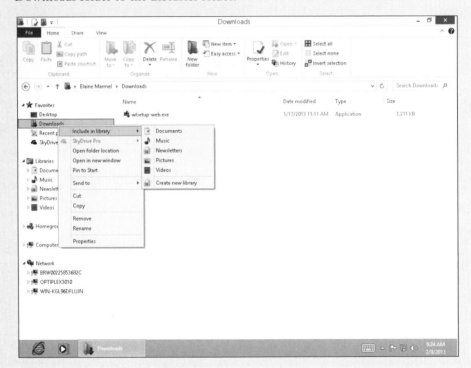

Adding the Downloads folder to your library.

Adding folders to a library

To make use of the library, you need to add folders to it. When you add a folder, remember that you aren't moving or copying files; instead, you are creating a link from the library location to a folder's physical location to help you use the information in that folder more easily.

1   In the right-hand contents pane, tap or click Include a Folder. The Include Folder in *library name* dialog box appears (where *library name* is the name of the library you created in the previous exercise); use this dialog box to include folders in your library. For this example, we will add the Newsletter-2013 folder in the My Documents folder and the Newsletter folder in the My Pictures folder.

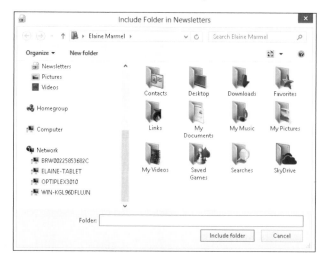

Use this dialog box to select a folder to include in your library.

2   Double-tap or double-click My Documents.

3   Select the **Newsletters–2013** folder to include in the library.

Adding a folder to the library.

4   Tap or click the Include Folder button. File Explorer redisplays the new library and shows that it contains one folder.

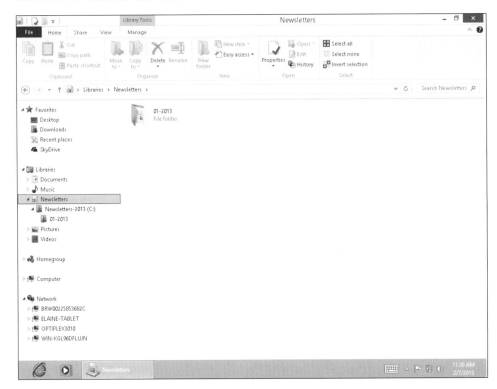

The selected folder and its contents appear in the new library.

You can add more folders to a library in the same basic way, but you'd start from a different place because there'd no longer be an Include Folder button in the right-hand contents pane for the library. To add another folder to a library, follow these steps:

1 Tap or click the library to which you want to add a folder.

2 Tap or click the Manage tab on the Ribbon.

3 Tap or click the Manage Library button. The *library name* Library Locations dialog box appears, where *library name* is the name of the library you selected in Step 1.

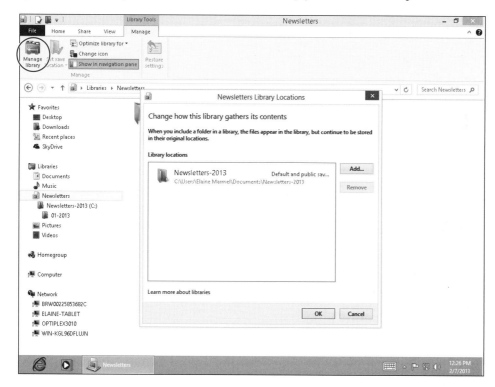

Adding more folders to a library.

4 Tap or click the Add button to redisplay the Include Folder in *library name* you saw in the preceding set of steps.

5 Navigate to the folder you want to include, for example, Libraries\Pictures\My Pictures\Win8LessonPictures\Lesson 6 Pictures.

Navigating to include another folder in the library.

6 Tap or click Include Folder. File Explorer updates the included locations for the library.

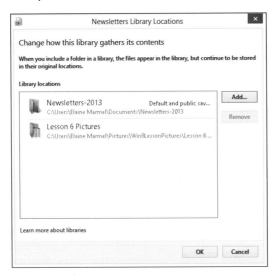

The library now includes two locations.

7 Repeat Steps 4 through 6 to add more folders to the library.

8   When you finish adding folders to the library, tap or click OK. The library's contents appear in the right-hand contents pane.

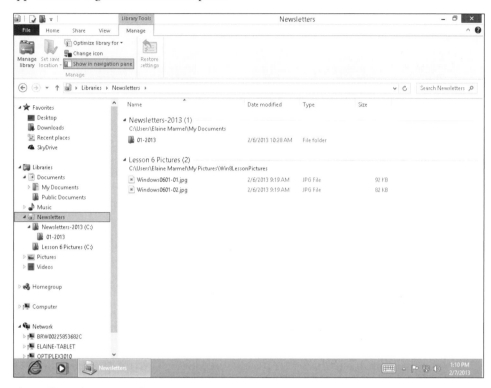

The new library after adding two folders to it.

Libraries and deletions

It's important to understand how your actions can affect files and folders in a library.

First, if you delete a library, File Explorer moves the library to the Recycle Bin—but that action doesn't affect the files and folders in the library, because they are accessible elsewhere on your hard drive. Deleting a library does not delete any files or folders included in the library.

If you accidentally delete one of the four default libraries—Documents, Music, Pictures, or Videos—you can restore it. Tap and hold or right-click Libraries in the Navigation pane, and from the shortcut menu that appears, tap or click Restore default libraries.

Deleting files or folders that you included in a library has a different effect. If you delete files or folders while working in a library, File Explorer also deletes them from their original locations. Similarly, if you include a folder in a library and then delete the folder from its original location, the folder disappears from both the original location and the library. This occurs because the library entry is really a link to the original location.

If you want to eliminate a folder from a library but keep it in its original location, you should remove the folder containing the item from the library. Removing a folder from a library eliminates the folder from the library but doesn't delete any items in the folder.

To remove folders from a library:

1   Tap or click the library from which you want to remove a folder.

2   Tap or click the Manage folder on the Ribbon.

3   Tap or click the Manage Library button. The *library name* Library Locations dialog box appears, where *library name* is the name of the library you selected in Step 1.

4   Tap or click the folder you want to remove from the library.

5   Tap or click the Remove button. File Explorer removes the folder from the library.

Remember, removing a folder from a library does not affect the folder's contents; the action simply disconnects the folder from the library.

6   Repeat Steps 4 and 5 for each folder you want to remove from the library.

7   Click OK.

Searching for files in File Explorer

You can use the Search box in the upper-right corner of File Explorer to help you locate a file on which you need to work.

You can open a file in File Explorer by double-tapping or double-clicking it. The program used to create the file opens, along with the file.

You can limit a search and get the best and most reliable results if you tap or click the folder in the Navigation pane that you think contains the file. For example, if you search from the Newsletters library for filenames containing the word Windows, File Explorer displays results using those files found in the folders included in the Newsletters library.

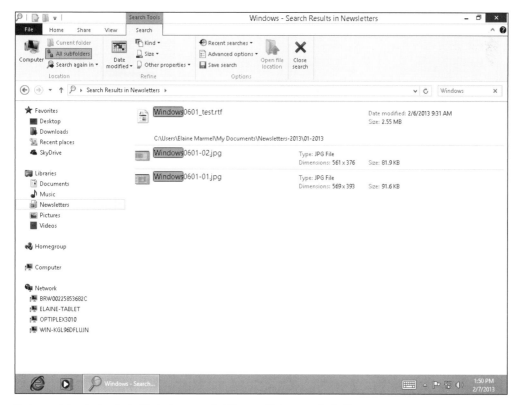

Start a search by selecting, in the Navigation pane, the folder most likely to contain the file.

If your search returns many possible files, try narrowing your search further by first selecting a folder further down the path. In this example, you can narrow the search further by selecting a folder in the Newsletters library and then searching.

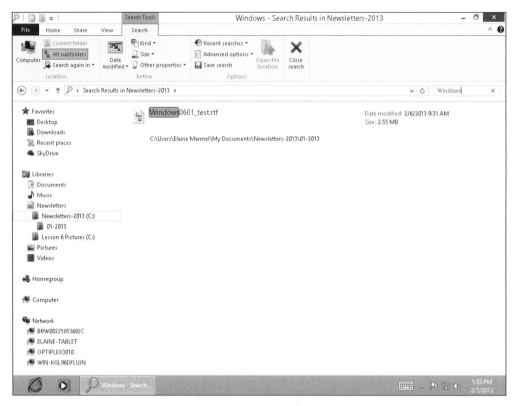

Selecting a folder inside the Newsletters library narrows the search to just that folder.

Self study

1 Practice selecting multiple files using the method most often available for your computer. That is, if you're working on a touch device, use touch techniques. If you're working instead with a keyboard and mouse, use the keyboard and mouse. Make sure you practice selecting groups of contiguous files and groups of non-contiguous files.

2 Practice moving and copying files.

3 Create a library and add three folders to it (preferably folders from different libraries, such as one from the Documents library and one from the Pictures library). Then, copy a file into the library from a folder not included in the library. Finally, check the contents of the original folder to see if they match.

Review

Questions

1 Describe the two panes visible in File Explorer and their functions.

2 How do you use File Explorer's Navigation pane?

3 How do you create a new folder?

4 How do you rename a file or folder?

5 When you copy files, what buttons on the Ribbon do you use? When you move files, what buttons on the Ribbon do you use?

Answers

1 The pane on the left side of the screen is called the Navigation pane and enables you to move through the folders on your hard drive or any external drive you attach. The right-hand contents pane displays the contents of the folder you select in the Navigation pane.

2 Tap or click a right-pointing caret beside a folder name to view folders stored inside that folder. Tap or click a downward-pointing caret beside a folder name to hide folders stored inside that folder. Tap or click a folder name to display its contents in the right-hand contents pane.

3 In the Navigation pane, tap or click the folder in which you want to create the new folder. Then, on the Home tab of the Ribbon, tap or click the New Folder button and type a name for the folder.

4 Select the file or folder. Then, using a keyboard and mouse, press F2, type a new name, and press Enter. Or, using a touch device, tap the Rename button, type a new name, and then tap a blank area on the screen.

5 Use the Copy and Paste buttons when you copy files and the Cut and Paste buttons when you move files.

What you'll learn in this lesson:

- Understanding the World Wide Web

- Understanding the two versions of Internet Explorer

- Working with the Windows 8 native version of Internet Explorer

- Using the Desktop version of Internet Explorer

- Managing Internet Explorer settings

Surfing the Web

In this lesson, you will learn how to use a web browser to view web pages on the Internet using the two versions of Internet Explorer available in Windows 8.

Starting up

You will not need to work with any files for this lesson.

See Lesson 7 in action!

Use the accompanying videos to gain a better understanding of how to use some of the features shown in this lesson. The video lesson for this tutorial can be found at www.DigitalClassroomBooks.com/Windows8.

Understanding the World Wide Web

The World Wide Web, often referred to as *the Web* or *the Internet*, is a collection of computers called *web servers* that are located around the world and contain massive amounts of information. These web servers are powerful computers connected to each other and to a system of computers that share their information with anyone who can connect to the web. The term *web* refers to a spider web, which offers a good way to visualize the connected web servers.

You can connect to the Internet as long as your computer contains a network card and you have signed up with an Internet Service Provider (ISP). Your ISP will provide you with the information you need to connect your computer to the Internet.

There are five web-related concepts to master to get the most out of using the web:

- Web browsers
- Web pages
- Web addresses
- Websites
- Links

Web browsers

You can view information from the Internet using an app called a *web browser*, or *browser*, for short. Windows 8 comes with Internet Explorer, Microsoft's browser. You also can use any number of other popular browsers, such as Firefox, Safari, or Google Chrome. Browsers are typically free and you can download them from the Internet and install them.

Web pages

Web pages present the information you view when you browse the Internet. Each web page can present its information using a combination of text, images, and sounds, including music and videos.

Web addresses

Web addresses uniquely identify each web page. A web address is also called a *URL* (pronounced using its letters), and URL stands for *Uniform Resource Locator*. A typical web address might look like *http://www.example.com*. If you know a web page's address, you can type that address into your browser's address bar to view that page.

Websites

Websites are collections of related web pages. Typically, a website is associated with—and controlled by—a particular person, business, or government organization. You can often identify the type of owner for a site by looking at the last part of the site's address. For example, .com is usually a commercial site, while .gov is a government site, and .org usually indicates the site is controlled by a non-profit organization.

Links

You'll often find links, also called hyperlinks, on a web page. These links connect one web page to another. If you tap or click a link on a web page, your browser displays the page to which the link refers. Links can have different appearances, but they often appear underlined or in a different color than other text on the page.

The Two Versions of Internet Explorer

Two versions of Internet Explorer 10 ship with Windows 8: a Windows 8 native version and a legacy Desktop version. Although the two versions of Internet Explorer share settings and other technological features, the way they work feels very different to the user who has used the legacy Desktop version in the past.

Does one version of Internet Explorer have advantages over the other? That depends on circumstances and what you consider important. For example, the Windows 8 native version operates much faster than the legacy version because the Windows 8 native version doesn't allow you to use plugins or add-in programs, extensions, or toolbars. In particular, the native Windows 8 native version of Internet Explorer doesn't display Flash animations on websites unless Microsoft has added the site to a list of sites allowed to display Flash animations. In addition, the entire screen of the Windows 8 native version is devoted to the webpage you're viewing, with no visible address bar, tabs, or menus unless you choose to display them.

On the other hand, the legacy version of Internet Explorer keeps visible commonly-used browsing tools such as tabs, the address bar, a "favorites" navigational bar, and the capability to run add-ons, plugins, and toolbars.

The Windows 8 native version of Internet Explorer.

The legacy Desktop version of Internet Explorer.

Using the Windows 8 native version of Internet Explorer

To open the Windows 8 native version of Internet Explorer, tap or click its tile on the Start screen. By default, when you open the Windows 8 native version, you see a full screen of the web page you've set as your Home page. You don't see an address bar or any toolbars at the top of the screen.

The Home page is a web page that you can set to be the default web page that displays when you open your web browser. For information on setting a Home page, see "Managing settings" at the end of this lesson.

Navigating through web pages

Switch web pages by typing the address of a new page in the address bar. The address bar appears at the bottom of the screen when you display Internet Explorer's App bar by slightly sliding your finger down from the top of the screen, sliding your finger up from the bottom of the screen, or by right-clicking anywhere on the screen.

The address bar appears at the bottom of the screen when you display the App bar.

If you accidentally display the App bar, you can hide it by repeating the motion you used to display it; either slightly slide your finger down from the top of the screen or up from the bottom of the screen, or right-click anywhere outside the App bar.

The Windows 8 native version of Internet Explorer supports tabbed browsing so you can open multiple web pages and switch among them. To open a new tab and display a second web page, display the App bar and then tap or click the plus sign in the upper-right corner. The screen changes to display a tiled list of favorites—you can tap or click one to visit that page—and a blank address bar. You can type an address in the address bar and tap or click the Go arrow to the right of the address bar to go to that page.

Opening a new tab in Internet Explorer.

As you type, Internet Explorer searches for website names that match what you type; if you see the one you want before you finish typing, tap or click it to display the website.

To switch among Internet Explorer tabs, display the App bar. At the top of the screen, images appear representing each open tab. Tap or click one to view that web page.

Open tabs appear at the top of Internet Explorer.

You can close a tab by tapping or clicking the X that appears in the tab image when you display open tabs on the App bar.

If you've visited several web pages using one tab, you can travel forward and backward between those pages by tapping or clicking the Forward and Back arrows on either side of the address bar.

Pinning a site

If you've used any browser in the past, you've probably learned about establishing shortcuts to web pages you visit frequently. Internet Explorer calls these shortcuts "Favorites" and you can create a favorite in the Windows 8 native version of Internet Explorer using these steps:

1   Display the page you want to establish as a favorite.

2   Display the App bar.

3   At the bottom of the screen, tap or click the Pin Site button.

Click the Pin Site button to add the web page to your favorites.

4 Tap or click Add to Favorites. Internet Explorer adds the site to your list of favorites.

To visit a favorite site, display the App bar. Then, tap or click in the address bar to view sites you visit frequently and Favorite sites. The newest favorite appears at the right edge of tiles. To display a favorite or frequently visited site in a new tab, tap and hold or right-click the tile, and from the shortcut menu that appears, tap or click Open in New Tab.

Favorites appear when you tap or click in the address bar.

To remove a frequent site or a Favorite site, tap and hold or right-click the tile for the site. When the shortcut menu appears, tap or click Remove.

You might have noticed that the shortcut menu gives you the option to pin the site to the Start screen; when you select this option, a tile for the site appears on the Start screen and you can open the site directly from the Start screen.

Browsing privately

By default, when you browse using Internet Explorer, it allows websites leave cookies on your computer. Cookies are small text files that contain pieces of relatively harmless data containing information about a user's activity on the website. In addition, Internet Explorer keeps track of the web pages you visit—known as *history*—and also stores temporary files on your computer.

If you use Internet Explorer's InPrivate mode, you can visit websites without leaving a trail of the visit. When you browse using InPrivate mode, Internet Explorer allows no cookies or temporary files to be stored on your computer and keeps no record of pages you visit.

Cookies can be viewed as an invasion of privacy, but they can serve a valuable purpose. For example, some cookies are designed to notify a website of your activity on a prior visit, and other cookies help websites determine whether to allow you to send sensitive information.

If you want to browse the Internet privately, use InPrivate mode:

1 Display the App bar.

2 At the top right edge of the screen, tap or click the Tab Tools button.

Opening an InPrivate browsing tab.

3 From the shortcut menu that appears, tap or click New InPrivate Tab. Internet Explorer displays a screen telling you that InPrivate mode is enabled and Internet Explorer won't store any information about your browsing session from the current tab.

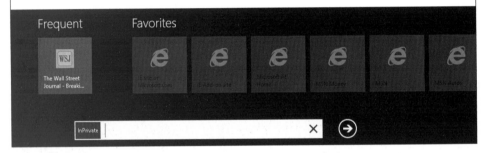

Internet Explorer informs you that InPrivate mode is turned on.

4 In the address bar, type a web address or tap or click a frequently visited or favorite site.

Remember, the private session applies only to the current tab. If you want to open a new tab but continue private browsing, repeat the preceding steps to open that new tab using InPrivate mode.

You can always tell when you're browsing privately: display the App bar and look for the InPrivate button to the left of the address bar and in the image for the browser tab.

Searching the Internet

You've already seen how to use the Windows 8 native version of Internet Explorer to search for websites; as you start typing in the address bar, the default search engine displays tiles for websites with names that contain the letters you type. You can click one to view that page.

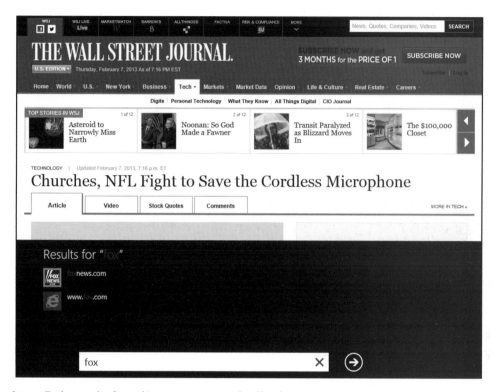

Internet Explorer searches for matching sites as you type in the address bar.

If you keep typing and don't supply a website ending such as .com or .org, Internet Explorer assumes you want to search for the item. The default search engine, Bing, displays a list of possible websites for you to visit.

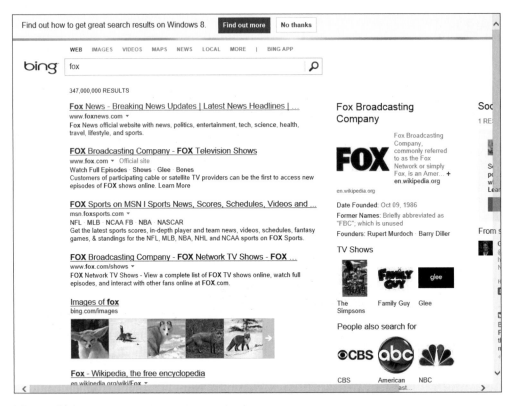

A Bing search page.

 To change the default search engine, see "Manage settings and defaults" at the end of this lesson.

You also can search for information on a page:

1 Press Ctrl+F or display the App bar.

2 Tap or click the Page Tools button on the right side of the address bar (it looks like a wrench).

3 From the shortcut menu that appears, tap or click Find on Page. Internet Explorer replaces the address bar with a Find box, where you can type search text.

Searching for text on a web page.

Printing and sharing web pages

You can print a web page using the Devices charm. Display the page and then display the Charms bar to select the Devices charm. Select a printer and Windows 8 prints the web page.

Use the Devices charm to select a printer while viewing a web page you want to print.

To share a web page, you can use the Mail app or, if you've set up links to a social networking site, you can use the People app. Display the Charms bar and select the Share charm to select an app.

You can share a web page via e-mail or using a social networking site.

Changing your Internet settings

The Windows 8 native version of Internet Explorer uses many of the settings established for the legacy Desktop version of Internet Explorer; for example, both versions of the browser use the same Home page, but you can establish a Home page only from the legacy Desktop version of Internet Explorer. To change those settings, you need to work in the Desktop version of Internet Explorer. Later in this lesson, in the "Managing settings " section, you'll explore some of those settings.

You can, however, change the following settings from the Windows 8 native version of Internet Explorer:

- Delete browsing history.
- Turn on or off whether Internet Explorer reports your physical location to websites.
- Set the zoom level for all pages.
- Turn on or off the Flip Ahead feature.
- Manually switch the language encoding on a web page if Internet Explorer doesn't seem to correctly interpret it.

The Flip Ahead feature is a navigation tool. While reading a multi-page article, using Flip Ahead, you can use a flipping gesture like the one you might use while reading a book to navigate ahead to a subsequent page. The Flip Ahead feature doesn't increase your browsing speed, but it does send information to Microsoft on the pages you view so that Microsoft can improve the Flip Ahead feature.

To change settings for the Windows 8 native version of Internet Explorer, follow these steps:

1   Open the Windows 8 native version of Internet Explorer.

2   Display the Charms bar.

3   Select the Settings charm.

4   Tap or click Internet options to display and change the options listed previously.

Use the Settings charm while viewing the Windows 8 native version of Internet Explorer to change its settings.

On the Settings charm panel for Internet Explorer, you also can select:

• About, which displays the version of Internet Explorer you're using.

• Help, which displays a website with answers to frequently asked questions about Internet Explorer.

• Permissions, which lets you opt to hide or display notifications from Internet Explorer on the Start screen and the Desktop.

Switching to the Desktop view

When using the Windows 8 native version of Internet Explorer, you could come across a website that displays incorrectly. The most likely reason for the page not displaying correctly could be that the site is using Adobe Flash, but Microsoft hasn't included that site in the list of sites permitted to display Flash in the Windows 8 native version of Internet Explorer. In such cases, you can switch to the legacy Desktop version. When you make the switch, the Desktop version of Internet Explorer automatically displays the page you were viewing in the Windows 8 native version, so you don't need to do any additional browsing.

To switch from the Windows 8 native version of Internet Explorer to the Desktop version of Internet Explorer, follow these steps:

1 On the current web page, display the App bar.

2 To the right of the address bar, tap or click the Pages Tools button (the wrench icon).

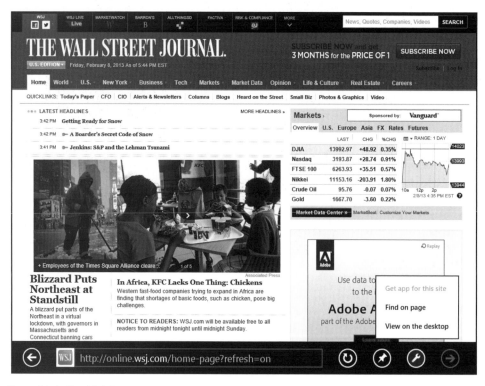

Tap or click the Page Tools button.

3 From the shortcut menu that appears, tap or click View On The Desktop. The legacy Desktop version of Internet Explorer opens and displays the same page you were viewing in the Windows 8 native version of Internet Explorer.

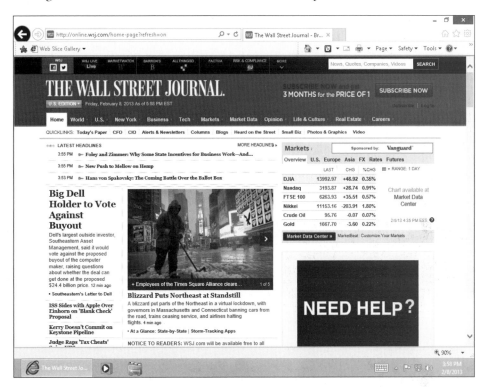

The legacy Desktop version of Internet Explorer displays the same page you were viewing in the Windows 8 native version of Internet Explorer.

By the way, making this switch doesn't close or affect the Windows 8 native version of Internet Explorer; it's still running and you can switch back to it to continue browsing or to close it.

Using the Desktop version of Internet Explorer

In Windows 8, the legacy version of Internet Explorer is available from the Desktop app.

Navigating through web pages

When you open the legacy version of Internet Explorer, you see familiar toolbars and navigational aids. To work with the legacy Desktop version of Internet Explorer, tap or click the Desktop app from the Start screen or press WinKey (⊞)+D. Then, tap or click the Internet Explorer button on the Desktop taskbar.

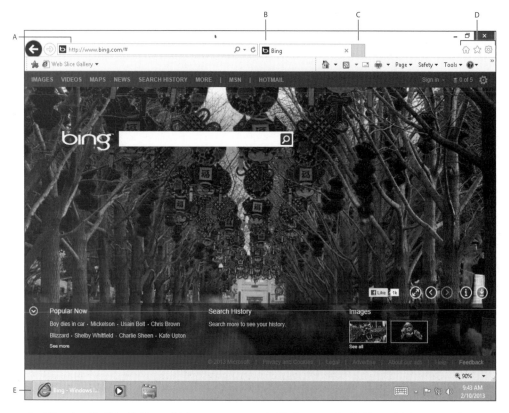

A. Address bar. *B. Tab.* *C. Tap or click here to open a new tab.* *D. Browser tools.* *E. Tap or click here to open Internet Explorer.*

You can switch web pages by typing the address of a new page in the address bar at the top of the screen. You can open additional tabs to browse multiple web pages by tapping or clicking the gray square beside the X at the right edge of the address bar. The screen changes to display a list of favorite sites you have visited. You can tap or click one to visit that page, or you can type in the blank address bar and tap or click the Go arrow to the right of the address bar to visit a page. As you type, Internet Explorer searches for website names that match what you type; if you see the website you want before you finish typing, tap or click the name to display the page.

A. *Forward and Back buttons.* **B.** *Go arrow.*

To close a tab, tap or click the X at the end of the address bar.

If only one X appears at the end of the address bar, tapping or clicking it closes Internet Explorer. You also can close Internet Explorer by tapping or clicking the red X in the upper-right corner on the Internet Explorer window.

To switch among Internet Explorer tabs, tap or click a tab to view that web page. If you've visited several web pages using one tab, you can travel forward and backward between those pages by tapping or clicking the Forward and Back arrows on either side of the address bar.

Creating and managing favorites

In the legacy Desktop version of Internet Explorer, you can also create favorites to web pages you visit frequently. Follow these steps:

1 Display the page you want to establish as a favorite.

2 Tap or click the Favorites button at the right edge of the address bar. (The Favorites button looks like a star.)

3 Tap or click the Add To Favorites button that appears just below the Favorites button. Internet Explorer adds the site to your list of favorites.

Creating a favorite.

To visit a favorite site, tap or click the Favorites button and then tap or click one of the favorites in the list. The newest favorite appears at the bottom of the list.

To remove a Favorite site, tap or click the Favorites button and then tap and hold or right-click the site in the list. When the shortcut menu appears, tap or click Delete.

You also can pin web pages to the Desktop taskbar; you can then display the site without first opening Internet Explorer and navigating to the site. Drag the icon just to the left of the web page address—called the *favicon*—to the task bar.

A. Favicon. *B. This button appears as you drag.*

Navigating using your site visit history

You can navigate to web pages you've visited using the Forward and Back buttons in Internet Explorer, or you can jump directly to a site you've recently visited using your browsing history. When you display the Favorites list, tap or click the History tab. The History tab displays the sites you've visited, which are organized, by default, by date (you can switch to view your history in alphabetical order by site name or ordered by most visited). You also can search through your site visit history by supplying a keyword.

Searching the Internet

In the legacy Desktop version of Internet Explorer, as in the Windows 8 native version, you can search for information on the Internet by typing in the address bar. As you type, Internet Explorer suggests websites that match the characters you type. If you supply a website extension, such as .com or .org, and press Enter or tap or click the Go arrow, Internet Explorer takes you to the site you typed, assuming you typed a valid web address.

If you don't supply a valid website extension, Internet Explorer assumes you want to search the Internet for the phrase you typed, and Bing, the default search engine, displays a list of potential websites for you to visit.

You can tap or click the Search button in the address bar, but if you haven't supplied a valid website extension, Internet Explorer defaults to searching.

Browsing privately

By default, when you browse using Internet Explorer, Internet Explorer allows websites to leave cookies on your computer. Cookies are small text files containing pieces of relatively harmless data containing information about a user's activity when visiting a website. In addition, Internet Explorer tracks the web pages you visit and saves them as part of your browsing history. Last, Internet Explorer stores temporary files on your computer.

When you browse privately, you visit websites without leaving a trail of the visit; Internet Explorer allows no cookies or temporary files to be stored on your computer and keeps no record of pages you visit.

If you want to browse the Internet privately, use InPrivate mode:

1   Open Internet Explorer on the Desktop.

2   At the top right edge of the screen, tap or click the Tools button (the one that looks like a gear).

3   From the shortcut menu that appears, tap or click Safety.

Opening an InPrivate browsing session.

4   Tap or click InPrivate Browsing. Internet Explorer opens a new instance of itself—you'll see two Internet Explorer buttons on the Desktop taskbar. The window that appears contains the InPrivate button at the left edge of the address bar; a message appears explaining that InPrivate mode is enabled; and Internet Explorer doesn't store any information about your browsing session.

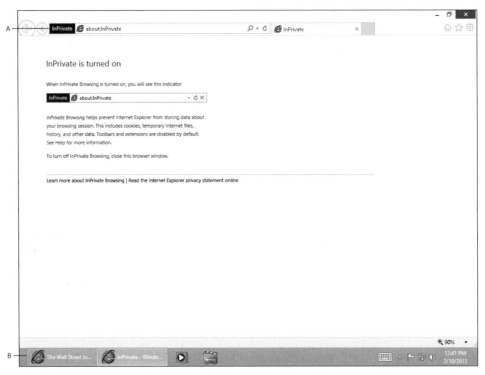

A. InPrivate button. B. Two Internet Explorer sessions.

5   In the address bar, type a web address or use the Favorites button to tap or click a frequently visited or a favorite site.

The private session applies only to the current InPrivate instance of Internet Explorer, but you can open new tabs in the session as you browse privately.

As long as the InPrivate button appears at the left edge of the address bar, you know that you're browsing privately.

Managing settings

As you learned earlier in this lesson, you can manage some browser settings from the Settings charm when you open the Windows 8 native app version of Internet Explorer. You can control many more of Internet Explorer's settings from the legacy Desktop app.

Changing interface settings

You can customize the default appearance of the legacy Internet Explorer app. For example, the legacy Internet Explorer doesn't display the Command bar or the Favorites bar, but you can add these screen elements.

1 Tap and hold or right-click the Internet Explorer title bar to display a shortcut menu.

2 Tap or click a screen element you want to add. In this example, add the Command bar; it helps you quickly print web pages, start an InPrivate browsing session, and change Internet Explorer settings, so you'll use it in the rest of this lesson.

A. Command bar. *B. Screen elements you can add.*

The Favorites bar can display buttons for favorites you've established. To do so, display the Favorites bar. Then, tap or click the Favorites button to display your favorites. You'll see a folder called Favorites at the top of the list. Drag any listed favorite into that folder, and a button for it appears on the Favorites bar.

Setting your home page

The home page is the web page that appears when you open Internet Explorer (or any browser). The default home page is Bing, Microsoft's search engine but, you can change the home page to any web page you want.

Both versions of Internet Explorer use the same home page.

1   Display the web page you want to use as your home page.

2   Tap or click the Tools button to display a menu. (The Tools button looks like a gear and it's located in the upper-right corner; you can also use the Tools button on the Command bar.)

A. Home button. B. Tools button.

You can tap the Home button in the upper-right corner or on the Commands bar to quickly redisplay your home page at any time.

3 Tap or click Internet Options to display the Internet Options dialog box.

4 In the General tab, tap or click the Use Current button. The address for your home page changes to the address of the page you're currently viewing.

If you don't tap or click the Use Current button and instead tap or click the Use New Tab button, Internet Explorer sets a blank tab as your home page; starting with a blank page can considerably speed up browsing.

5 Tap or click OK.

Tap or click the Use Current button to set the current web page as your home page.

You can set Internet Explorer to open several pages (and therefore have several different home pages) by listing the page addresses in the box at the top of the General tab. After you list each page, don't tap or click the Use Current button; instead, just tap or click OK.

Adding a search engine

Internet Explorer's default search engine is Bing, owned by Microsoft. If you prefer a different search engine, you can choose to set that search engine as the default engine Internet Explorer uses. When you choose a search engine, you choose it for both the Windows 8 native version and the legacy version of Internet Explorer. Follow these steps:

1   With Internet Explorer open, tap or click the down arrow beside the Search magnifying glass in the address bar. Tap or click the Add button in the lower-right corner of the menu that appears. Internet Explorer opens the Internet Explorer Gallery web page in a new tab.

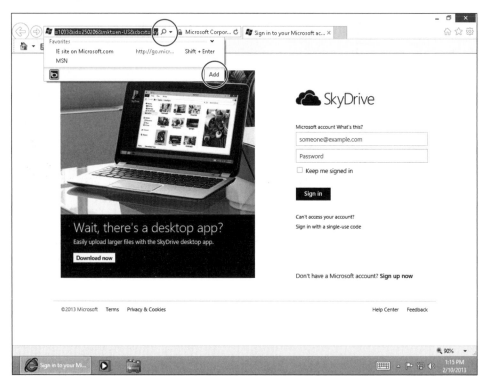

Tap or click the down arrow to add another search engine.

2 Scroll down, look for the search engine you want to use, and tap or click it. In this example, tap or click Start Page (Start Page is a search engine that protects your privacy by not keeping track of your searches). The search engine you choose appears on a new web page.

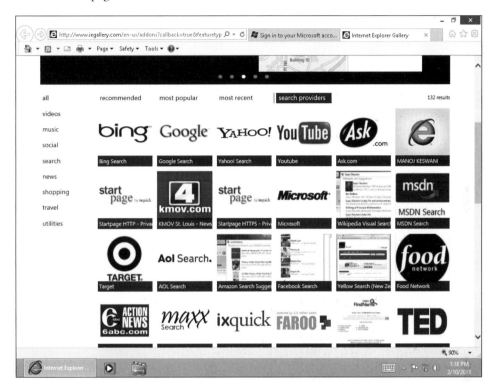

Tap or click a search engine.

3   Tap or click Add to Internet Explorer. The Add Search Provider dialog box appears.

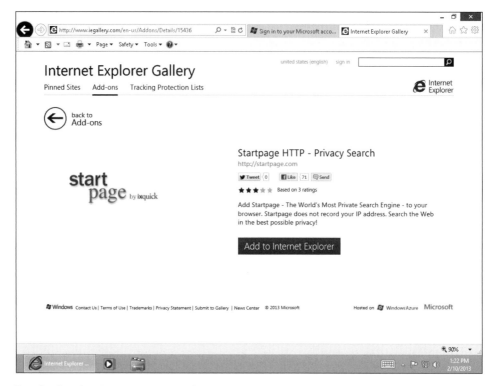

Your selected search engine appears on a new web page.

4 In the Add Search Provider dialog box, tap or click the Add button. Internet Explorer adds the search engine and sets it as the default search engine. It then redisplays the web page where you added the search engine.

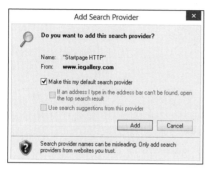

Use this dialog box to add a search engine, and if you want, set it as the default search engine.

To set the new search engine as the default search engine, tap or click the Make This My Default Search Provider checkbox.

5 Tap or click the tab's X to close it.

The next time you type in the address bar, notice that two search engines appear; the one on the left is the one you selected as the default search engine.

Changing the default search engine

If you've added several search engines, tested each of them, and now you've decided on one that you want to use as the default search engine. Here's how to change the default search engine:

1   On the Commands bar, tap or click Tools.

2   Tap or click Manage add-ons. The Manage Add-ons window appears.

3   On the left side, tap or click Search Providers. Your installed search providers appear; the default search engine displays "Default" in the Status column.

4   Tap or click the search engine you want to use by default.

5   In the lower-right corner, tap or click the Set as Default button.

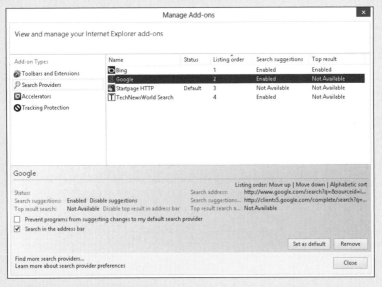

Selecting a new default search engine.

6   Tap or click the Close button.

   You also can remove a search engine you no longer need by tapping the Remove button.

Setting your default browser

Windows 8 contains two versions of Internet Explorer; the version that opens when you click a link depends on where you are in Windows 8. If you're working in a Windows 8 native app and click a link, then the Windows 8 native version of Internet Explorer opens. If you're working on the Desktop using a legacy app and you click a link, the legacy version of Internet Explorer opens.

Windows 8 allows you to change this behavior by choosing one of them to be the default browser at all times.

1   Open legacy Internet Explorer on the Desktop.

2   Tap or click the Tools button in the upper-right corner (the one that looks like a gear) or tap or click the Tools button on the Command bar.

3   Tap or click Internet Options to display the Internet Options dialog box.

4   Tap or click the Programs tab.

5   In the first section of the tab, tap or click the list box to choose how you open links. Choose Always in Internet Explorer to use the Windows 8 native version or Always in Internet Explorer on the Desktop to use the legacy version.

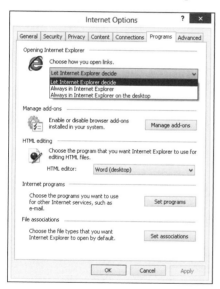

Decide which version of Internet Explorer opens when you tap or click a link.

6   Tap or click OK.

Housekeeping

To ensure your browsing experience runs smoothly, you should consider deleting, from time to time, temporary files, browsing history, and cookies.

Internet Explorer stores temporary files—copies of web pages you visit—in the Temporary Internet Files folder on your hard drive. Internet Explorer uses those files to speed up your browsing experience; when you visit a page you've visited in the past, Internet Explorer loads the copy stored in the Temporary Internet Files folder instead of loading a new copy. This process saves lots of time, especially if you're using a slow Internet connection, but it also takes up lots of room on your hard drive—250 MB, by default.

Browsing history, on the other hand, doesn't take up much space on your hard drive. Even if you surf voraciously, your history file will probably not exceed 1 MB. But it does contain a list of every site you've visited and you might not want that list available to anyone who sits down at your computer.

Last, as mentioned previously, cookies are typically innocuous, but there are companies out there that exploit them. After a while, as you visit websites, you might start seeing advertising that seems surprisingly aware of your interests—almost as if it were targeted at you. If you find that disconcerting, you can delete your cookies. Be aware that cookies will replenish themselves as you continue browsing.

It's also possible that your bank's website will no longer recognize you if you delete cookies—and then you'll need to go through the bank's process of re-establishing you as a valid visitor. While the process is rarely difficult, you might find it annoying.

To delete information that Internet Explorer stores, follow these steps:

1   Open legacy Internet Explorer.

2   Tap or click the Tools button on the Command bar.

3   Tap or click Internet Options.

4   In the Browsing History section of the General tab, you can tap or click the Delete Browsing History on Exit checkbox to always clear your browsing history.

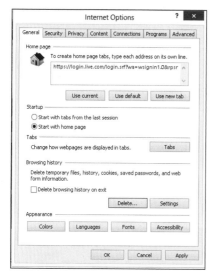

You can delete browsing history every time you close Internet Explorer.

5   Tap or click the Delete button to display the Delete Browsing History dialog box.

Once you've set your preference for deleting browsing history when you close Internet Explorer, you can skip Steps 1–5 and open the Delete Browsing History dialog box directly. Tap or click the Safety button on Internet Explorer's Command bar and then tap or click Delete Browsing History.

6   Tap or click the checkboxes beside the browsing history elements you want to delete. Read the descriptions under each item to decide if you want to delete that type of information.

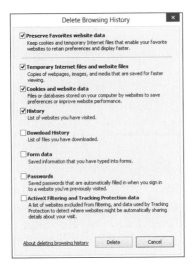

Use this dialog box to select the types of information you want to delete.

To keep Internet Explorer working quickly, make sure a checkmark appears in the Preserve Favorites Website Data checkbox. Deleting Download History and Form Data probably won't get you into any trouble, but if you store passwords in Internet Explorer, read the sidebar, "Passwords and Browsers" before you delete passwords.

Passwords and Browsers

It's really not safe to allow your browser to remember passwords, because then anyone sitting at your computer could log onto, for example, your bank's website. It's also unsafe to use the same password everywhere; if anyone ever gets that password, all your protected information is compromised.

To avoid the problem of saving passwords in your browser and using multiple passwords, consider using a password manager browser plug-in app like RoboForm or LastPass. However, be aware that the Windows 8 native version of Internet Explorer doesn't permit plug-in apps—only legacy Internet Explorer (along with non-Microsoft browsers like Firefox and Chrome) supports plug-ins. So, if you're going to avoid allowing your browser to save passwords, you'll need to use legacy Internet Explorer—and a password manager plug-in—when you visit sites that require passwords.

If you decide to store passwords in Internet Explorer, be careful about deleting them unless you have another source that can provide them to you after you delete them from Internet Explorer.

7   Tap or click the Delete button and then tap or click OK to close the Internet Options dialog box.

Self study

1 Using both the Windows 8 native version and the legacy Desktop version of Internet Explorer, practice navigating to a website and then pinning the website or "creating a favorite."

2 Review how to manage settings for both the Windows 8 native version of Internet Explorer and the legacy Desktop version of Internet Explorer.

Review

Questions

1 Are the settings for the two versions of Internet Explorer that come with Windows 8 independent of each other?

2 Describe how to browse privately in both versions of Internet Explorer.

3 Describe how to pin a site from the Windows 8 native version of Internet Explorer.

4 Describe how to add a favorite to the legacy Desktop version of Internet Explorer.

5 How can you view a web page in the Windows 8 native version of Internet Explorer and then easily view it in the legacy Desktop version?

6 How can you delete Internet temporary files, browsing history, and cookies and why might you want to do so?

Answers

1 No. The settings you set—such as your home page—will affect both versions of the browser.

2 In the native Windows 8 version, display the App bar and tap or click the Tab Tools button. From the menu that appears, tap or click New InPrivate tab. In the legacy Desktop version of Internet Explorer, tap or click the Safety button on the Command bar and then tap or click InPrivate Browsing. Or, tap or click the Gear tool, tap or click Safety, and then tap or click InPrivate Browsing.

3 Navigate to the site you want to pin; then tap or click the Pin Site button and choose whether to pin the site to the Start screen or to add it to Internet Explorer favorites.

4 Navigate to the site you want to add as a favorite. Then, tap or click the Favorites button (it looks like a star) in the upper-right corner of the window. Last, tap or click the Add to Favorites button. You can edit the favorite's name; when you finish, tap or click the Add button.

5 While viewing the page in the Windows 8 native version of Internet Explorer, display the App bar. Then, tap or click the Page Tools button (it looks like a wrench) and tap or click View on the Desktop.

6 You'll save lots of hard drive space if you periodically delete Internet temporary files. Deleting browsing history deletes the trail of sites you have visited; you might want to delete browsing history to preserve your privacy. Cookies are relatively harmless, but if you don't want your website activities to be tracked, you can delete them; they will, in all likelihood, reappear. To delete these browser elements, open legacy Internet Explorer. Then, tap or click the Safety button on the Command bar and tap or click Delete Browsing History.

What you'll learn in this lesson:

- Setting up an e-mail account
- Changing account settings
- Receiving, reading, creating, and sending e-mail
- Importing contacts into the People app
- Creating contacts

E-mail and Contacts

You can use the Windows 8 Mail and People apps to communicate with others via e-mail. The Mail app shares the contacts you store in the People app.

Starting up

You will not need to work with any files for this lesson.

For all the Windows 8 native apps discussed in this lesson to work, you must sign in to them using a Microsoft account. If you are signed in to your computer using a local account, you'll be prompted to provide a Microsoft account when you open one of these apps. If you haven't yet set up a Microsoft account, see Lesson 1, "Getting Started with Windows 8."

See Lesson 8 in action!

Use the accompanying videos to gain a better understanding of how to use some of the features shown in this lesson. The video lesson for this tutorial can be found at www.DigitalClassroomBooks.com/Windows8.

Running the Mail App

Electronic mail—*e-mail*—has changed the way people communicate. Using e-mail, you can send a message or a file almost instantly to any place in the world. An e-mail message travels from your computer, over the Internet, to the recipient at another computer. To send and receive e-mail messages, you use an e-mail account, typically set up through an Internet Service Provider (ISP). Each e-mail message contains an electronic address used to identify the recipient the same way the US Postal Service uses printed addresses on mail pieces to deliver paper mail.

To create and send e-mail messages, you use an e-mail program. The program you use can be one that you install on your computer—such as the Mail app that comes with Windows 8—or you can use your browser to view your e-mail, as do users of Gmail.com, Yahoo.com, or Outlook.com accounts. Some ISPs, such as Cox Communications, also offer a browser-based interface that you can use to work with e-mail.

There is one primary difference between e-mail programs installed on a computer and those accessible from browser-based interfaces: When you use a program installed on your computer, your e-mail messages are stored on a server and also on your computer. However, when you use a web-based interface program, your e-mail messages are stored only on a server and not on your computer.

Many people use multiple e-mail addresses, often for different purposes. Some people use different e-mail addresses to segregate different types of mail, using one for shopping and another for business communication, and even a third for personal communication.

The point is that you might have multiple e-mail addresses for which you want to collect e-mail, and the Windows 8 native Mail app lets you collect e-mail from a variety of e-mail addresses. You just need to identify the various e-mail addresses you use for the Mail app.

By using a program installed on your computer—such as the Mail app—you can collect e-mail from several different accounts. Some, but not all, web-based services also enable you to collect e-mail from several different accounts.

Meet the Mail app

To access the Mail app, tap or click its tile on the Windows 8 Start screen.

If you have signed in to your computer using a local account, you'll see a prompt asking you to provide a Microsoft account. Supply your Microsoft account username and password and tap or click the Sign In button.

If you signed in to your computer or the Mail app using a Microsoft account that's also a Hotmail.com or Outlook.com e-mail address (@hotmail.com, @live.com, or @outlook.com), the Mail app automatically downloads the last two weeks' worth of messages, and your screen might look similar to the one shown in the figure.

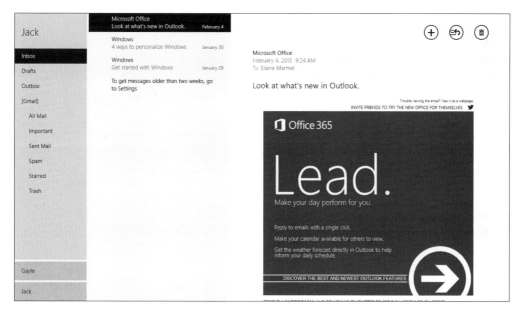

A typical screen in the Mail app.

If your screen resolution is less than 1366 x 768, you'll see only two columns rather than the three columns shown in the figure.

The accounts you have set up will appear at the bottom of the left column. When you select an account, its name appears at the top of the left column and all its corresponding information appears in the set of folders below. Note that the folder names can change when you select a different account.

To view the messages in a folder, click a folder; the list of messages appears in the middle column. Finally, the right column displays the contents of the message selected in the middle column.

Setting up an e-mail account in the Mail app

You can set up an e-mail account from within the Mail app, and you can set up the Mail app to collect e-mail from the following types of accounts:

- Hotmail (which include Hotmail.com, Live.com, and MSN)
- Outlook.com
- Exchange server
- Office 365
- Google mail (Gmail.com)
- AOL
- Yahoo

1   Open the Mail app.

2   Display the Charms bar.

3   Tap or click Settings.

4   Tap or click Add An Account. The types of accounts you can add appear.

 If you already have an account here, you will have to tap or click on Accounts before you can see the "Add an Account" button.

Select a type of account to add to the Mail app.

5 Tap or click the type of account you want to add.

The Other Account option enables you to add IMAP e-mail accounts that aren't already listed. If you select Other Account, you'll see an option to add a POP3 account. Note, however, that the Mail app doesn't support POP3 accounts presently; you'll see an error message if you select POP3.

6 Supply the e-mail address and password for the account you want to add to the Mail app and any other information for which the account type prompts you.

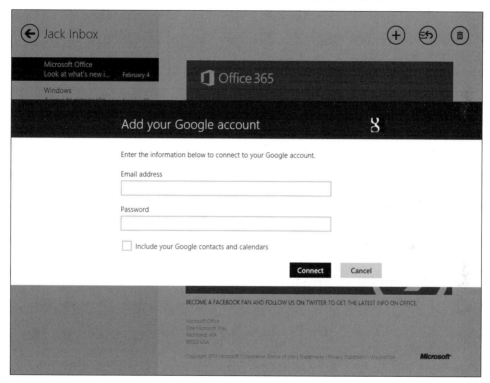

Supply e-mail address information for the account you're adding.

If you add a Google account (Gmail), you can opt to also add your Google contacts to the Windows 8 People app and your Google calendars to the Windows 8 Calendar app.

7 Tap or click the Connect button. Mail creates your account and assigns it a generic name based on the type of account you added.

Changing Mail app settings

While you probably don't want to make changes to too many Mail app settings, there are three settings worth examining: the name of your e-mail account, whether the Mail app automatically downloads external images, and the length of time you want the Mail app to use when downloading new messages.

To change these settings, you need to display the Mail app's Settings pane.

1 Display the Charms bar.

2 Tap or click the Settings charm.

3 Tap or click Accounts.

4 Tap or click the account you want to change. The settings for the account you selected appear.

Making changes to your account.

To change the account name to something more meaningful, type the name you want to appear in the left column of the Mail app in the Account Name box. We suggest that you change the Your Name entry to something more meaningful than your e-mail address; the information in the Your Name box appears when you send an e-mail from the Mail app.

By default, the Mail app downloads only the last two weeks' worth of messages, but you can change that setting; to change the amount of e-mail you want downloaded, open the Download e-mail from list box and make a selection.

Last, you might want to change the way the Mail app behaves when downloading images contained in e-mail messages because, by default, Mail downloads images. Many messages sent by spammers contain *web beacons*, which are graphics that notify the message sender when you open a message. If you don't change Mail's default setting for downloading images, you could potentially receive lots of spam. To change the setting, tap or click the Automatically Download External Images option to Off. Then, when you receive a message containing images, you'll see a prompt that you can tap or click to display those images. That way, you choose the images you see (and the information you might accidentally send back to the sender).

Receiving and reading mail

Incoming e-mail messages appear in the Mail app in the Inbox of the account that received the message. By default, the Mail app checks for messages every so often while you are online, but you can force the Mail app to check for messages whenever you want.

To change the frequency with which the Mail app checks for new messages, display the Account options panel and select a frequency for the Download New Mail option. This option works independently for each account you set up.

To check for messages and read them, follow these steps:

1 In the Mail app, display the App bar by swiping down slightly from the top of the screen or by right-clicking anywhere on the screen.

2   Tap or click the Sync button. In the upper-right corner, an indicator appears to let you know that the Mail app is checking for messages.

The "Syncing…" message appears when you check for new e-mail.

3   To read a message, tap or click the message in the middle pane; its content appears in the right pane. You can tap or click the message in the right pane and then scroll vertically to read additional content.

Creating and sending an e-mail

You can use the buttons in the upper-right corner of the Mail app to either create a new mail message or respond to a message you've received. Whether you reply or create a new message, the basic steps are the same:

1   In the upper-right corner of the Mail app window, tap or click the Plus sign button to create a new message or the button immediately to its right to reply to a message.

Use the New, Respond, and Delete buttons when creating or responding to messages.

If you tap or click the Reply button, the Mail app gives you the option to reply to the message sender, reply to everyone who originally received the message, or forward the message to recipients you identify.

2   If you created a new message, fill in the e-mail addresses of the recipient(s) in the To and Cc boxes; if you want to send blind copies or set the message priority, tap or click the Show More link below the Cc box.

When you create a message, you can tap or click the plus sign beside the To, Cc, or Bcc boxes to select recipients from the People app. Or you can type in e-mail addresses.

3   To type your message, tap or click the right side of the message window and start typing. You can do any of the following as you create message text:

Available message formatting options.

- You can format text if you select it; formatting options automatically appear when you select text.

- To add an emoticon, display the App bar by swiping down slightly from the top of the screen or by right-clicking anywhere on the screen. Then, tap or click the Emoticons button.

- You can tap or click the More button to create a bulleted list, a numbered list, or to use the Undo and Redo commands.

- You can add an attachment by tapping or clicking the Attachments button; the Mail app displays a screen that helps you select the file you want to attach. By default, the Mail app assumes the file is a picture, but you can navigate to any folder on your computer.

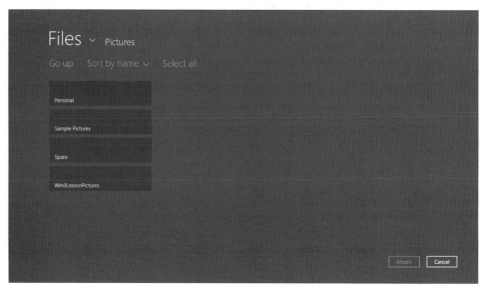

The Mail app allows you to send a file in an e-mail as an attachment.

4 When you're ready to send your message, tap or click the Send button in the upper-right corner of the message window.

If you change your mind and don't want to send the message, tap or click the X in the upper-right corner and choose Delete Draft. You can choose Save Draft to place the message in your Drafts folder, where you can work on it at a later time.

Searching through e-mail

You can search for mail in the Mail app. Follow these steps:

1 Tap or click the folder you want to search.

2 Display the Charms bar.

3 Tap or click the Search charm.

4 Type your search term.

5 Tap or click the magnifying glass beside the search term, and the Mail app searches through the selected folder for e-mail containing your search term.

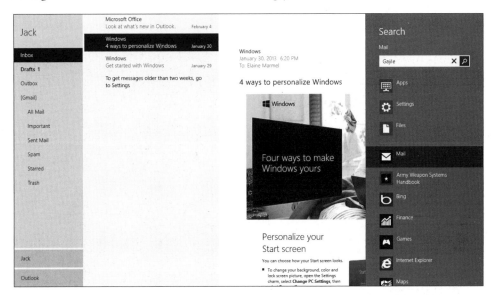

Deleting e-mail

Once you've handled a message—read it and responded to it or forwarded it, or determined it required no further action on your part—you can delete it. Select the message in the middle pane and then tap or click the Delete button (it contains an image of a trash can) in the upper-right corner of the Mail app window.

Using the People app

Use the People app to store contacts. You can use the contacts stored in the People app when you create an e-mail message or a calendar appointment.

You can create contacts in the People app or you can import contacts—from e-mail accounts you set up in the Mail app or from social networks to which you belong.

Importing contacts into the People app

Be aware that importing contacts into the People app can affect other apps. For example, if you import your friends from your Facebook account, the People app adds them as contacts, and your Facebook photos also appear in the Photos app.

In addition, if you maintain a contact in more than one social network, you might end up with duplicates in the People app, even though the People app will try to identify duplicates and avoid importing them.

To import contacts from a social network, follow these steps:

1   From the Start screen, tap or click the People app to open it.

2   Display the Charms bar by sliding in slightly from the right side of the screen, pressing WinKey (⊞)+C, or placing your mouse in the upper- or lower-right corner of the screen.

3   Tap or click the Settings charm.

4   Tap or click Add an account to display the available social networks from which you can import contacts.

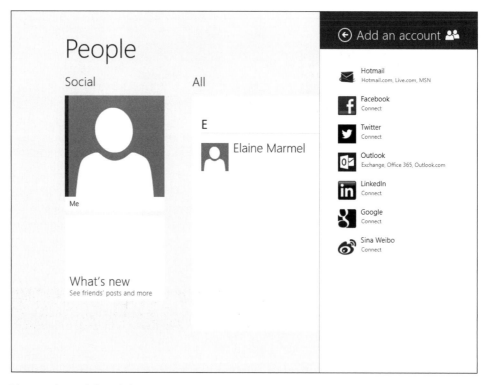

Select a social network from which to import contacts.

5   Tap or click a social network.

6   Supply the information requested by the selected social network. The People app imports your contacts from that network.

Creating a contact

You don't need to import contacts, you can create them. To create a contact in the People app, follow these steps:

1   In the People app, display the App bar by swiping down slightly from the top of the screen or by right-clicking anywhere on the screen.

2   Tap or click the New contact button.

Tap or click the New contact button.

3 On the New contact screen that appears, fill in the information for the contact.

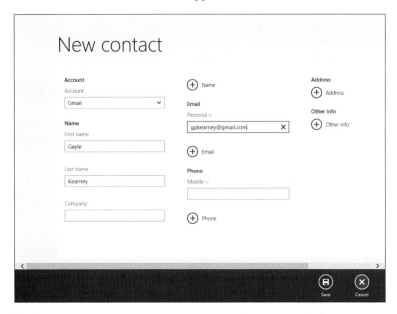

Creating a new contact.

4 When you finish, tap or click the Save button.

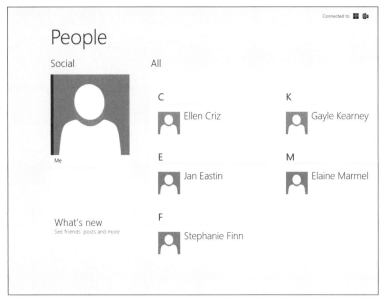

Use the People app to keep all your contacts organized.

By default, the People app sorts your contacts by first name. You can change to sorting by last name from the People app's Options screen. Display the Charms bar by sliding in slightly from the right side of the screen, pressing WinKey (⊞)+C, or placing your mouse in the upper- or lower-right corner of the screen. Then, tap or click Settings and tap or click Options.

You can view any contact's information from the main window of the People app by tapping or clicking the contact's name. To redisplay your list of contacts, display the App bar by swiping down slightly from the top of the screen or by right-clicking anywhere on the screen. Then, tap or click the Home button.

You will notice a placeholder image box appears at the left side of the main screen of the People app, just above the What's New block; the placeholder box is labeled "Me." If you set up a login picture for Windows 8, that picture will replace the placeholder. And, if you tap or click the Me box, you see information about you, including a link to your public Facebook profile, a list of your Facebook status updates and tweets, and the Facebook photos that appear in the Photos app.

You can tap or click the What's New block to display the What's New screen, which includes a tile for each Facebook or Twitter contact, Facebook status updates, and tweets.

Self study

1 Add an e-mail account to the Mail app.

2 Add a contact to the People app.

Review

Questions

1 How do you change the frequency with which the Mail app downloads an e-mail?

2 How do you force the Mail app to download e-mail?

3 How do you create a new e-mail?

4 How do you reply to an e-mail?

5 How do you display formatting tools for an e-mail you're creating?

6 How do you create a new contact?

Answers

1 While using the Mail app, display the Charms bar by sliding in slightly from the right side of the screen, pressing WinKey (⊞)+C, or placing your mouse in the upper- or lower-right corner of the screen. Then, tap or click the Settings charm and tap or click Accounts. Select the account for which you want to set the frequency for downloading e-mail and change the Download New E-mail setting.

2 While using the Mail app, display the App bar by swiping down slightly from the top of the screen or by right-clicking anywhere on the screen. Then, tap the Sync button.

3 While using the Mail app, tap or click the plus button in the upper-right corner of the screen.

4 While using the Mail app, tap or click the middle button in the upper-right corner of the screen.

5 While working on a message (after choosing to create a new message or respond to an existing message), display the App bar by swiping down slightly from the top of the screen or by right-clicking anywhere on the screen.

6 While working in the People app, display the App bar by swiping down slightly from the top of the screen or by right-clicking anywhere on the screen. Then, tap or click the New Contact button.

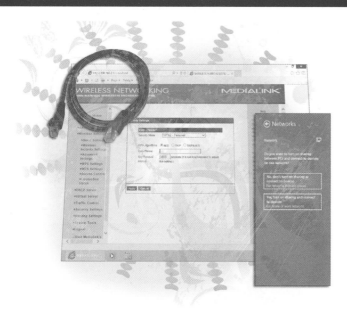

What you'll learn in this lesson:

- The basics of networking
- Networking and hardware
- Networking and share files

Networking with Windows 8

If you use more than one computer, you can network those computers together so they share information. In this lesson, you learn about the hardware and software settings to make to share information on your computers.

Starting up

In this lesson, you will work with several files from the Windows09lessons folder. Make sure that you have loaded the files from the Win8Lessons folder onto your hard drive from *www.DigitalClassroomBooks.com/Windows8*. For more information, see "Loading lesson files" in the Starting Up section of this book.

See Lesson 9 in action!

Use the accompanying videos to gain a better understanding of how to use some of the features shown in this lesson. The video lesson for this tutorial can be found at www.DigitalClassroomBooks.com/Windows8.

The basics of networking

A network of computers is composed of two or more computers that are connected so they can share information and devices. After you network your computers, you can, for example, copy pictures from your tablet PC to your desktop PC or to the external hard drive attached to your desktop PC. You also can print documents from your tablet PC to the printer attached to your desktop PC.

Sharing without networking

Windows automatically sets up some public folders for each account on a computer; you'll find a public folder in each of the default libraries: Public Documents, Public Music, Public Pictures, and Public Videos.

If multiple people share the same computer and each person has his or her own account on the computer, you can use the public folders to share information across accounts—no networking required. For example, suppose that your husband, who uses one account on your home computer, took some pictures of your dog and cat. You use a different account on the same home computer, and you want to include your husband's photos in the family Christmas greeting card. Your husband can copy the pictures to the public folder, and you can then use them.

 You also can share files using SkyDrive; see Lesson 10, "Sharing Device Settings and Content."

In this example, we'll copy two pictures from the Win8Lessons folder for this lesson to the Public Pictures folder. As you saw in Lesson 6, "Using Files and Folders," copying files is a two–part operation: you first select and copy a file or multiple files, and then paste.

1   Make sure you are in the Desktop app by tapping or clicking on it from the Start screen or pressing WinKey (⊞)+D on your keyboard.

2   Tap or click the File Explorer in the task bar at the bottom of the screen and in File Explorer, use the Navigation pane to navigate to the Windows09lessons folder that you saved to your hard drive.

3   Select the files named **Windows0901-01.jpg** and **Windows0901-02.jpg**.

 To select both files using the keyboard and mouse, click the first file and then press and hold Ctrl as you click the second file. To select both files using a touch device, display Item Check Boxes using the View tab on the Ribbon; then, tap each file to check the boxes beside the file names.

4   On the Home tab of the Ribbon, tap or click the Copy button.

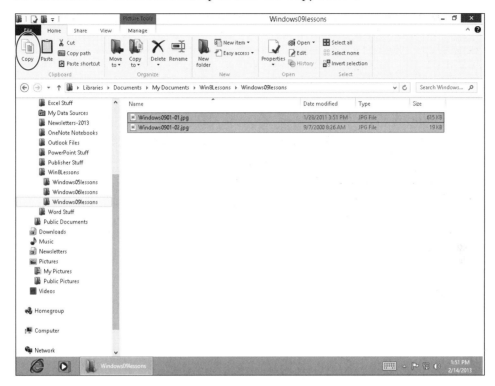

Select the files you want to copy and tap or click the Copy button on the Ribbon.

5   In the Navigation pane, tap or click the caret beside the Pictures folder.

6   Tap or click the Public Pictures folder.

7   Tap or click the Paste button on the Ribbon. A copy of each file appears in the Public Pictures folder.

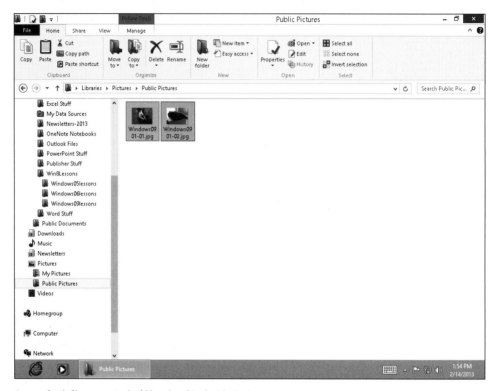

A copy of each file appears in the folder selected in the Navigation pane.

To verify that the originals still appear in the Windows09lessons folder, use the Navigation pane to redisplay that folder.

Anyone using a computer connected to your network can see, copy, delete, move, or edit the files in the Public Pictures folder.

Establishing a network is a two-part process:

• You must set up the network using hardware.

• You must share files among the computers on the network.

Networking and hardware

To establish a network, each computer that you intend to connect to the network must contain a network card (most modern computers do come with network cards). In its simplest form, you can create a network between two computers by connecting their network cards using a network cable.

A typical network cable.

Remember the title of this section: it covers the basics of networking. In a large network, you'll find a number of devices not discussed here. The discussion in this lesson focuses primarily on a simple network you might find in a small office or a home office; such a network can function with three basic pieces of equipment: a network card in each computer, a router, and if you want to connect to the Internet, a modem.

For example, you may want to create a network between three or four computers, and have all the computers in the network share information with each other. For this type of setup, you need a *router*, which is a device that routes information between computer networks. If you intend to connect devices wirelessly, which is the ideal way to connect a mobile device such as a tablet PC, the router you use must also include functions that enable it to serve as a wireless access point. Most routers sold today include these functions.

A router.

You can purchase a router at a local retailer, such as Staples, Best Buy, or Walmart, or you can buy a router online. Routers commonly used in the small office/home office environment contain four *ports* (places where you can plug in a network cable) so using one router, you can connect up to four devices using wires. Most routers also contain a special fifth port that you can use to connect your router to the Internet so that all the computers connected to the router can use the same Internet connection.

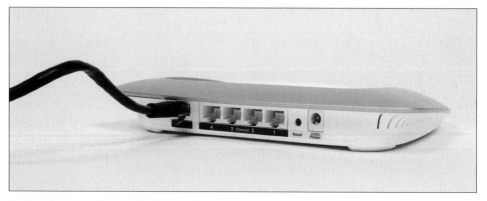

The back of a router typically contains four ports that you can use to connect devices and a fifth port to connect to the Internet.

Setting up your router

To use a router to create a network, plug the router into an electrical outlet. Then, connect each of your computers to the router. If you're connecting a desktop PC to a network, you'll probably run a network cable from the network port on the back of the computer to one port on the router. For details on connecting a portable device wirelessly to the network, see "Connecting wirelessly to the router" later in this lesson.

When you first establish a network connection, Windows will ask you whether you want to turn on sharing and connect to devices. If you turn on sharing, your PC can join a HomeGroup. You will read more about HomeGroups later in this lesson. If you see this prompt, choose to turn on sharing.

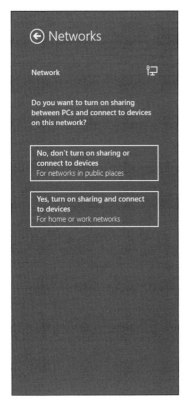

Turn on sharing to enable your PC to join a HomeGroup.

Some printers can serve as network printers; if you have such a printer, you can connect it to a port on the router to make it available to all computers on the network. If your printer doesn't have the capability to serve as a network printer, you can still make it available to all computers on the network by sharing it through your HomeGroup. See "Setting up a HomeGroup" later in this lesson.

If you're planning to connect any wireless devices to your network, read the next section, but do not connect your router to the modem you'll use to connect to the Internet. You will carry out this connection later in this lesson.

Once you've established connections between your computers and the router, you'll see an icon in the Desktop app system tray and when you display the Settings charm; the name of the network to which the computer is connected appears below the icon. (There are two different icons that could appear: one that represents wired network connections, and another that represents wireless network connections. The icon you see depends on the type of network connection you use.)

On computers using wired network connections, this icon appears in the System Tray of the Desktop app and when you display the Settings charm.

On computers using wireless network connections, this icon appears in the System Tray of the Desktop app and when you display the Settings charm.

Securing your wireless network

If you plan to wirelessly connect any devices to your network, you should secure your network before doing so. If you don't secure your wireless network, anyone with a wireless device within range of your network will be able to connect to it. For example, someone could park a car in front of your home or office and connect to your (or any) available unsecured wireless network. Once connected, that person can go through your files, steal information from you, and even plant a virus.

When you secure a wireless network, you set up a password for the network. Any devices that want to join your network are prompted to supply the password. That way, you control the devices that are allowed to connect to your network and have access to your files.

Securing a wireless network is not difficult; you open a web browser and navigate to the IP address for your router. You can find the IP address in the documentation that came with your router; it is typically 192.168.0.1 or 192.168.1.1. You'll probably be prompted for the username and password to edit your router's setting; that information will also appear in your router's documentation.

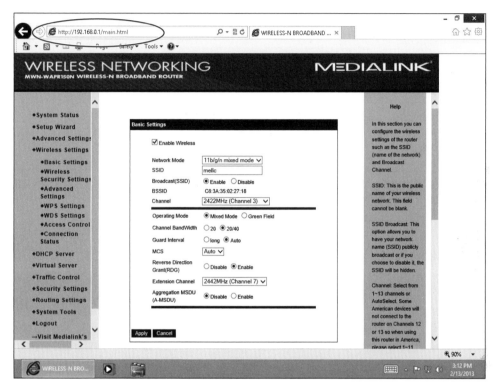

A typical opening page for adjusting router settings.

Although different routers require different instructions, here are some basic steps to follow for a typical set up. Always refer to the documentation that comes along with your specific router.

Once you've navigated to the IP address for your router and have successfully logged on, follow these steps:

1   Navigate to your router's wireless settings using the links either above or on the left side of the page.

2   Make sure a checkmark appears in the box that enables wireless communication.

3   Establish a service set identification (SSID) name for your network; you'll use this name to identify the correct network to select when connecting a wireless device.

4   Opt to broadcast your SSID.

5 Find the setting for establishing wireless security.

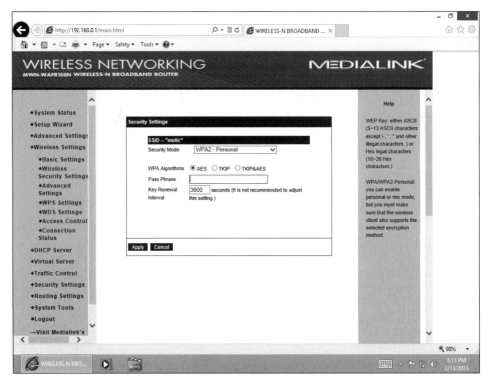

Selecting an encryption method and establishing a network password.

6 Select an encryption method; your router's documentation will identify for you the encryption methods your router supports. WPA and WPA2 are commonly available and considered to be secure.

7 Supply a password (also called a pass phrase by some router manufacturers) for your network. This password or pass phrase should be:

a. At least eight characters long and consist of both letters and numbers so it's strong enough to resist any attempts at identifying it.

b. Be something you can remember easily, since you'll need to supply it each time you connect a wireless device to your network.

When you later supply this password or pass phrase while connecting a wireless device to your network, you'll need to supply the password exactly as you type it here, including upper- and lower-case letters.

8   Look for a setting that enables you to control WPS settings, and if possible, disable WPS; this option isn't always available. Read more about why you should disable WPS in the sidebar, "Disable WPS."

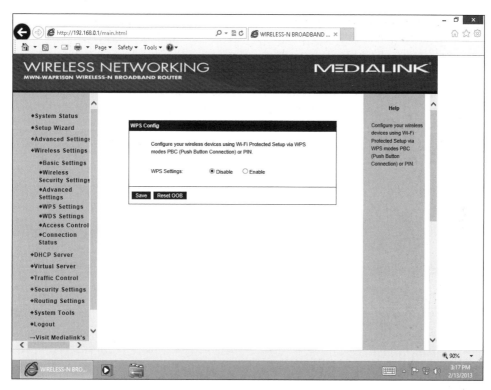

Disable WPS if possible.

9   Look for a setting that enables you to change the password you use to access your router's settings and change the password. Be sure to put the new password in a safe place.

After you establish wireless security, it's a good idea to change the password used to adjust your router's settings. That way, nobody else can use the factory-default password to access your router's settings and make unauthorized changes.

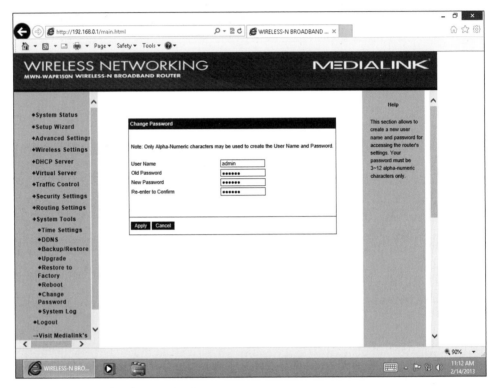

Change the password used to adjust your router's settings.

10 Save your changes and close your browser.

Disable WPS

WPS stands for Wi-Fi Protected Setup and it's a method used by some router manufacturers to make setting up, securing, and adding devices to a wireless network easy without the need to supply a password or pass phrase.

The idea is a good one, but experts have determined that WPS can be easily hacked; that is, a remote hacker can access a router using WPS and recover the WPS password in just a few hours. Using the WPS password, the same hacker can access any WPA/WPA2 keys.

Most routers come with WPS enabled, and on some routers, you can't disable WPS. But if you can disable WPS on your router, you should.

Connecting your router to the Internet

To connect your network to the Internet, use a network cable to connect your router to the modem provided or recommended by your Internet Service Provider (ISP). By connecting your router to your modem, all the computers connected to the router can share one Internet connection.

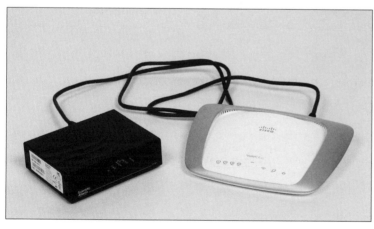

A router connected to a modem.

The back of the modem typically has only one place where you can connect the network cable. On the back of the router, look for a port that's labeled WAN or Internet: that's the port into which you should place the other end of the network cable.

Connecting wirelessly to the router

Now that you've set up your router and wireless security, you can safely connect wireless devices to your network. To make the connection, use your wireless device and follow these steps:

1 Display the Charms bar by sliding slightly in toward the center of the screen from the right side of the screen, pressing WinKey (⊞)+C, or placing your mouse in the upper- or lower-right corner of the screen.

2 Tap or click the Settings charm.

Tap or click the network icon.

3 Tap or click the network icon. A list appears of the SSIDs for the available networks.

4   Tap or click the SSID of the network to which you want to connect.

Click the Connect button to connect to the selected network.

5   Tap or click the Connect button.

If you want the wireless device to always connect to your network whenever it's within range of your network, tap or click the Connect Automatically box to place a checkmark in it.

6 When you're prompted for a password or pass phrase, supply the one you established earlier in this lesson when you set up security for your wireless network. It is case-sensitive, so type the password exactly as you originally entered it.

Your mobile device is now connected to your network. When you redisplay the Settings charm, the Network icon displays bars; the more bars you see, the stronger the connection between the wireless device and your router.

When you display the Settings charm on a mobile device connected to a network, the Network icon displays bars indicating signal strength.

If your printer can connect wirelessly to your network and you want to set it up to do so, follow the printer manufacturer's instructions to set up the connection. Typically, you need to supply the password or pass phrase to attach the printer, and the manufacturer's instructions will explain how to supply the information.

Networking and sharing files

Now that you've established the hardware setup of your network, you need to make files available to various network users using a technique called *sharing* files or folders. When you share files or folders, use Windows to identify the files and folders that should be visible and available to everyone using the network.

The *HomeGroup* is Microsoft's solution to sharing files easily. Introduced in Windows 7, you create a HomeGroup on one networked computer and establish a HomeGroup password. Then, users on the other computers on the network can join the HomeGroup by supplying the HomeGroup password.

HomeGroup limitations

HomeGroups work only on computers using Windows 7 or Windows 8 that also have turned on sharing as described earlier in the section, "Setting up your router." In addition, computers running Windows 7 must be part of a network designated as a "Home" network. The term "Home" has nothing to do with the geographic location of the computer; it is simply the term Microsoft chose to use to identify Windows 7 computers that can participate in a HomeGroup. If you intend to add a computer running Windows 7 to a HomeGroup, follow these steps on that Windows 7 computer to make sure its network type is Home:

1 Tap or click the Start button.

2 Tap or click Control Panel.

3 Under the Network and Internet heading, tap or click the View Network Status and Tasks link.

4 In the View Your Active Networks box, if your network type is anything other than Home, tap or click the link that mentions the network type you currently use.

5 In the window that appears, tap or click Home.

6 Tap or click OK.

Now your computer running Windows 7 can join a HomeGroup.

Computers using other versions of Windows or other operating systems cannot join a HomeGroup, but they can be part of your network. You must share the files and folders on these computers in a different way. You can place files and folders on these computers in their Public folders as described at the beginning of this lesson, or you can establish sharing permissions for their files and folders; check your operating system's Help files for information on establishing sharing permissions for files or folders.

Setting up a HomeGroup

You can create a HomeGroup using the tiled interface of Windows 8 or using File Explorer in the legacy Desktop app.

To use the tiled interface, follow these steps:

1   Display the Charms bar by sliding slightly in toward the center of the screen from the right side of the screen, pressing WinKey (⊞)+C, or placing your mouse in the upper- or lower-right corner of the screen.

2   Tap or click the Settings charm.

3   Tap or click Change PC Settings at the bottom of the Settings charm pane.

4   On the left side of the PC Settings interface, tap or click HomeGroup.

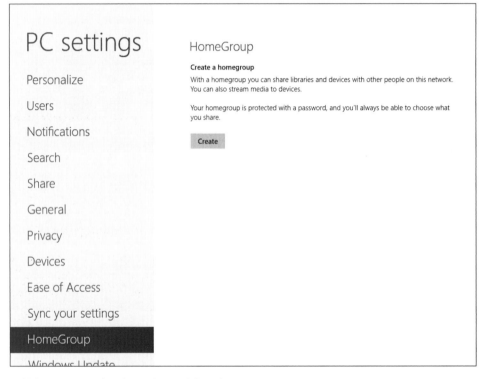

Establish a HomeGroup from the Windows 8 tiled interface.

5   On the right side of the screen, tap or click the Create button. Once Windows 8 creates the HomeGroup, the screen will change to help you select libraries to share.

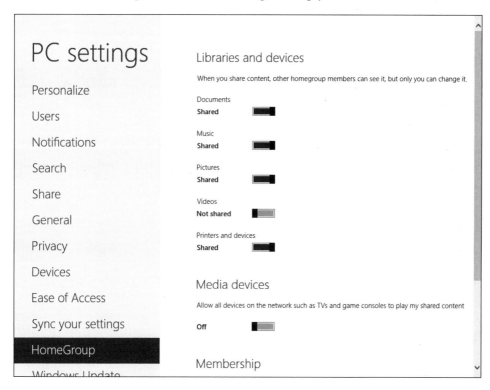

Select libraries to share from the available list.

6   Tap or click the button beside each library or device that you want to share.

You can scroll down the screen to view the HomeGroup password, but since other computers on the network will need the password to join the HomeGroup, we'll change it to make it more meaningful. Close the PC settings window by pressing Alt+F4, or by sliding your finger or dragging the mouse down the screen from the top to the bottom.

Changing the HomeGroup password

Use File Explorer in the legacy Desktop app to change the HomeGroup password. Follow these steps:

1 From the Start screen, tap or click the Desktop app.

2 On the Desktop taskbar, tap or click the File Explorer button.

3 In the Navigation pane, tap or click Homegroup. The Ribbon changes to display HomeGroup options.

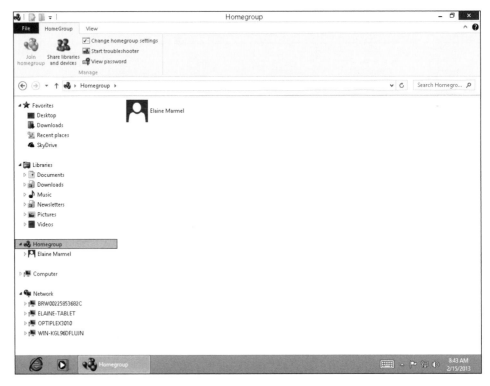

Using File Explorer to change HomeGroup settings.

4   Tap or click the Change HomeGroup Settings button on the Ribbon to display the HomeGroup window.

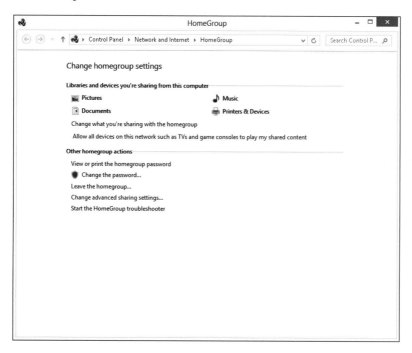

Tap or click the Change The Password link.

5   Tap or click the Change The Password link to display the Change Your HomeGroup Password dialog box, which warns you that changing the password will disconnect any current members from the HomeGroup.

6   Tap or click the Change The Password button.

7   In the window that appears, type a new password and tap or click Next.

Type a new password for the HomeGroup.

Windows changes your HomeGroup password and displays a window that suggests that you write down the password, along with a link you can use to print the password. You don't need to write down or print the password because you can view it at any time from either the tiled Windows 8 PC Settings screen or by selecting the HomeGroup in File Explorer, and on the Ribbon, tapping or clicking the View Password button.

Tap or click the Finish button in that window. You also can close the HomeGroup window, the File Explorer window, and the Desktop app.

Connecting to a HomeGroup

You can join a Home Group using either the tiled Windows 8 interface or using File Explorer. To join using the tiled Windows 8 interface, follow these steps:

1 Display the Charms bar by sliding slightly in toward the center of the screen from the right side of the screen, pressing WinKey (⊞)+C, or placing your mouse in the upper- or lower-right corner of the screen.

2 Tap or click the Settings charm.

3 Tap or click the Change PC Settings link.

4 On the left side of the screen that appears, tap or click HomeGroup.

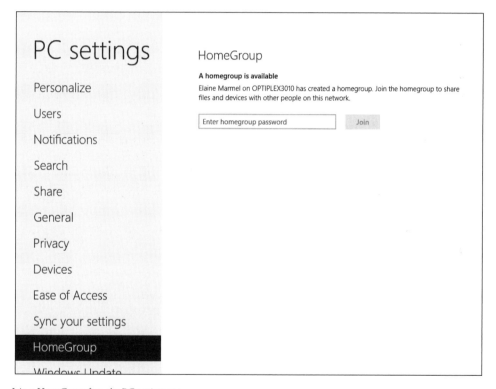

Join a HomeGroup from the PC settings screen.

5   Type the HomeGroup password and tap or click the Join button. Windows changes your networking settings to join the HomeGroup and then displays a screen where you can decide what to share.

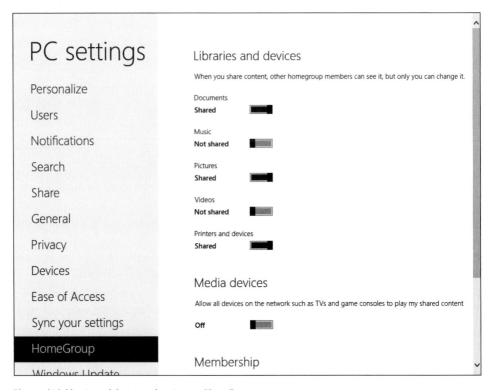

Choose which libraries and devices to share in your HomeGroup.

6   Tap or click the button beside each library or device that you want to share.

7 You can close the PC Settings screen by pressing Alt+F4, or by sliding your finger or dragging the mouse from the top to the bottom of the screen.

If you display File Explorer in the legacy Desktop app and you tap or click HomeGroup in the Navigation pane, you will see icons representing the computers that have joined the HomeGroup.

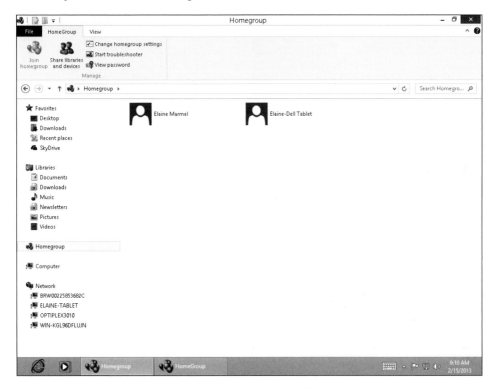

Other computers that have joined your HomeGroup will display as icons in File Explorer.

If you double-tap or double-click a computer, you can view the shared folders on that computer; you can double-tap or double-click any folder to drill down and use files in that folder.

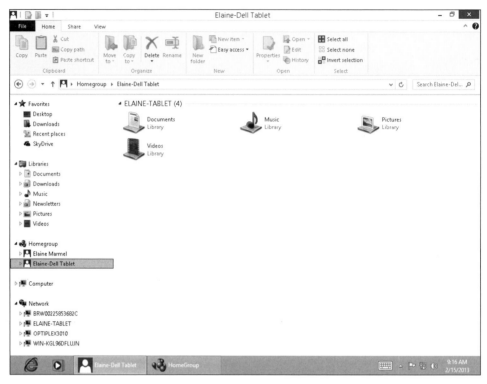

The shared folders on a computer connected to the HomeGroup.

Windows 7 users who want to join a HomeGroup or Windows 8 users who want to use File Explorer to join a HomeGroup should use these steps:

1   Open Windows Explorer, and in the Navigation pane, tap or click HomeGroup.

2   Tap or click the Join Now button. Windows updates your network settings to make your computer part of the HomeGroup.

3   In the window that appears, choose the libraries to share.

Self study

1   Name the hardware you'll need to network three computers, one of which will connect to the network wirelessly.

2   Describe the process of networking on a Windows 7 or Windows 8 computer.

Review

Questions

1   How do you connect a computer to a router?

2   How do you set up security for a wireless network?

3   How do you connect networked computers to the Internet?

4   How do you connect a wireless device to a network?

5   How do you create a HomeGroup?

6   How do you join a HomeGroup?

Answers

1   Connect a computer to a router by using a network cable or by connecting wirelessly.

2   To set up security for a wireless network, use a browser to navigate to the router's IP address, and in the router's settings, establish the type of security you want to use and a password or pass phrase to be used by devices that want to connect to the network.

3   To connect networked computers to the Internet, start by connecting the computers to the router (either by using a network cable or a wireless connection). Then, connect the router to the modem provided or recommended by your Internet Service Provider (ISP).

4   To connect a wireless device to a network, start on the wireless device by displaying the Charms bar and selecting the Settings charm. Next, tap or click the Network icon to display a list of available networks. Then, tap or click the network to which you want to connect and tap or click the Connect button. If prompted, supply the password or pass phrase to connect to the network.

5   Create a HomeGroup by first displaying the Charms bar and selecting the Settings charm. Then, tap or click the Change PC Settings link. On the left side of the PC Settings screen, tap or click HomeGroup. On the right side of the screen, tap or click the Create button. After Windows creates the HomeGroup, select the libraries and devices you want to share.

6   To join a HomeGroup, begin by displaying the Charms bar and selecting the Settings charm. Next, tap or click the Change PC Settings link. On the left side of the PC Settings screen, tap or click HomeGroup. On the right side of the screen, enter the HomeGroup password and tap or click the Join button. After Windows finishes setting up your computer to join the HomeGroup, select the libraries and devices you want to share.

What you'll learn in this lesson:

- Synchronizing settings across devices

- Understanding cloud storage

- Using the Windows 8 native SkyDrive app

- Using SkyDrive in a browser

Sharing Device Settings and Content

In this lesson, you learn how Windows 8 makes it easy to share settings across Windows 8 devices, keeping your Windows 8 experience friendly and familiar. You'll also learn how to take advantage of cloud storage to easily share information.

Starting up

In this lesson, you will work with several files from the Windows10lessons folder. Make sure that you have loaded the files from the Win8Lessons folder onto your hard drive from *www.DigitalClassroomBooks.com/Windows8*. For more information, see "Loading lesson files" in the Starting Up section of this book.

See Lesson 10 in action!

Use the accompanying videos to gain a better understanding of how to use some of the features shown in this lesson. The video lesson for this tutorial can be found at www.DigitalClassroomBooks.com/Windows8.

Synchronizing Windows 8 settings across devices

Windows 8 introduces the Microsoft account, a new type of log in account that you can use when you start your computer. Each time you log in to Windows 8 using a Microsoft account, you connect your computer to the cloud. By connecting to the cloud, you can use the same settings on all your Windows 8 devices to make your Windows 8 experience a familiar one.

By default, when you connect to the cloud from your desktop PC Windows 8 automatically synchronizes some settings to the cloud (for example, your pictures, your backgrounds, your Internet Explorer history and favorites, and more). If you later sign in to another device (such as to a tablet PC) using the same Microsoft account, Windows 8 synchronizes the settings from your desktop PC to your tablet PC to make your Windows 8 experience familiar on all your devices. If, while working on your tablet PC, you make any change to the settings that Windows 8 synchronizes, those new settings will appear on your desktop PC the next time you log in using your Microsoft account.

Although the default behavior for Windows 8 is to synchronize settings between devices on which you use the same Microsoft account when you sign in, you can change that default behavior and control synchronization. To make changes to the Windows 8 device synchronization settings, you need to log in to your Windows 8 device using your Microsoft account. If you've been using a local account, you can switch to your Microsoft account using these steps:

If you haven't established a Microsoft account, see Lesson 1, "Getting Started with Windows 8."

1   Display the Charms bar by sliding slightly in toward the center of the screen from the right side of the screen, pressing WinKey (⊞)+C, or placing your mouse in the upper- or lower-right corner of the screen.

2   Tap or click the Settings charm.

3   Tap or click Change PC Settings.

4   On the left side of the PC Settings screen, tap or click Users.

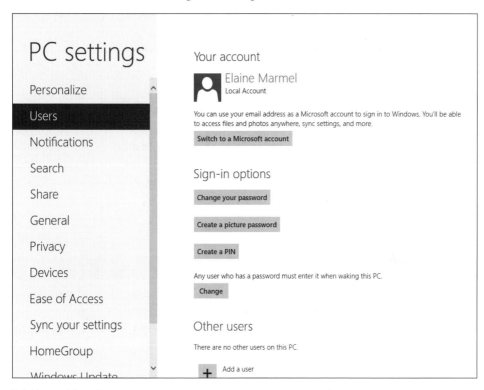

Switching to a Microsoft account.

5   Tap or click the Switch To A Microsoft Account button.

6 Provide the password for your local account and tap or click Next.

Provide the password for your local account.

7 Supply your Microsoft account e-mail address and tap or click Next.

8   Supply the password to your Microsoft account. Remember, this password is not necessarily the same as the password you use to collect e-mail for this address.

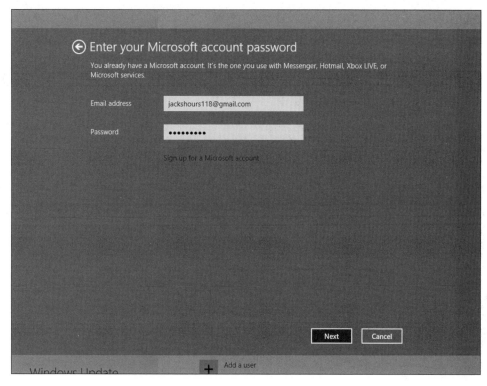

Supply your Microsoft account e-mail address and password.

9   Tap or click Next to display the last screen of the wizard that switches you to your
Microsoft account.

*You might be prompted to supply security information at this point. If so, provide the information
and tap or click Next.*

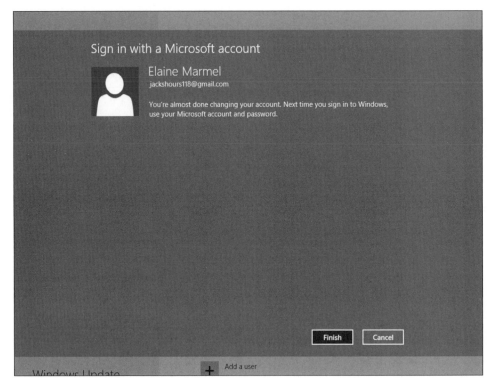

The final screen for switching to your Microsoft account.

10 Tap or click Finish.

Windows 8 switches to your Microsoft account and redisplays the PC Settings screen. Notice that you now have the option to switch to a local account; after you set synchronization settings, you can repeat the preceding steps to switch back to a local account.

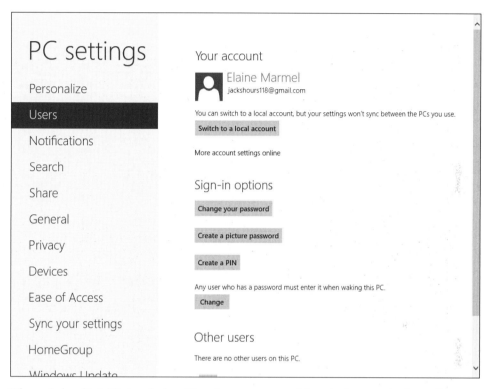

When you're logged in to Windows 8 using a Microsoft account, you can switch to a local account using the preceding steps.

Next, review and make changes to your Windows 8 synchronization settings. Follow these steps:

1 Scroll down the left side of the PC Settings screen and tap or click Sync Your Settings. The settings you can synchronize appear.

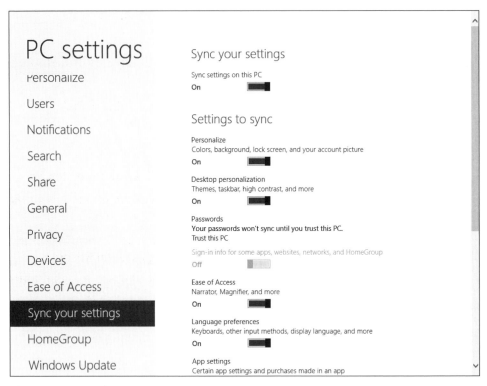

The settings you can synchronize.

2 Tap or click a setting to turn it off.

To turn off all synchronization, tap or click the first option.

3 Scroll down the right side of the screen to view additional synchronization settings you can control and make changes to them as needed.

4 Close PC Settings by pressing Alt+F4 or by dragging your finger or the mouse down from the top of the screen to the bottom of the screen.

The basics of cloud storage

Storing your files in the cloud (that is, on a remote server operated by a company you typically pay for the storage space) has both advantages and disadvantages. Among the advantages:

- You can access files at any time, from anywhere, using any computer.
- You can easily share files you select with remote users.
- If you store important information remotely, it will still be available to you if your home or office is robbed or burns down.
- Most companies that offer remote storage provide a free amount of storage, so you might not need to pay for your remote storage.

Among the disadvantages:

- You must have a working Internet connection to use your remotely stored files.
- A hacker could breach the security of the remote server and gain access to your private files.
- The company operating the remote server has programs that can scan your private information, and employees of the company can see your private information.
- By law, the company operating the remote server must comply with any court orders it receives from law enforcement officials to turn over or copy your data.

Weigh the pros and cons of storing information remotely and make your own decision.

Introducing SkyDrive

If you opt to use remote storage, Microsoft, among others, offers remote storage and provides you with up to 7 GB of storage for free. You can easily access Microsoft's remote storage, called SkyDrive, using a Microsoft account and any browser or the Windows 8 native SkyDrive app.

The Windows 8 native SkyDrive app.

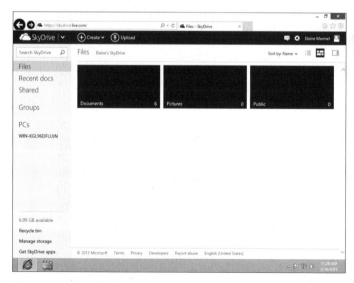

The browser version of SkyDrive shown in the legacy Desktop app Internet Explorer.

> *There is a legacy Desktop SkyDrive app that you can install; it gives you the most powerful of all cloud features: the ability to remotely download a document that you haven't uploaded to your SkyDrive. See the section, "Using the legacy Desktop SkyDrive app" later in this lesson.*

SkyDrive is more than just online storage. In addition to uploading and downloading documents, you can open and edit documents. If you use the Windows 8 native version of SkyDrive, you will be able to open documents using a locally installed app. For example, if you open a word-processing document, SkyDrive will open the document in WordPad or Microsoft Word, if you have installed Microsoft Word.

If you use the browser version of SkyDrive and you open a document, SkyDrive attempts to use one of the Office Web Apps: Word, Excel, PowerPoint, or OneNote.

The browser version of SkyDrive has more capabilities than the Windows 8 native version of SkyDrive. For example, you can create documents in the browser version of SkyDrive, and you can then download them to your hard drive.

Although you can't create documents in the Windows 8 native SkyDrive app, you can accomplish a lot using it.

Using the Windows 8 native SkyDrive app

You don't need to be signed in to Windows 8 using a Microsoft account to use the Windows 8 native SkyDrive app. If you're signed into Windows using a local account and you tap or click the SkyDrive app on the Start screen, you're prompted to provide your Microsoft account information. Once you fill in this information, the SkyDrive app saves it. Then, all you need is a working Internet connection to use the SkyDrive app.

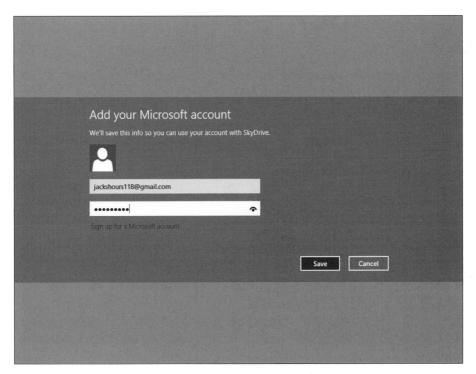

If you try to launch the SkyDrive app while signed in to Windows 8 under a local account, this screen appears.

When the Windows 8 native SkyDrive app appears, some see three folders by default, and these folders are represented by tiles: Documents, Pictures, and Public.

The folders shown are an example of what you might see; your SkyDrive might show different folders.

The default screen for the Windows 8 native SkyDrive app.

Adding a folder

You aren't limited to these three folders, but you might prefer to add folders inside the default folders. For example, in the Documents folder, you might want to create folders for the different types of documents you create, and then tap or click the folder to access a file.

Initially, your SkyDrive default folders won't contain any folders. To add a folder, follow these steps:

1   From the location where you want to add the folder (either the opening SkyDrive screen or inside one of the default folders), display the App bar by swiping down slightly from the top of the screen or by right-clicking anywhere on the screen.

2   Tap or click the New Folder button.

3   In the window that appears, type the name of the new folder.

4　Tap or click the Create Folder button.

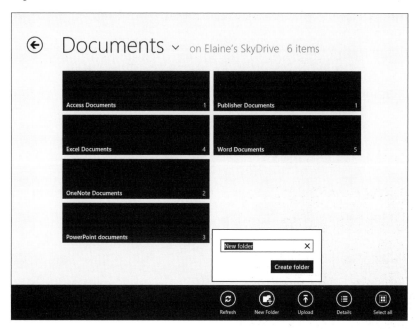

Creating a new SkyDrive folder.

As mentioned, you open a folder by tapping or clicking it. After you've added folders inside folders and you've drilled down into a folder, you navigate up to a higher folder level using the Back button.

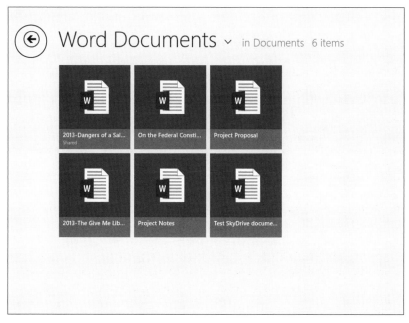

Use the Back button to navigate up the folder tree.

Uploading files

You can upload files from your hard drive to your SkyDrive. For this example, you use the following steps to upload the Windows10lessons files from the My Pictures folder on your hard drive to your SkyDrive:

1   Place the lesson files for this lesson into your my Pictures folder.

2   In the native Windows 8 SkyDrive app, tap or click the Public folder (or other preferred folder).

2   Display the App bar by swiping down slightly from the top of the screen or by right-clicking anywhere on the screen.

To upload a file from your hard drive to your SkyDrive, navigate to the SkyDrive folder where the file should appear.

3   Tap or click the Upload button. SkyDrive suggests that you select files from your hard drive's Documents folder.

4   To select a different folder, tap or click Files to display a list of locations on your hard drive that you can search for files to upload to your SkyDrive.

Select the location on your hard drive containing the files you want to upload to your SkyDrive.

5   For this example, tap or click Pictures to display the contents of the Pictures folder.

6   For this example, tap or click **Windows1001-01.jpg**. A checkmark appears beside the selected file.

Selecting a file to upload to your SkyDrive.

7   Tap or click the Add to SkyDrive button. The SkyDrive app uploads
Windows1001–01.jpg to the Public folder.

File uploaded to SkyDrive.

When you redisplay the main screen of the Windows 8 native SkyDrive app, the
number of files in the folder you selected in Step 1 above updates to reflect the new
addition.

Downloading files

You can download files from your SkyDrive to your hard drive. For this example, you'll download the **Windows1001-01.jpg** file you just uploaded since it's the only file you have available on your SkyDrive. Follow these steps:

1   In the native Windows 8 SkyDrive app, tap or click the Public folder (or the folder chosen in Step 1 of the previous exercise).

2   Select the **Windows1001-01.jpg** file you want to download by tapping and holding and dragging down slightly or right-clicking. A checkmark appears beside the file.

3   Display the App bar by swiping down slightly from the top of the screen or by right-clicking anywhere on-screen.

Select the file you want to download and display the App bar.

4   Tap or click the Download button. SkyDrive suggests that you download the file to your hard drive's Documents folder.

5 To select a different folder, tap or click Files to display a list of locations on your hard drive where you can download files from your SkyDrive.

Select the location on your hard drive where you want to place the files you download from your SkyDrive.

6 For this example, tap or click Desktop.

7 Tap or click the Choose This Folder button. A button for the Desktop folder appears at the bottom of the screen.

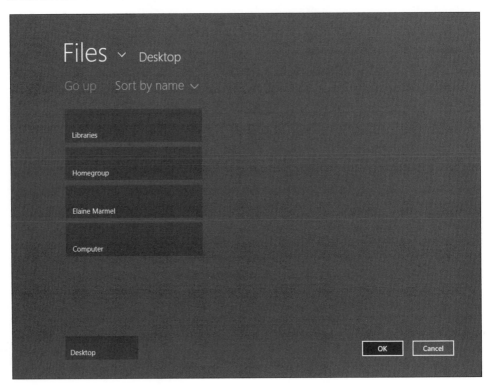

Selecting the Desktop as the download location.

8 Tap or click OK. The SkyDrive app downloads the **Windows1001-01.jpg** file to the Desktop and displays its progress in the upper-right corner of the SkyDrive app screen.

Downloading a file from SkyDrive.

9 Display the Desktop app, and you'll find **Windows1001–01.jpg** on the Desktop.

The file you downloaded from your SkyDrive now appears on your Desktop.

Signing out of SkyDrive

There is no formal sign out procedure in the Windows 8 native SkyDrive app. Close the app by pressing Alt+F4 or by dragging your finger or the mouse down the screen from the top of the screen to the bottom.

Browsing with SkyDrive

You can also work with your SkyDrive space using any Internet browser. The browser version of SkyDrive is more powerful than the Windows 8 native SkyDrive app. For example, using the browser version of SkyDrive, you can create documents and folders.

In this example, we'll use the Windows 8 native version of Internet Explorer to run the browser version of SkyDrive. Open the Windows 8 native version of Internet Explorer and navigate to *www.skydrive.com*. On the sign-in screen, supply your Microsoft account user name and password.

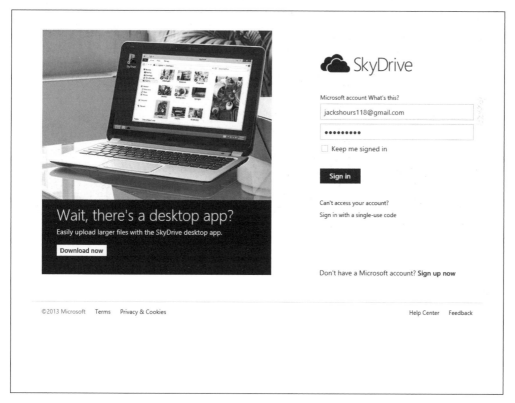

Signing in to SkyDrive using a browser.

When you tap or click the Sign In button, the browser version of SkyDrive appears. Navigate this interface by using the links along the left side of the screen. To search for a file on your SkyDrive, tap or click in the Search SkyDrive box above the links in the left column. If you know the folder that contains the file you want, you can tap that folder.

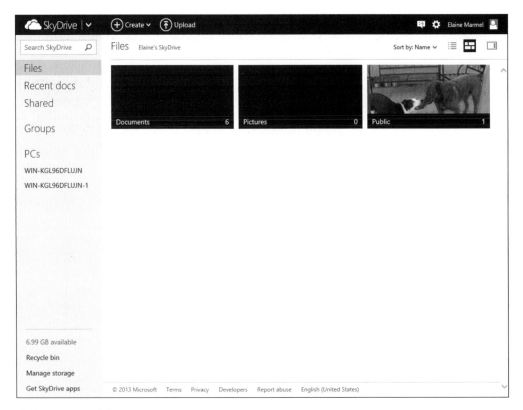

The browser version of SkyDrive.

Creating folders and documents

Using the browser version of SkyDrive, you can create folders as well as Word, Excel, PowerPoint, and OneNote documents using the Web App versions of these programs. To see your choices, tap or click the Create button at the top of the screen.

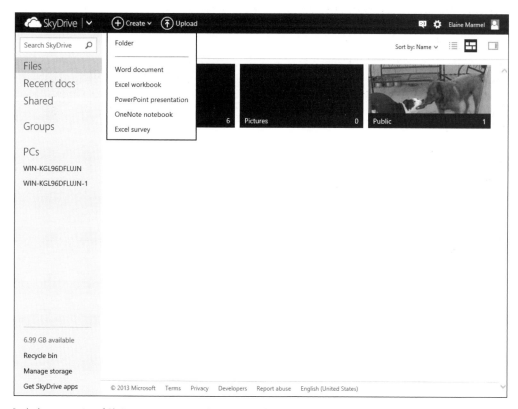

In the browser version of SkyDrive, you can create documents and folders.

Creating a new a folder in the browser version of SkyDrive is done in much the same way as creating a folder in the Windows 8 native SkyDrive app: begin by tapping or clicking the Create button; then tap or click Folder. A new folder appears that will let you type a name for it. After typing a name, press Enter or tap or click anywhere outside the folder to save the name.

Navigating in the browser version of SkyDrive is done a little differently than navigating in the Windows 8 native SkyDrive app. After you've added folders inside folders and you've drilled down into a folder, navigate up to a higher folder level using the path that appears beside the folder name; the folder name appears below the Create button. The last entry in the folder path matches the folder name below the Create button. You can navigate back up the folder tree one folder at a time by tapping or clicking the portion of the folder name to the left of the caret (>).

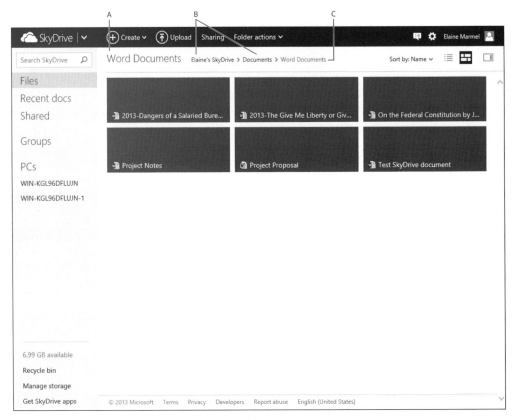

*A. Folder name. **B.** Tap to navigate up the folder tree. **C.** Folder path.*

To create a new document, follow these steps:

1   Tap or click the Documents folder (or another preferred folder.)

2   Tap or click the Create button.

3   Tap or click the type of document you want to create (for example, Word document). The browser version of SkyDrive prompts you for a file name.

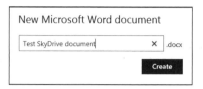

Supply a file name for the new document.

4   Tap or click the Create button. The browser version of SkyDrive opens the appropriate Office Web App.

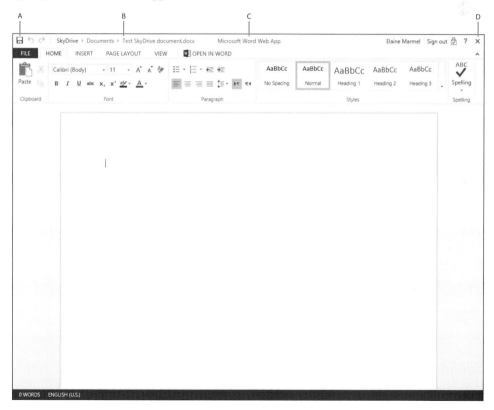

A. *Save button.* **B.** *The document you are creating.* **C.** *Working in a web app.* **D.** *Close button.*

5   Create your document.

6   To save your document, tap or click the Save button.

7   To close the Web App, tap or click the Close button.

Uploading files

You can upload files stored on your hard drive to SkyDrive using the browser version of SkyDrive. In this example, make sure that **Windows1002-01.jpg** is loaded onto your hard drive in the Pictures folder. Then, follow these steps:

1 From the main SkyDrive screen, tap or click the Pictures folder.

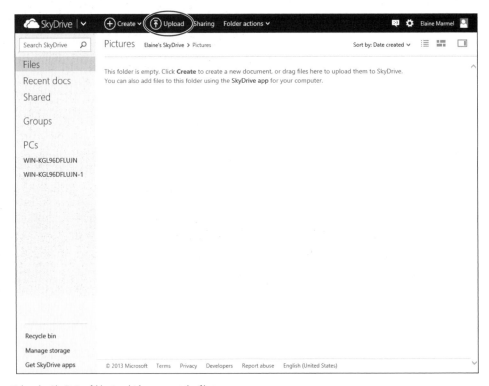

Select the SkyDrive folder in which you want the file to appear.

In the native Windows 8 SkyDrive app, tap or click the folder where you want the pictures to appear. This example uses the Public folder, but you can select any folder.

2 Tap or click the Upload button at the top of the screen. The SkyDrive app suggests that you upload a file from your hard drive's Documents folder.

3   Tap or click Files to display a list of folders you can use to upload a file.

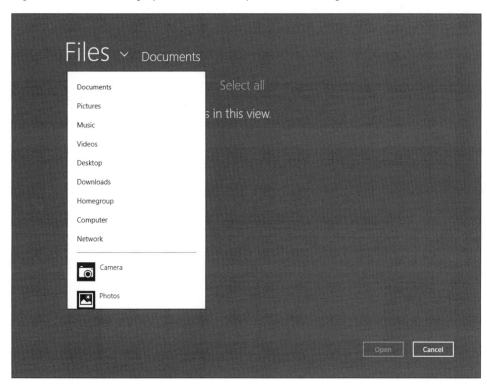

Select the folder containing the file you want to upload.

4   Tap or click Pictures.

5   Tap or click **Windows1002-01.jpg**. A checkmark appears beside the selected file.

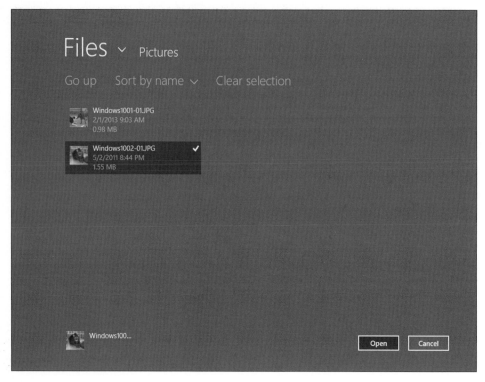

Selecting a file to upload.

6   Tap or click the Open button. The browser version of SkyDrive uploads the file.

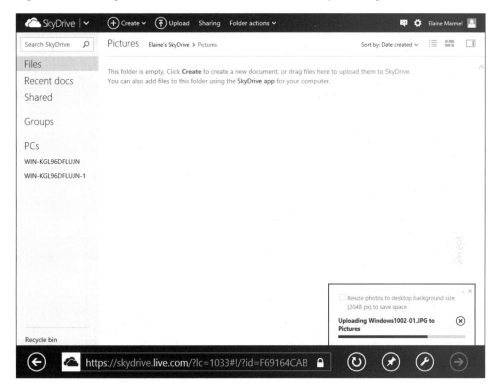

Uploading a file to SkyDrive.

For photos, the browser version of SkyDrive offers to resize the file to save space on your SkyDrive. You can tap or click the box to resize the file.

Downloading a file

You can download files to your hard drive using the browser version of SkyDrive. By default, Internet Explorer downloads files to your Downloads folder, and the Windows 8 native version of Internet Explorer doesn't permit you to select a different location. To control where the browser version of SkyDrive places a file you download, use the legacy Internet Explorer app. For this example, you'll download the **Windows1002-01.jpg** file you just uploaded to the Desktop. Follow these steps:

1 In legacy Internet Explorer, log in to SkyDrive.

2 Tap or click the Pictures folder.

3 Select the **Windows1002-01.jpg** file by tapping and holding or right-clicking. A checkmark appears beside the file and a menu appears.

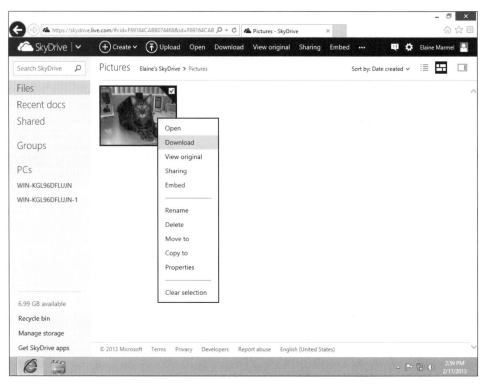

Select the file you want to download.

4 Tap or click Download. The legacy version of Internet Explorer displays a box at the bottom of the screen.

5   Tap or click the down arrow beside the Save button.

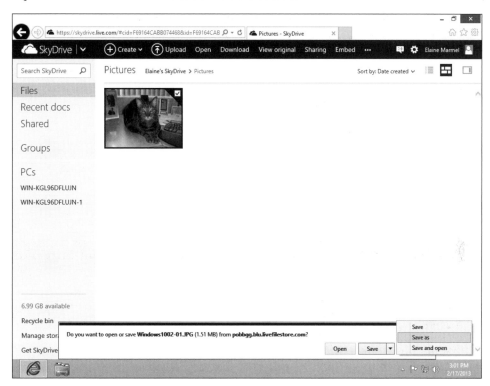

Tap or click the arrow beside the Save button.

6   Tap or click Save As to display the Save As dialog box.

7   In the Navigation pane on the left, tap or click Desktop.

Select the location on your hard drive where you want to place the files you download from your SkyDrive.

8 Tap or click the Save button. The browser version of SkyDrive downloads the **Windows1002-01.jpg** file to the Desktop and displays its progress in the box at the bottom of the screen.

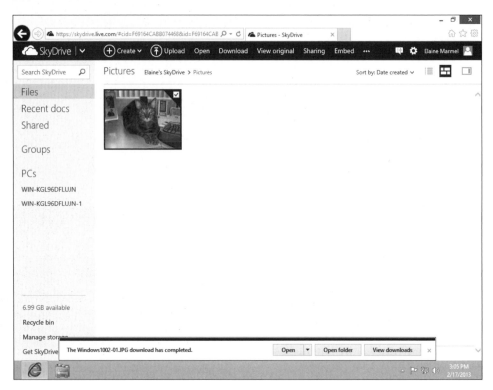

Downloading a file from SkyDrive.

Tap or click Open folder to display the Desktop in File Explorer. Or switch to the Desktop. In both places, you'll see **Windows1002-01.jpg**.

The file you downloaded from your SkyDrive now appears on your Desktop.

Sharing files

Using the browser version of SkyDrive, you can easily share files stored on your SkyDrive with other users through any of the following methods:

- By sending an e-mail containing a link to the shared document. This is the default method suggested by SkyDrive.
- By creating a link for the document and distributing the link as necessary.
- By posting the document to Facebook, Twitter, or LinkedIn.

In this section, you learn how to use the default e-mail sharing method.

When you use the default e-mail sharing method, you provide the recipient's e-mail address and write an optional personal message. SkyDrive sends the message, which contains a link to a web page. When the recipient clicks the link in the e-mail, the web page opens, displaying the file you shared. As you create the link, you have the option of allowing the recipient to edit the shared document. You also can opt to have the recipient sign in to a Microsoft account that matches the e-mail address to which you sent the message before he or she can view the shared document.

Follow these steps to share a file:

1 Navigate to the file you want to share.

2 Tap and hold or right-click the file.

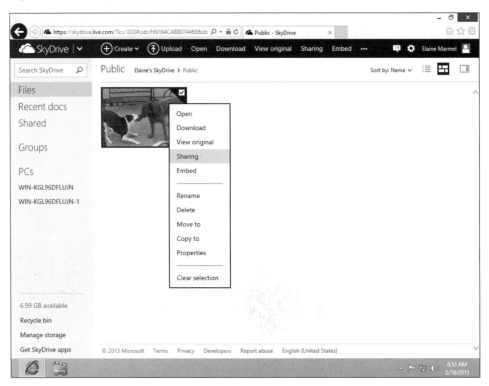

Select a file to share.

3   From the menu that appears, tap or click Sharing. SkyDrive displays the window where you set up the e-mail message for the shared file.

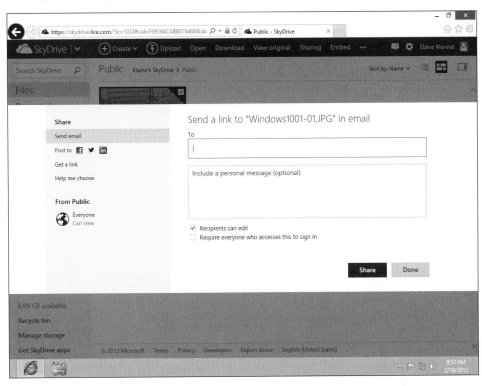

Set up the e-mail message you want the recipient to see.

4   Supply the recipient's e-mail address and write a message. If you don't want to offer editing privileges, deselect the Recipient Can Edit checkbox. If you want the recipient to sign in to the Microsoft account associated with the e-mail address you supply, select the Require Everyone Who Accesses This To Sign In checkbox.

5   Tap or click the Share button.

SkyDrive sends a message to the recipient containing a link to the file. When you're finished sharing the document, you can stop sharing it using these steps:

1 Navigate to the file you want to stop sharing.

2 Tap and hold or right-click the file. SkyDrive displays the window where you set up the e-mail message for the shared file. At the bottom of the window on the left side, you'll find a list of those with whom you have shared the file.

3 Tap or click a name in the Permissions list.

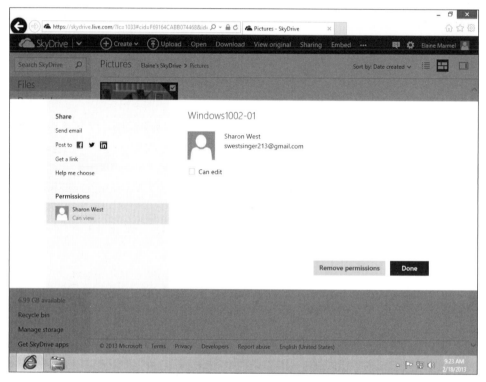

Select a person whose sharing privileges you want to remove.

4 Tap or click the Remove Permissions button. SkyDrive removes the sharing privileges.

5 Tap or click the Done button to return to SkyDrive.

Synchronizing and fetching files using the legacy Desktop SkyDrive app

In addition to being able to access your SkyDrive using the Windows 8 native SkyDrive app and any browser, you can install the legacy SkyDrive app that works with File Explorer on the Desktop. The legacy SkyDrive app gives you two additional features that you don't have using the Windows 8 native SkyDrive app or a browser:

- You can synchronize files across multiple computers.

- You can use the "fetch" feature to remotely access files that you didn't upload to SkyDrive. This feature works as long as the computer on which the files reside is running using your Microsoft account.

The legacy SkyDrive app isn't a typical app in the sense that you don't need to run it once you install it. Installing the legacy SkyDrive app places a new folder on your computer: the SkyDrive folder. It appears in File Explorer and you work with it in File Explorer just as you work with any other folder on your computer:

- Placing a file in the SkyDrive folder automatically uploads it to your cloud SkyDrive.

- Deleting a file from your SkyDrive folder automatically deletes it from your cloud SkyDrive.

- You can add, delete, or remove folders inside the SkyDrive folder; doing so adds, deletes, and removes the same folders in your cloud SkyDrive.

- You can copy and move files among your SkyDrive folders and the results also appear in your cloud SkyDrive.

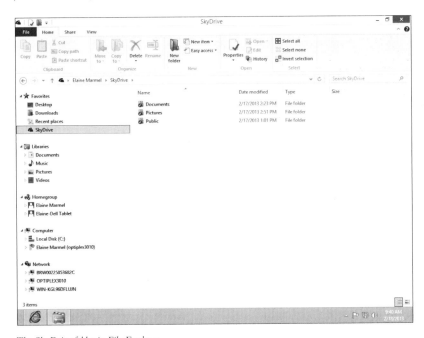

The SkyDrive folder in File Explorer.

To install the legacy SkyDrive app, follow these steps:

1   Log into your SkyDrive using a browser.

2   At the bottom of the left pane, tap or click the Get SkyDrive Apps link. SkyDrive apps for available platforms appear.

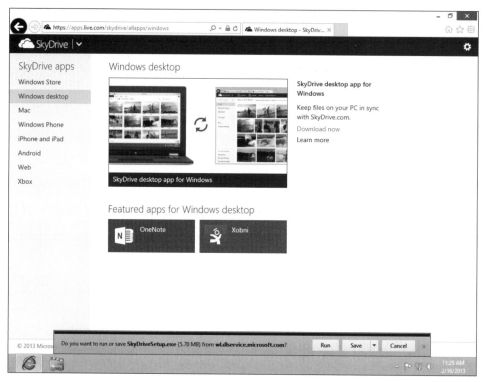

SkyDrive apps for available platforms.

3   In the left pane, tap or click Windows Desktop.

4   In the right pane, tap or click the Download Now link. A message appears at the bottom of the screen, asking if you want to run or save.

5 Tap or click the Run button. The legacy SkyDrive app installs itself and prepares for its first use.

6 In the Welcome to SkyDrive dialog box that appears, tap or click the Get Started button.

7 In the Sign In dialog box, provide your Microsoft account e-mail address and password and tap or click the Sign In button.

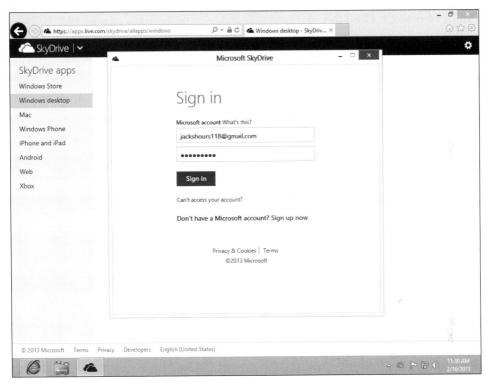

Provide your Microsoft account sign in information.

8 A message appears, showing you the location of your local SkyDrive folder. You can change the folder; for this example, tap or click the Next button.

9 The legacy SkyDrive app asks you to identify the cloud SkyDrive folders that you want to synchronize to your PC. For this example, tap or click All Files And Folders On My SkyDrive and tap or click the Next button.

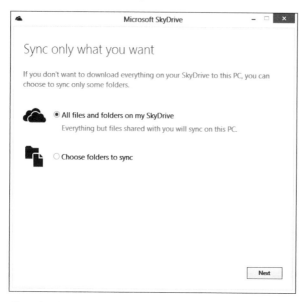

Choose the SkyDrive files and folders to synchronize to your desktop computer.

10 The legacy SkyDrive app lets you decide whether to enable the "fetch" feature. For this example, make sure a checkmark appears in the Let Me Use SkyDrive To Fetch Any Of My Files On This PC checkbox.

Choose to enable the "fetch" feature.

11 Tap or click the Done button. The SkyDrive legacy app opens File Explorer, shows you your SkyDrive folder, and displays an explanatory message.

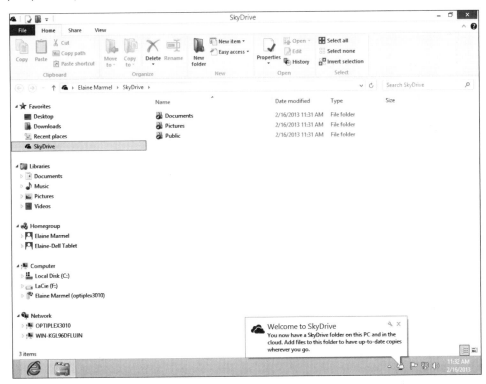

The legacy SkyDrive app shows you your SkyDrive folder.

To synchronize files between your computer and your SkyDrive cloud storage, place the files into your SkyDrive folder. When you make a change locally to the file, the legacy SkyDrive app automatically uploads the changed file to your cloud SkyDrive. If you make a change to the document from the cloud SkyDrive, the legacy SkyDrive app automatically downloads the changed file to your SkyDrive folder on your computer.

For example, if you're planning to travel out of town and use a tablet PC while you're away from home or the office. Before you leave, you upload files you expect to need to your SkyDrive. Once you're on the road, you discover that you forgot a file. You can use the legacy SkyDrive app's "fetch" feature to get the file as long as:

• Your home or office computer is running.

• You signed into it using your Microsoft account.

To fetch a file, follow these steps:

1 On your tablet PC, log into the browser version of SkyDrive.

2 In the PCs list in the left pane, tap or click the computer to which you want to connect. SkyDrive displays a tiled representation of all the folders and libraries on your computer.

3 Navigate to the file you want to retrieve and tap or click it. A representation of the file appears on the screen.

4 Tap and hold or right-click the file, and at the top of the screen, tap or click the Upload to SkyDrive button.

5 When you're prompted for a folder on SkyDrive for the file, select a folder and then tap or click the Upload button to copy the file to your SkyDrive. You can then download the file to your tablet PC.

Signing out of SkyDrive

When you're done using the browser version of SkyDrive, you can sign out of your SkyDrive account. Tap or click your name in the upper-right corner of the screen to display a menu. At the bottom of the menu, tap or click Sign Out.

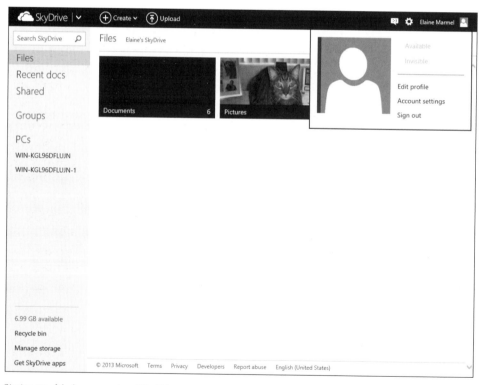

Signing out of the browser version of SkyDrive.

Self study

1 Review your synchronization settings and make any changes you deem appropriate.

2 Log into the native and legacy version of SkyDrive and upload a file.

Review

Questions

1 How do you upload a file to your SkyDrive using the Windows 8 native SkyDrive app?

2 How do you download a file from your SkyDrive using the Windows 8 native SkyDrive app?

3 How do you upload a file to your SkyDrive using the browser version of SkyDrive?

4 How do you download a file from your SkyDrive using the browser version of SkyDrive?

5 How do you send an e-mail to share a file?

6 List some of the ways in which you can use the legacy SkyDrive Desktop app and some of its advantages.

Answers

1 To upload a file to SkyDrive using the Windows8 native Sky Drive app, tap or click the folder where you want the files to appear. Then, display the App bar and tap or click the Upload button. Tap or click Files to display a list of locations on your hard drive that you can search for files to upload to your SkyDrive. Select the file you want to upload, and then tap or click the Add to SkyDrive button.

2 To download a file from SkyDrive using the Windows8 native SkyDrive app, tap or click the folder containing the file you want to download and select the file. Then, display the App bar and tap or click the Download button. Select a folder in which to place the downloaded file by tapping or clicking Files. Then, tap or click the Choose This Folder button and tap or click OK.

3 To upload a file to SkyDrive using the Windows8 native SkyDrive app, tap or click the folder in which you want to place the file you upload. Then, tap or click the Upload button at the top of the screen. To display a list of folders you can use to upload a file, tap or click Files and select the folder location that contains the file you want to upload. Tap or click the file you want to upload and tap or click the Open button. The browser version of SkyDrive uploads the file.

4 To download a file to SkyDrive using the Windows8 native SkyDrive app, use the legacy Internet Explorer to log in to SkyDrive. Then, tap or click the folder containing the file you want to download and select the file you want to download by tapping and holding or right-clicking to display a shortcut menu. Tap or click Download; a box appears at the bottom of the screen. Tap or click the down arrow beside the Save button to select a folder into which the downloaded file will appear. Then, tap or click the Save button.

5 To share a file by sending an e-mail, use the browser version of SkyDrive to navigate to the file you want to share, and then tap and hold or right-click the file. From the menu that appears, tap or click Sharing. SkyDrive displays the window where you set up the e-mail message for the shared file. Supply the recipient's e-mail address and write an optional message. Decide whether to allow the recipient to edit the shared file and tap or click the Share button.

6 Some of the ways and advantages of using the legacy SkyDrive Desktop app are:

- Using File Explorer, you can make changes to the SkyDrive folder on your local hard drive.

- The legacy SkyDrive Desktop app makes it easy to manage files between your local drive and your cloud storage.

- Placing a file in the SkyDrive folder automatically uploads it to your cloud SkyDrive.

- Deleting a file from your SkyDrive folder automatically deletes it from your cloud SkyDrive.

- You can add, delete, or remove folders inside the SkyDrive folder; doing so adds, deletes, and removes the same folders in your cloud SkyDrive.

- You can copy and move files among your SkyDrive folders; the results appear in your cloud SkyDrive.

What you'll learn in this lesson:

- Using the Windows 8 Music app

- Getting acquainted with the Windows 8 Video app

- Examining Windows Media Player

Using Audio and Video in Windows 8

In this lesson, you'll learn how to use both the Windows 8 app as well as the legacy Windows Media Player Desktop app to play and manage your Music and Video library.

Starting up

In this lesson, you will work with several files from the Windows11lessons folder. Make sure that you have loaded the files from the Win8Lessons folder onto your hard drive from *www.DigitalClassroomBooks.com/Windows8*. For more information, see "Loading lesson files" in the Starting Up section of this book.

See Lesson 11 in action!

Use the accompanying videos to gain a better understanding of how to use some of the features shown in this lesson. The video lesson for this tutorial can be found at www.DigitalClassroomBooks.com/Windows8.

Working with the Windows 8 Music app

Let's explore the native Windows 8 Music app, called the Xbox Music app. Tap or click it from the Start screen. The Xbox Music app works with your Music library, and the My Music section at the left side of the screen displays tiles for some of the albums stored there. By default, the Xbox Music app downloads information from the Internet about your albums.

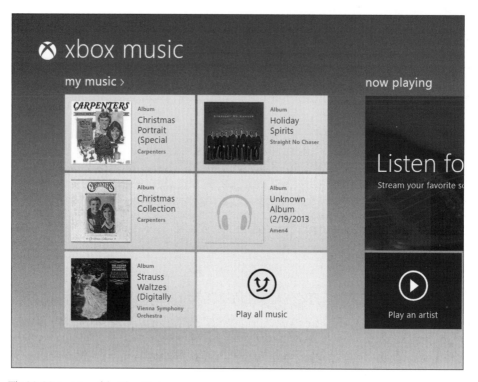

The My Music section of the Xbox Music.

Sample Music Files

If you don't have any music of your own in your Music library, copy the files provided in the Windows11lesson folder to your Music library. They will appear on the screen under the heading "Gary."

1   From the Start screen, tap the Desktop app.

2   Tap or click File Explorer.

3   In the Navigation pane, navigate to the Windows11lessons folder that you saved to your hard drive and select all the files in it.

4   On the Home tab of the Ribbon, tap or click the Copy button.

5   In the Navigation pane, tap or click the Music library.

6   Tap or click the Paste button on the Ribbon.

Playing music

When you tap or click an album, the songs on that album appear; you can tap or click an individual song to play it, or you can play the entire album using the Play Album button on the left side of the window.

Viewing songs on an album.

When you select an album or a song to play, the Xbox Music app automatically displays the App bar so that you can control playback. For example, using Playback Options, you can option to repeat or shuffle songs or you can add a song to a playlist, which you'll read about later in this lesson.

To control playback volume, use the volume control on your external speakers or display the Settings charm on the Charms bar and then tap or click the Volume button at the bottom of the Settings pane.

If you tap or click the album cover that appears in the App bar, the Xbox Music app displays biographical information about the artist and a list of the albums produced by the artist.

While playing, you can read about the artist.

As a song plays, you can scroll to the right to see the title of the current selection in the Now Playing section.

The Now Playing section displays the currently playing song.

The My Music section doesn't contain tiles for all your albums, but you can view a list of all your music and select music to play by tapping or clicking My Music. You can tap or click the Back button to redisplay the main screen of the Xbox Music app.

The list of all music stored in your My Music library.

You can tap or click a selection to play it or tap or click the Back button to return to the main screen of the Xbox Music app.

Buying music

As you scroll to the right beyond the Now Playing section, you see titles that might interest you; to buy an album or a song, tap or click either All Music or Top Music, or in the Now Playing section, tap or click Play An Artist. Locate the album or song you want to buy by working your way through a genre. You can tap or click a song or an album to preview it. When you don't own a song or album, an option to buy it appears on the left side of the window as you play the selection.

When you play a title you don't own, you have the option to buy it.

Tap or click the Buy Album button, and when prompted, confirm your purchase. The Xbox Music Store will download your purchase and make it part of your Music library.

If you don't see the title or artist you want, use the Windows 8 Search charm to search for music. While working in the Xbox Music app, display the Charms bar by sliding slightly in toward the center of the screen from the right side of the screen, pressing WinKey (⊞)+C, or placing your mouse in the upper- or lower-right corner of the screen. Then, tap or click the Search charm. In the Search box, type the name of the song title or artist and tap or click the magnifying glass. The search results for music in the Windows Store appear; you can then preview and buy as described.

If you're looking for music to buy, you'll find a lot of options on the web. Just search for your favorite song or artist. Windows 8 will play any song you buy and download using either Music app (the Windows 8 native Xbox Music app or Windows Media Player) as long as you place the song in your Music library.

Creating a playlist

You can create a *playlist* of the songs you want to hear. The songs in the playlist can come from different albums. Effectively, when you create a playlist, you're creating your own version of an album by combining songs you want to hear.

If you intend to use Windows Media Player as well as Windows 8 native Xbox Music app, you might prefer to create your playlist in Windows Media Player and then import it into the Windows 8 native Xbox Music app. See "Creating and playing a playlist" later in this lesson for details.

To create a playlist, follow these steps:

1 Tap or click My Music on the left side of the Xbox Music app.

2 In the list on the left, tap or click playlists.

3 Tap or click the plus sign on the right beside Start a new playlist.

Tap or click the plus sign beside Start a new playlist.

4 In the small box, type a name for the playlist and tap or click the Save button.

5 On the left side of the screen, tap or click Songs.

6 Tap or right-click a song in the list on the right.

7   Open the App bar at the bottom of the screen then, tap or click Add to playlist and add this song to the playlist you created in Step 4.

Adding a song to a playlist.

8   Repeat Steps 6 and 7 for each song you want to add to the playlist.

9   When you finish, you can tap or click the Back button to redisplay the main screen of the Xbox Music app. Your playlist appears in the My Music section.

Your play list appears in the My Music section.

10   Tap or click your playlist to play it.

Using the Windows 8 Video app

The native Windows 8 Video app, called the Xbox Video app, operates in much the same way as the Xbox Music app. To open Xbox Video, tap or click the Video app.

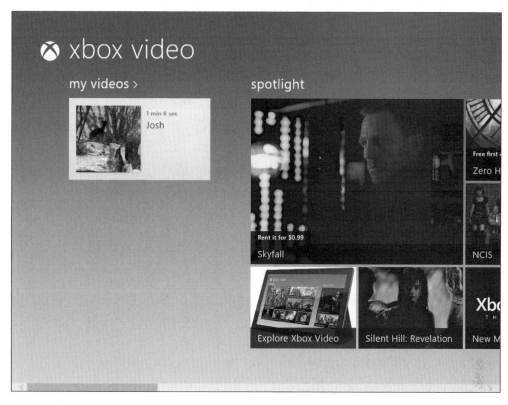

The Xbox Video app.

If you have any videos in your Videos library, they appear on the left side of the Xbox Video screen in the My Videos section. To watch a video, tap or click the video you want.

If you store videos from your phone or camera in the Pictures library, the Xbox Video app won't find them. You need to move your videos to the Videos library for the Xbox Video app to find them.

As you scroll to the right, you'll find available videos that you can preview and buy or rent divided into three sections: Spotlight, Movies Store, and Television Store. When you opt to buy or rent a video, the Xbox Video store asks you to confirm your purchase and then downloads the video to your Videos library.

If you don't see the video you want, use the Search charm to find it. While working in the Xbox Video app, display the Charms bar by sliding slightly in toward the center of the screen from the right side of the screen, pressing WinKey (⊞)+C, or placing your mouse in the upper- or lower-right corner of the screen. Then, tap or click the Search charm. In the Search box, type the name of the video and tap or click the magnifying glass. The search results for videos in the Windows Store appear.

Working with Windows Media Player

You can use the legacy Windows Media Player on the Desktop to listen to music and watch videos. The legacy Windows Media Player has the ability to do more than play music and videos and create playlists. You also can use it to rip and burn music and to control your privacy settings.

1   Display the Start screen.

2   Start typing Windows Media Player.

3   When it appears highlighted on the left, tap or click it.

Later in this lesson, you'll learn how to make Windows Media Player the default player. If you don't intend to make it the default player but want it easily available, pin it to the Desktop taskbar: search for Windows Media Player, display the App bar, and then choose Pin to Taskbar.

4   The first time you open Windows Media Player, it prompts you for setup information. To establish privacy controls, tap or click the Custom Settings option and tap or click Next.

The first time you open Windows Media Player, you will be asked to choose the initial settings for the player.

5 On the Select Privacy Options screen, select or deselect options based on your personal preferences. Then, tap or click Next.

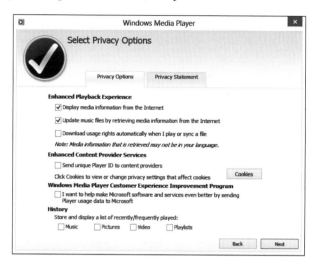

Select privacy-related options.

6 Choose whether you want Windows Media Player to be the default media player. By default, Windows 8 uses the Xbox Music and the Xbox Video apps as the default apps and opens them when you select a music or video file without first opening an app. Since you can still use them to play music or videos, opt to make Windows Media Player the default media player. Tap or click the Finish button.

Set Windows Media Player as the default media player.

If you don't set Windows Media Player as the default media player, you can select the types of files that Windows Media Player will play, and more screens in this setup wizard will appear.

Windows Media Player opens in Library view and populates its screen with albums that appear in the My Music library and the Public Music library on your computer, and if your computer is part of a Homegroup, Windows Media Player also searches other Homegroup computers for music.

A. *Address Bar.* **B.** *Task controls.* **C.** *Built-in playlist.* **D.** *Switch to Now Playing mode.* **E.** *Controls for playing media.* **F.** *Navigation pane.*

To select a task you want Windows Media Player to perform, use the three tabs in the upper-right corner of the Windows Media Player window: the Play, Burn, and Sync tabs. When you play music or a video, use the controls at the bottom of the screen. To select a location on your computer that contains media, use the Navigation pane running down the left side of the screen. The current location appears in the address bar.

You can connect an external music player and use the Sync tab to synchronize music on your computer with music on your external music player.

Playing music

In the center of the window, you see albums along with the songs they contain. The right side of the window acts as a built-in playlist when you start playing media. If you tap the Play button in the controls at the bottom of the screen, Windows Media Player fills the built-in playlist with all the songs on all the albums in your Music library, and starts playing media in the order they appear in the middle of the window.

> *If you're looking for music to buy, you have lots of options on the web. Just search for your favorite song or artist. Windows 8 will play any song you buy and download using either the Windows 8 native Xbox Music app or using Windows Media Player as long as you place the song in your Music library.*

Playing a CD

If you want to play a CD containing music, insert it into your device. If it doesn't start playing automatically, you'll see a notification asking what you want Windows to do when you insert an audio CD. If you opt to play the CD using Windows Media player, all future music CDs will play using Windows Media Player. If you opt to take no action, you can choose how to handle every audio CD you insert. If you choose to handle audio CDs individually, tap or click your CD/DVD drive in the Windows Media Player Navigation pane and then tap or click the Play button at the bottom of the Windows Media Player window.

Ripping music

You can copy music (called *ripping*) from an audio CD to your computer. When you rip music from a CD to your computer, Windows Media Player converts the audio tracks on the CD to a format that your computer can understand. By default, Windows Media Player uses the .WMA music file format, but that format is not as universally recognized as .MP3. To change Windows Media Player's settings to rip to the MP3 format, follow these steps:

1   Tap or click the Organize drop-down menu in the upper-left corner and choose Options from the list.

2 When the Options dialog box appears, tap or click the Rip Music tab.

On the Rip Music tab, you can change the format
Windows Media Player uses when it rips music.

3 In the Rip Settings section, open the Format list and select .MP3.

4 Tap or click OK.

Ripping music from a CD to your computer is a simple process:

1   Insert a music CD into your computer's CD drive. It will probably begin playing.

2   At the top of the screen, tap or click the Rip CD button. The Rip button changes to the Stop Rip button and the status of each track on the CD appears in the Rip Status column.

Ripping a CD to your computer.

Burning music to a CD

You can create a backup copy of a music CD or you can create your own CD made up of audio tracks you own. This section describes how to create an audio CD that works on most computers and players. This type of audio CD holds approximately one album's worth of music.

To help ensure success, you should check and modify Windows Media Player's Burn settings by following these steps:

1 Tap or click the Organize drop-down menu in the upper-left corner and choose Options from the list.

2 When the Options dialog box appears, tap or click the Burn tab.

Setting Burn options.

3 Set the Burn Speed to slow to help ensure that you produce a usable CD.

4 Change the Add a List Of All Burned Files To The Disc In This Format option to M3U, which is a more universal format.

5 Tap or click OK.

For this exercise, you'll need the files you downloaded to your hard drive from the Windows11lesson folder. Place these files in the Music library. If you want, place them in their own folder.

You'll also need a blank CD/DVD to burn music. To ensure that your CD works on any computer or music-playing device, use a CD-R or a DVD-R disc and not a read/write (RW) disc.

If you're creating a backup copy of a CD, start by ripping the tracks to your computer as described in the preceding section. Then, burn a new CD using the steps that follow.

1 Insert your blank CD into your CD/DVD drive. If you've never inserted a blank CD, Windows will display a notification asking how to handle blank CDs. You can safely tap or click Take No Action so that you can always decide how to handle a blank CD.

2 In Windows Media Player, tap or click the Burn tab.

3 Drag the tracks you want on your CD from the center of the window into the Burn list on the right side of the screen. For this exercise, drag the files you downloaded from the Windows11lesson folder into the Burn list. In Windows Media Player, the songs appear under the heading "Gary." As you select songs, the amount of free space remaining on the CD appears above the Burn list.

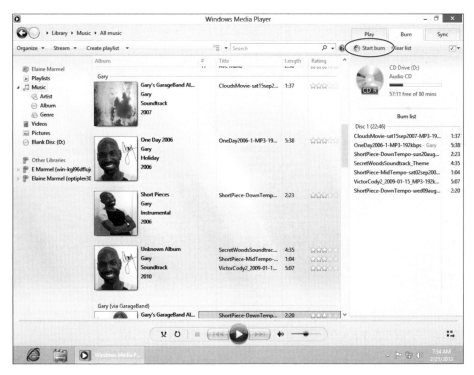

Creating a Burn list.

You can reorder a song in the Burn list by dragging it up or down.

4 When you finish adding songs to the Burn list, tap or click the Start Burn button above the Burn list. Windows Media Player burns the songs to the CD. You can watch the progress bars above and below the Burn list. When burning finishes, Windows Media Player ejects the CD.

Copying .MP3 files to a CD

A standard CD can hold many more .MP3 files than a CD formatted as an audio CD. But CD players, especially older ones, might not be able to interpret and play the .MP3 file format. If you know that you're going to be using your CD in a player that can play the .MP3 format, you can create a Data CD of .MP3 files. Follow the preceding steps to burn a CD, but before you perform Step 4, tap or click the button at the right edge of the Burn tab to display a menu of choices. From that menu, tap or click Data CD or DVD.

Select Data CD or DVD.

Then, tap or click the Start Burn button; Windows Media Player burns your CD. To play the CD, insert it into your device; File Explorer opens to display its content. You can double-tap or double-click the .M3U file to play it. You also can open Windows Media Player and use its Navigation pane to select the CD, and in the center pane, double-tap or double-click Music. Then, double-tap or double-click Album and use the Play button at the bottom of the screen to start playing the CD.

Creating and playing a playlist

If you have a favorite set of tracks in your Music library that you want to hear in an order of your choosing, you can create a playlist. If you don't have any music of your own in your Music library, you can use the files provided in the Windows11lesson folder for this exercise. They will appear in Windows Media Player under the heading "Gary."

If you created a custom CD in the preceding section with songs of your choosing from various albums, you can save your Burn list as a playlist. Tap or click the words "Burn List" above the songs you placed in the Burn list. Then, type the name you want to assign to the songs as a playlist.

1   Tap or click the Play tab.

2   Drag the songs you want to include in the playlist from the middle of the screen to the list on the right side of the screen. As you place songs in the playlist pane, Windows Media Player begins playing them.

You can reorder the songs in the list by dragging them up or down in the playlist, and you can remove a song by tapping and holding or right-clicking it and selecting Remove From List.

3   When you've got the list the way you want it, tap or click the Save list button above the list.

4 Type a name for the playlist.

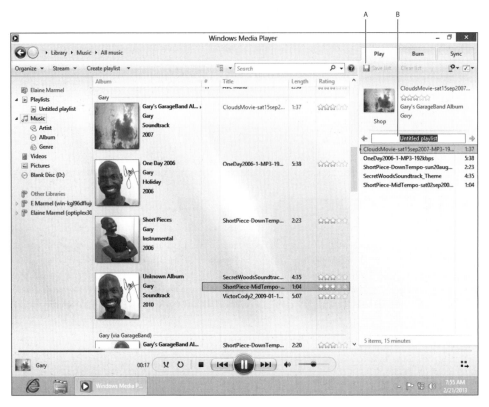

A. Tap or click here. **B.** *Type the playlist name here.*

Windows Media Player saves the playlist and displays it in the Navigation pane under the Playlists entry, even when you're playing other music.

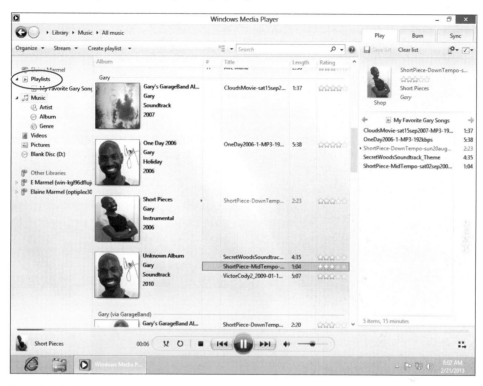

You can find playlists in the Navigation pane.

To play a playlist, double-tap or double-click it.

Importing a playlist from Windows Media Player to the Windows 8 native Xbox Music app

Although the Windows Media Player and the Windows 8 native Xbox Music app use your Music library, the two apps don't communicate directly. When you create a playlist in one, it doesn't appear by default in the other. There is no way to create a playlist in the Windows 8 native Xbox Music app and then make it appear in Windows Media Player, but you can go the other direction and create a playlist in Windows Media Player that you then import into the Windows 8 native Xbox Music app.

1   After you create a playlist in Windows Media Player, open the Windows 8 native Xbox Music app.

2   Tap or click My Music.

3   On the left side of the screen, tap or click Playlists.

4   Display the App bar by swiping down slightly from the top of the screen or by right-clicking anywhere on the screen.

Importing a playlist.

5   In the App bar, tap or click Import Playlists.

(continues)

Importing a playlist from Windows Media Player to the Windows 8 native Xbox Music app (continued)

6   In the message box that appears, tap or click the Import Playlists button. The Windows 8 native Xbox Music app adds any playlists you created with Windows Media Player to the playlists in the Windows 8 native Xbox Music app.

The Windows 8 native Xbox Music app adds playlists created in Windows Media Player.

Watching videos

You can use Windows Media Player to watch videos and play music by following these steps:

1 In the Windows Media Player Navigation pane, double-click or double-tap Videos. Your available videos appear in the center page.

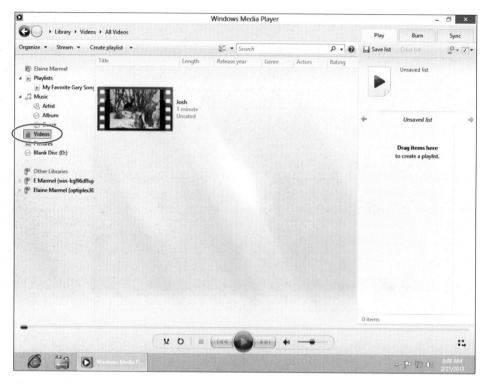

Selecting a video to play.

2   Double-tap or double-click the video you want to play. Windows Media Player switches to Now Playing mode and displays your video almost full-screen.

The Now Playing mode.

To hide everything on the screen, except for the video and its controls, tap or click the button in the lower-right corner of the screen. Tap or click it again to redisplay screen elements such as the taskbar.

3 When the video finishes playing, Windows Media Player gives you the option to play the video again, go to the library or play a previous list. Tap or click Go to Library to redisplay the Windows Media Player's Library mode.

Tap or click Go to Library when the video finishes.

Setting the default media player

You can select the default media player at any time.

1 Tap or click the Desktop app or press WinKey (⊞)+D.

2 Tap or click File Explorer on the Desktop taskbar.

3 Tap or click your Music library.

4 Find any music file and tap and hold or right-click it.

5 From the shortcut menu that appears, tap or click Open With.

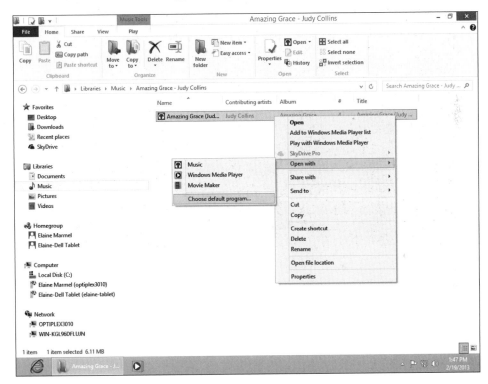

Tap and hold or right-click an audio file and select Open With from the shortcut menu.

If you see the program you want to use listed on the shortcut menu, tap or click it and skip Steps 6 and 7.

6 Tap or click Choose Default Program. File Explorer displays a window containing your options.

How do you want to open this file?

✓ Use this app for all .mp3 files

🎧 Keep using Music

🎞 Movie Maker

▶ Windows Media Player

More options

Select a default program to use for audio files.

7 Select a default program. In the future, Windows 8 will play the type of music file you selected in Step 4 using the default program you choose.

You can repeat these steps to set the default program you want to use for videos with the following changes:

• In Step 3, tap or click your Video library.

• In Step 4, tap and hold or right-click a video file.

Self study

1 Play a song using the Windows 8 native Xbox Music app.

2 Play a song using Windows Media Player.

Review

Questions

1 Where must you store music to be able to play it with the Windows 8 native Xbox Music app?

2 Where must you store music to be able to play it with Windows Media Player?

3 How do you create a playlist in the Windows 8 native Xbox Music app?

4 How do you create a playlist in Windows Media Player?

5 How do you rip music from a CD to your computer?

6 How do you burn music to a CD?

Answers

1 To be able to play music with the Windows 8 native Xbox Music app, you must store your music in the Music library on your computer or on a Homegroup computer.

2 To be able to play music with Windows Media Player, you must store your music in the Music library on your computer or on a Homegroup computer.

3 To create a playlist in the Windows 8 native Xbox Music app, tap or click My Music on the left side of the Xbox Music app, and in the list on the left, tap or click Playlists. On the right side of the screen, tap or click the plus sign beside Start A New Playlist. Provide a name for the playlist and tap or click the Save button. Then, on the left side of the screen, tap or click Songs; in the list on the right, tap or right-click a song. From the App bar, tap or click Add to *playlist name*, where *playlist name* is the name of the playlist you just created. Continue adding songs to the playlist. When you finish and redisplay the main screen of the Xbox Music app, your playlist appears in the My Music section.

4 To create a playlist in Windows Media Player, tap or click the Play tab. Then, drag the songs you want to include in the playlist from the middle of the screen to the list on the right side of the screen. When you've added all the songs you want in the playlist, tap or click the Save list button above the list and type a name for the playlist. Windows Media Player saves the playlist and displays it in the Navigation pane under the Playlists entry, even when you're playing other music.

5 To rip music from a CD to your computer using Windows Media Player, insert a music CD into your computer's CD drive. It will probably begin playing. At the top of the screen, tap or click the Rip CD button. The Rip button changes to the Stop Rip button and the progress for each track on the CD appears in the Rip Status column.

6 To burn music to a CD, open Windows Media Player and insert a blank CD into your CD/DVD drive. In Windows Media Player, tap or click the Burn tab. Then, drag the tracks you want on your CD from the center of the window into the Burn list on the right side of the screen. As you select songs, the amount of free space remaining on the CD appears above the Burn list. When you finish adding songs to the Burn list, tap or click the Start Burn button above the Burn list. Windows Media Player burns the songs to the CD, and you can watch the progress bars above and below the Burn list. When burning finishes, Windows Media Player ejects the CD.

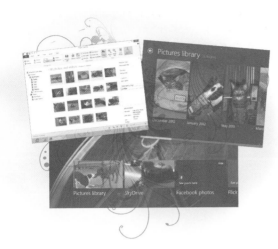

What you'll learn in this lesson:

- To work with the native Windows 8 Photos app

- To work with Windows Photo Viewer on the legacy Desktop

Photos and Pictures in Windows 8

In this lesson you will explore the Windows 8 native Photo app. You will also download and use the free Windows 8 Photo Gallery to browse and edit photos.

Starting up

In this lesson, you will work with several files from the Windows12lessons folder. Make sure that you have loaded the files from the Win8Lessons folder onto your hard drive. For more information, see "Loading lesson files" in the Starting Up section of this book.

See Lesson 12 in action!

Use the accompanying videos to gain a better understanding of how to use some of the features shown in this lesson. The video lesson for this tutorial can be found at www.DigitalClassroomBooks.com/Windows8.

The Windows 8 Photos app

The native Windows 8 Photos app helps you view photos from your computer, your SkyDrive account, Facebook, Flickr, and any devices you might have connected to your computer, all the while keeping the sources of your photos separate so you can determine where the photos are stored. The native Windows 8 Photos app can also help you search for a particular photo and organize your photos by date.

Browsing your photos

On the Start screen, the Photos app tile is a live tile, presenting a slideshow of the photos stored in your various picture sources.

The Photos app tile provides an ongoing slide show of your photos.

Tap or click the tile to open the Photos app and view its main screen.

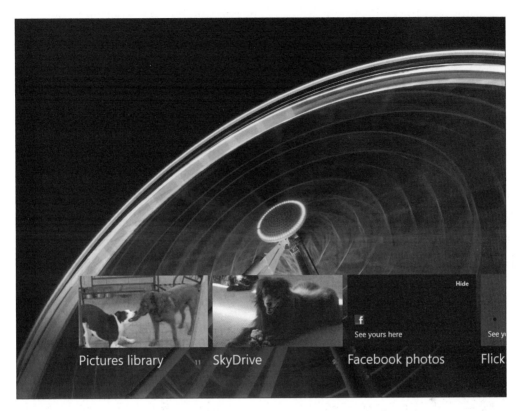

The Photos app showcases your photo libraries from SkyDrive, Facebook, Flickr, and from other devices.

Tap or click Pictures library to view the contents of both the local library and the Public Pictures folder. The Photos app presents tile representations for each folder you've set up in the Pictures library, displaying the folder name and the number of photos in the folder at the bottom of the tile. If your Pictures library contains photos not stored in a folder, the photos appear after the tiles that represent folders.

The contents of your Pictures library.

Photos available in the Photos app

The Photos app limits the display to just the photos in your Pictures library on your computer. If you're connected to a HomeGroup, you won't see the photos shared by other HomeGroup computers in the Photos app. You can see a still image of any video that you have stored in the Pictures library, but videos stored in the Videos library won't be represented in the Photos app. If you store a video in the Pictures library, you can play it from the Photos app; the video's representative image will contain a Play button you can tap or click.

To view photos stored in a folder in your Pictures library, tap or click that folder. To view a photo, tap or click it.

Working with a photo

While viewing a photo, display the App bar by swiping down slightly from the top of the screen or by right-clicking anywhere on the screen. The tools you can use while working with photos appear.

You can use the Photos app's tools to make some modifications to photos.

When you delete a photo, Windows 8 places the file in the Recycle Bin in the legacy Desktop app, where you can restore it if necessary. (For more information about using the Recycle Bin, see Lesson 6, "Using Files and Folders.")

If you tap or click the Set As button, you can set the picture to appear on the Windows 8 Lock Screen, the Photos app tile, or the Photos app background. Before you make these changes, consider carefully that you can easily change the image you assign to the Windows 8 Lock screen and you can re-establish a slideshow on the Photo app's tile, but it's difficult to return the Photos app's background to the default image because you must use the Refresh system recovery option.

To learn how to set the picture on the Windows 8 Lock screen and return the Photos app's background to the default image, see Lesson 13, "Customizing and Maintaining Windows 8."

To redisplay a slide show on the Photos app tile, follow these steps:

1   Display the Charms bar by sliding slightly in toward the center of the screen from the right side of the screen, pressing WinKey (⊞)+C, or placing your mouse in the upper- or lower-right corner of the screen.

2   Tap or click the Settings charm.

3   Tap or click Options.

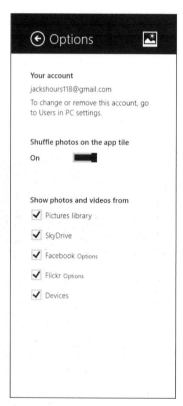

Select Options from the Charms bar.

4   Tap or click the Shuffle Photos On The App Tile option to turn it on.

Searching for photos

To search for a particular photo, you can use the Windows 8 Search charm. If you want to search in a particular folder, display that folder before you start the search. If you want to search all your photos in all locations, start the search from the main screen of the Photos app. This exercise uses the files found in the Windows12lessons folder, so make sure that you have loaded the files from the Win8Lessons folder onto your hard drive into the Pictures library.

1 In the Photos app, select the folder you want to search (for example, the Pictures library).

2 Display the Charms bar by sliding slightly in toward the center of the screen from the right side of the screen, pressing WinKey (⊞)+C, or placing your mouse in the upper- or lower-right corner of the screen.

3 Tap or click the Search charm.

4 In the Search box, type your search term (for example, type **Josh**).

Setting up a search in the Photos app.

5 Tap or click the magnifying glass beside your search term. The Photos app displays the results of your search. You can tap or click any blank space to hide the Charms bar.

The search results.

You can tap or click any photo to view it. To return to the Pictures folder, tap or click the Back button in the upper-left corner of the search results screen.

Displaying photos by date

You can browse through your photos by organizing them by date. The Photos app uses the date each photo file appeared on your computer (which is not necessarily the date you took the photo) to organize the photos in groups.

1 In the Photos app, tap or click the location you want to organize by date (for example, the Pictures library).

2 Display the App bar by swiping down slightly from the top of the screen or by right-clicking anywhere on the screen.

Setting up the Pictures library to browse by date.

3   Tap or click the Browse By Date button. The Photos app groups the photos in your Pictures library by month, displaying a large tile for each month.

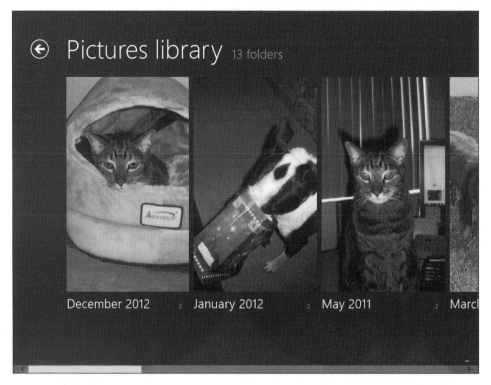

The Pictures library grouped by month.

You can tap or click any large tile to view the photos with file dates in the selected month. Use the Back button in the upper-left corner to navigate back up the folder structure. When you redisplay the main screen of the Photos app, the date groupings disappear.

Adding photos to the Photos app

You can add photos most easily to the Photos app by adding the photos to your Pictures library. If you are using SkyDrive as described in Lesson 10, "Sharing Device Settings and Content," any photos in the SkyDrive Pictures folder will also appear in the Photos app. You can add photos to the SkyDrive Pictures folder either by uploading them to SkyDrive or by placing them in the SkyDrive Pictures folder in File Explorer.

You also can connect Facebook or Flickr to the Photos app; if you do so, the Photos app will display all the images you've uploaded to either service. To connect the Photos app to your Facebook or Flickr accounts, you must:

- Use a Microsoft account; and
- Provide your Facebook and Flickr usernames and passwords so Microsoft can track your Facebook and Flickr information.

If you don't have any privacy concerns over Microsoft keeping your Facebook and Flickr passwords, then use these steps to connect the Photos app to your social networking accounts:

1   In the Photos app, tap or click either the Facebook Photos or Flickr Photos tile.

2   Tap or click the Connect button.

3   Provide your username and password.

4   Tap or click the Log In button.

When you connect a Flickr account, you have one additional step: Tap or click the OK, I'll Authorize It button on the page that appears after you log in.

Using Windows Photo Gallery

If you need photo management capabilities not offered by the Windows 8 native Photos app, you can download and install the free Windows Photo Gallery app, which is part of the Windows Essentials collection of free programs. Windows Photo Gallery works well on photo files commonly created by digital cameras, which are typically .JPG.

 If you have photo files of other types that you want to edit, you might be able to have Windows Photo Gallery make .JPG copies of them so you can edit them. Double-tap or double-click the photo and, on the Edit tab of the Ribbon, tap or click the Make A Copy button. In the dialog box that appears, open the Save As Type list and select JPG.

You can use Windows Photo Gallery to view, manage, share, and edit digital photos, and to a lesser extent, videos. Windows Photo Gallery displays all the photos in the Pictures library on your hard drive, including those that you import from a digital camera, memory card, or scanner.

Windows Photo Gallery makes it easy for you to find photos and videos and view them by name, date, tag, and other criteria. You also can use Windows Photo Gallery to combine photos into panoramic views, add captions, and edit photos or make movies and slide shows from still photos and videos, and more.

In this section, you'll explore some of the features that the Windows 8 Photo Gallery has to offer. Follow these steps to download and install Windows Photo Gallery:

1 Open Internet Explorer (either version) and type **download.live.com** in the address bar.

2 Scroll down the page and tap or click the Download Now button. A message appears at the bottom of the page, asking whether you want to run or save the Windows Essentials installation file.

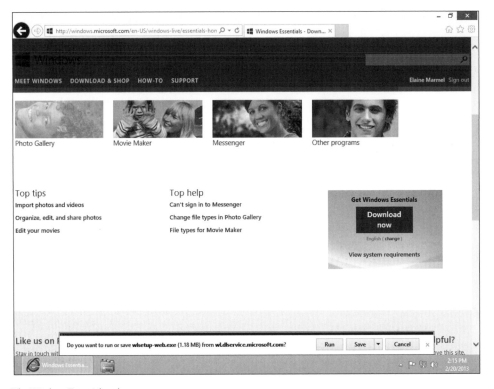

The Windows Essentials web page.

3 Tap or click the Run button.

If your PC does not have the .NET framework installed, you may receive a notification from Windows 8 indicating that it needs to be installed. Simply, press OK for the framework to be installed and the installation will begin. Once the installation is completed, Windows 8 will need to be rebooted. Once your PC has rebooted, you will need to go to http://download.live.com in Internet Explorer once again, and tap or click the Download Now button for the Windows Photo Gallery. You can now continue to follow the steps in this section.

4 On the first screen of the Windows Live Essentials installation wizard, tap or click Choose The Programs You Want To Install.

Choose to install only some Windows Essentials programs.

5 The installation program presents the programs you can install and places checkmarks beside all of them. Tap or click the check boxes beside each program you don't want to install. For this example, check only Photo Gallery and Movie Maker.

Select Windows Essentials programs to install.

6   Tap or click the Install button.

Windows installs the Windows Essentials 2012 programs for Windows Photo Gallery and Windows Movie Maker.

If you know you're going to use these programs frequently, you can pin them to the legacy Desktop app's taskbar or create a Desktop shortcut as described in Lesson 5, "Working with Desktop Apps."

Opening Windows Photo Gallery

To open the Windows Photo Gallery app, display the Windows 8 Start screen and type "Photo Gallery." When you see the entry for the Photo Gallery app, tap or click it. The first time you open the app, you'll need to read and accept the licensing agreement that appears; tap or click the Accept button.

Windows Photo Gallery then prompts you to sign in using your Microsoft account. You only need to sign in if you want to use Windows Photo Gallery with photos you've stored in your SkyDrive Pictures folder. If you want to sign in, supply your Microsoft account e-mail address and password and tap or click the Sign In button. Otherwise, tap or click the Cancel button to use Windows Photo Gallery without signing in and open Windows Photo Gallery.

The Windows Photo Gallery window functions in much the same way as File Explorer. On the left, you see the Navigation pane, and on the right, the contents pane displays the contents of the folder selected in the Navigation pane. When you first open Windows Photo Gallery, the contents pane displays thumbnails for the photos stored in your Pictures library, organized by the date you placed the photos in the Pictures library.

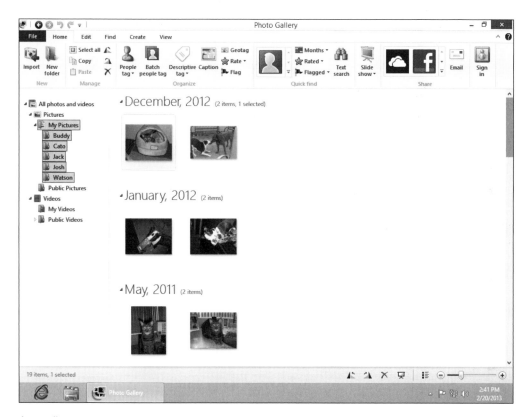

Photo Gallery's opening screen.

Working in Windows Photo Gallery on a touch device is not conducive to selecting multiple photos. We suggest that you use Windows Photo Gallery on a device that has a keyboard and mouse.

Viewing pictures

Use the Navigation pane on the left to control the images you view in Windows Photo Gallery. For example, to view only your videos, click the Videos library.

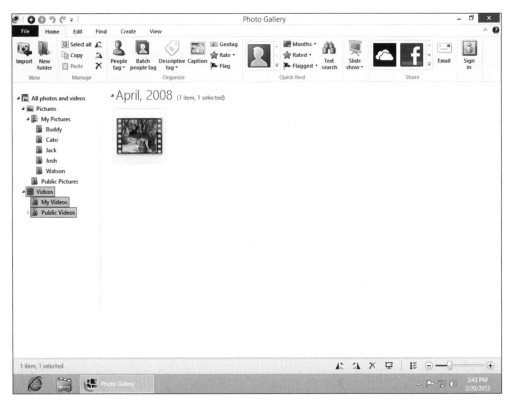

Use the Navigation pane to control the types of images you view.

If you click All Photos and Videos at the top of the Navigation pane, Windows Photo Gallery displays thumbnails for all images in both the Pictures library and the Videos library.

From the View tab on the Ribbon, you can use the Arrange List panel to change the way the photos appear in the contents pane.

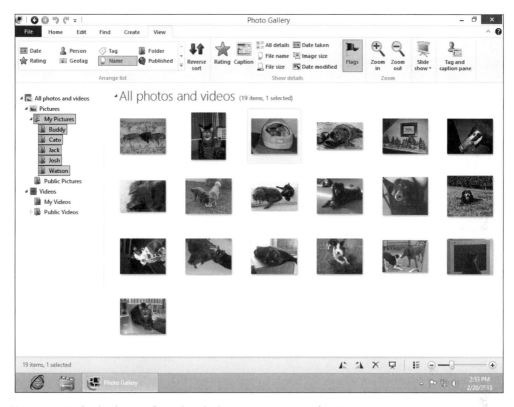

You can organize thumbnail images of your photos by date, name, type, or tag information.

You can use the Show Details section of the View tab to add information about each image to the view. For example, when you click the All details button, Windows Photo Gallery displays, for each image, the file name, the date you placed it on your computer, the file size, the image resolution, any rating you applied to the photo, and any caption you created for the photo.

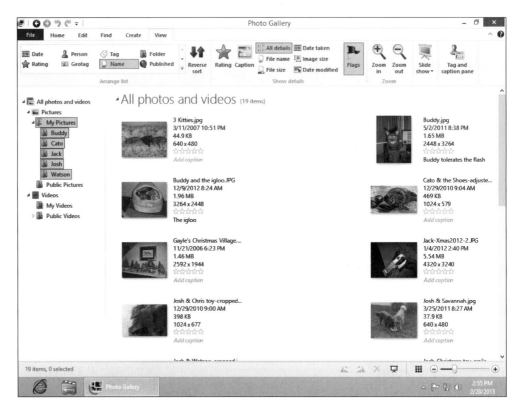

Click the All details button to display detailed information about your photos.

Adding tags and captions

You can add tags and captions to your photos to help you find and identify them. If you tag your photos with meaningful words and phrases, you can search for photos using those tags. Captions help identify a photo; you might provide a caption that helps you remember the people in the photo, the place where you took the photo, or the circumstances under which you took it.

You can assign the same tag to multiple photos simultaneously.

1   Select all the photos to which you want to assign the same tag. For images that appear contiguously in the contents pane, press and hold Shift as you click the first and last pictures. If the images don't appear contiguously, press and hold Ctrl as you click each image.

2   Click the View tab on the Ribbon.

3   Click the Tag and Caption Pane button to display the Tag and Caption pane.

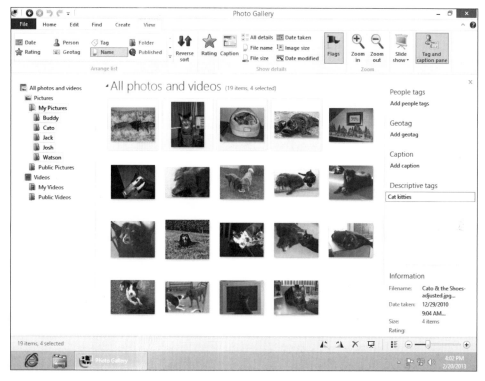

Use the Tag and Caption Pane to add tags, captions, and ratings to photos.

4   In the Tag and Caption pane, click one of the tag "add" buttons. You can add a "people" tag that identifies a person in the photo, a "geotag" that identifies the location where the photo was taken, and a "descriptive" tag for the photo.

In reality, all three types of tags are "descriptive" tags and you'll be able to search for photos using all three types of tags without differentiating the type of tag.

5   Type a word or phrase in the text field for the desired tag.

6   Press Enter or click anywhere outside the tag button.

You can add a caption to a photo the same way you add a tag, and you can add the same caption to multiple photos by selecting those photos before you assign the caption.

To use tags to find photos, click the Find tab. Then, click the Text Search button and supply a tag. If you supply more than one tag, Windows Photo Gallery finds only those photos that match all the tags you type.

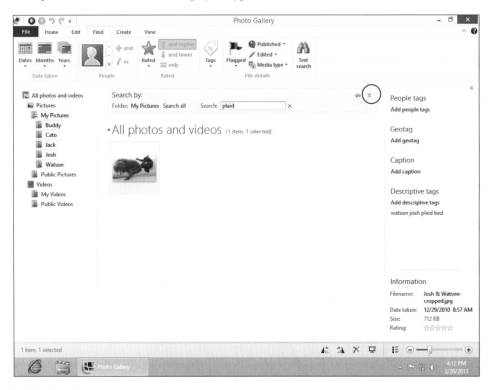

Searching for a photo.

When you use the Text Search, you can supply photo file name or caption information; you aren't limited to supplying tags.

To cancel a search, click the X beside the push pin.

If you find the Tag and Caption pane distracting, close it. Click the View tab on the Ribbon and then click the Tag and Caption Pane button.

Rotate a picture

Sometimes, when you take a digital photo, you might rotate your camera for a different angle. When you transfer the photo to your computer, the picture retains the rotated angle. You can use Windows Photo Gallery to turn the picture to view it on your computer screen.

1   In the Windows Photo Gallery Navigation pane, select the Jack folder.

2   In the right-hand content pane, click the image named **Jack and the squeaky snake.jpg** to select it.

3   At the bottom of the Windows Photo Gallery screen, click the Rotate Right button. Windows Photo Gallery rotates the image 90 degrees in a clockwise direction.

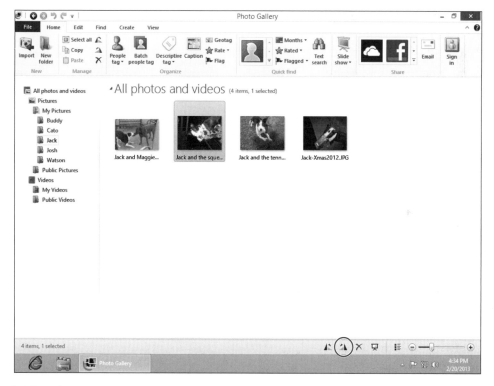

Rotating an image.

Resize a picture

Occasionally, you might find it useful to reduce the file size of a photo. For example, smaller photo files load onto web pages much more quickly than larger photo files. When you use resize a photo file using the following steps, Windows Photo Gallery creates a copy of the file in the new size and leaves the original photo file untouched on your hard drive.

Resizing a copy is important because smaller images load faster onto web pages, but larger images produce better physical prints.

1   In the Windows Photo Gallery Navigation pane, select the Buddy folder.

2   Click the image named **Buddy and the igloo.jpg**.

You can resize multiple images simultaneously by selecting all the images you want to resize.

3   Click the Edit tab on the Ribbon.

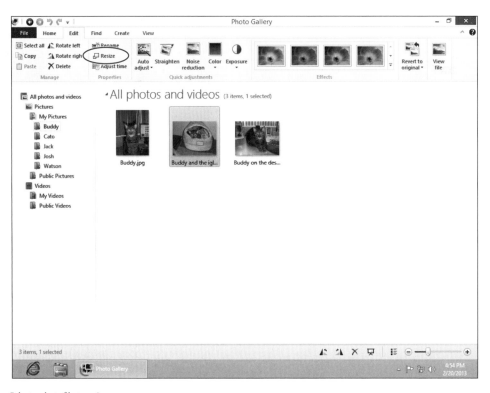

Select a photo file to resize.

4 Click the Resize button. The Resize dialog box appears.

Use this dialog box to resize an image.

5 From the Select a size drop-down menu, choose a size.

6 Click the Resize and Save button. Windows Photo Gallery creates a copy of the photo file and reduces its file size.

The copy appears in the same folder as the original, and Windows Photo Gallery adds the size you selected to the name of the copy; the size appears in parentheses after the file name. You can most easily distinguish between the two files if you select the File Size view on the View tab.

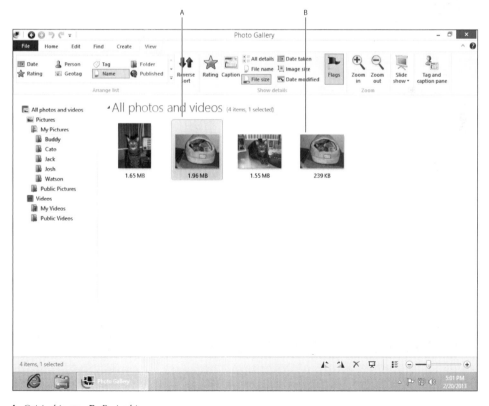

*A. Original image. **B.** Resized image.*

Print a picture

You can use Windows Photo Gallery to print a photo on your local printer.

1 In the Windows Photo Gallery Navigation pane, select the Josh folder.

2 Click the image named **Josh–headshot.jpg**.

3 Click the File tab.

4 Point the mouse pointer at Print.

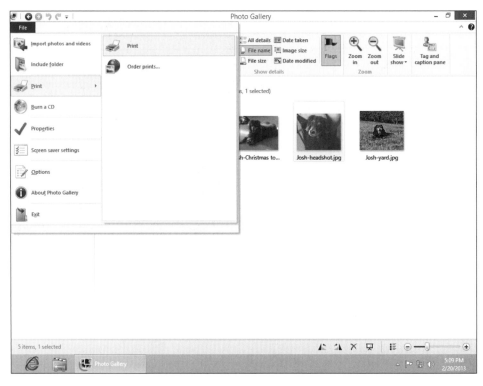

Printing a photo.

You can use the Order Prints option to upload selected photos to a photo printing company: CVS Pharmacy, Fujifilm, HP's Snapfish, Kodak, or Shutterfly. Each of these companies will print your photos for a fee.

5 Click Print. The Print Pictures dialog box appears.

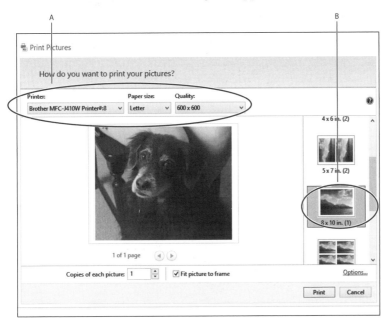

A. Select printer settings. B. Select a print size.

6 Select a printer, paper size, and print quality. Use the pane at the right to select a print size, and at the bottom, select the number of copies you want to print.

7 Click the Print button.

Burn pictures to a disc

You can share your pictures and all their metadata (tags, captions, and so on) if you burn the pictures to a CD or a DVD.

Some people store backups of photos on CDs, but note that CDs can fail without warning. We suggest that you store backups on external hard drives or flash drives, which are less likely to fail without warning.

1 Place a blank CD or DVD into your CD/DVD drive. If Windows displays a notification asking how to handle blank discs, ignore it.

2 In Photo Gallery, select all the pictures you want to place on the disc. For this example, select the Watson folder in Photo Gallery's Navigation pane. Then, on the Home tab of the Ribbon, click the Select All button in the Manage group.

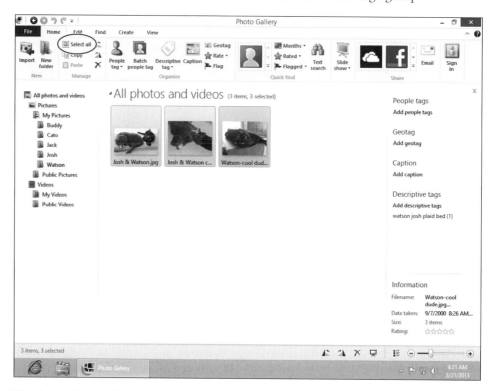

Select photos to place on a disc.

3 Click the File tab.

4   Click Burn a CD. File Explorer opens, offering to burn a disc. You can ignore the message in the lower-right corner of the Desktop that indicates you have files waiting to be burned.

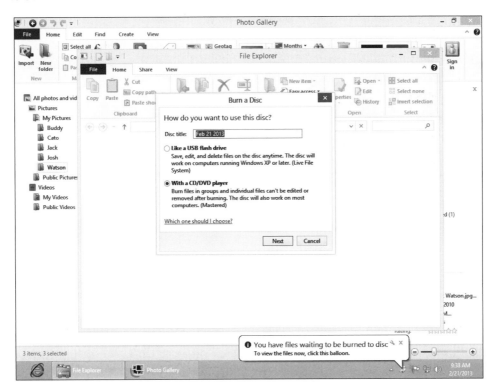

Click "Burn a Disc" then type in a title for your disc.

5   Optionally, type a title for the disc; select With A CD/DVD Player.

The CD/DVD Player option creates a disc that will work on most computers.

6   Click Next. File Explorer copies the files into memory, making them ready to be written to your disc.

7   Click the Manage tab.

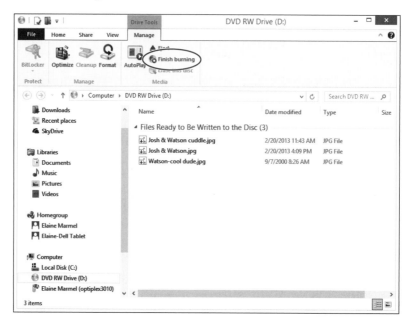

File Explorer displays the files waiting to be written to disc.

8   Click the Finish Burning button. File Explorer starts the Burn to Disc wizard. Once again, you have the opportunity to supply a disc title.

9   Select a recording speed; selecting a lower speed helps ensure that you'll burn the files successfully.

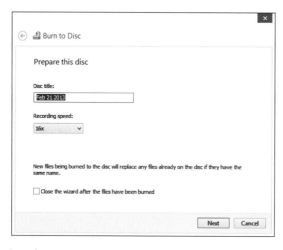

Set up burning parameters.

10   Click Next. File Explorer burns the files to the disc and displays a progress bar as it works.

11   When File Explorer finishes, click Finish. File Explorer also ejects the disc for you.

Self study

1 Select a photo in the native Windows 8 Photos app and display the App bar to identify the actions you can take.

2 Search for a photo while using the native Windows 8 Photos app.

3 Search for a photo while using Windows Photo Gallery.

Review

Questions

1 How do you display photos by date in the native Windows 8 Photos app?

2 How do you display photos by date in Windows Photo Gallery?

3 How do you add pictures to those already shown in the native Windows 8 Photos app? In Windows Photo Gallery?

4 How do you add tags to photos?

5 How do you resize a photo?

Answers

1 To display photos by date in the native Windows 8 Photos app, begin by selecting a location where you store pictures, for example, the Pictures library or your SkyDrive, and then display the App bar and tap or click the Browse By Date button.

2 To display photos by date in Windows Photo Gallery, click the View tab and then click Date in the Arrange List group.

3 To add pictures to those already shown in the native Windows 8 Photos app or Windows Photo Gallery, add pictures to the Pictures library. Adding pictures to SkyDrive, Facebook, or Flickr can also add photos to the native Windows 8 Photos app.

4 To add tags to photos, do the following: in Windows Photo Gallery, display the Tag and Caption Pane from the View tab on the Ribbon. Then, click any of the "Add Tags" buttons to add a People tag, a Geotag, or a Descriptive tag.

5 To resize a photo, do the following: in Windows Photo Gallery, select the photos you want to resize (you can simultaneously resize multiple photos) and click the Resize button on the Edit tab of the Ribbon. In the Resize dialog box, select a size and click the Resize and Save button. Windows Photo Gallery makes a copy of the photo and resizes the copy so you retain the original as well as the resized version.

What you'll learn in this lesson:

- Understanding how to change Windows 8 settings

- Personalizing Windows

- Handling misbehaving programs

- Backing up and restoring files

- An overview of system recovery options

Customizing and Maintaining Windows 8

This lesson explores the ways you can customize and maintain Windows 8 for both the native Windows 8 apps and the legacy Desktop apps.

Starting up

You will not need to work with any files for this lesson.

See Lesson 13 in action!

Use the accompanying videos to gain a better understanding of how to use some of the features shown in this lesson. The video lesson for this tutorial can be found at www.DigitalClassroomBooks.com/Windows8.

Understanding how to change settings in Windows 8

The Windows 8 operating system introduces an entirely new type of Windows to the world: a two-layered edition of Windows. In the simplest possible terms, users of past editions of Windows saw the Desktop when they started their computers, and they customized and maintained the Desktop using the Control Panel. Windows 8 continues to support the Desktop environment along with the apps that run on it, and Windows 8 users can customize and maintain the Desktop using the Control Panel.

But Windows 8 also introduces a new environment under which a new type of app can run, referred to as the "native Windows 8." It shouldn't be surprising that the new environment has its own tool for customization and maintenance: the PC Settings screen.

To summarize, you customize and maintain Windows 8 in two different ways:

- When you want to affect the native Windows 8 apps, work in the PC Settings screen.
- When you want to affect apps that run on the legacy Desktop, or the legacy Desktop app itself, use the Control Panel.

If you've used previous editions of Windows and are somewhat familiar with the Control Panel, we suggest that you think of Windows 8 as having two control panels: one that controls the native Windows 8 apps and the Start screen, and one that controls the Desktop and apps that run on it. If you visualize two control panels, we believe you'll find it easier to understand where to go when you want to make a change.

Personalizing Windows

You can personalize the two environments of Windows 8:

- For native Windows 8: the environment's Start screen, Lock screen, and account picture.
- For the Desktop app: the app's appearance.

Personalizing the Start screen

The Start screen is an element of the native Windows 8 environment; use the PC Settings screen to personalize it. You can personalize the Start screen by selecting a background color scheme and pattern for it.

1   Display the Charms bar by sliding slightly in toward the center of the screen from the right side of the screen, pressing WinKey (⊞)+C, or placing your mouse in the upper- or lower-right corner of the screen.

2   Tap or click the Settings charm.

Select the Settings charm.

3   Tap or click Change PC Settings at the bottom of the Settings charm panel. Windows 8 displays the PC Setting screen.

4   On the left side of the screen, tap or click Personalize.

5   At the top of the right side of the screen, tap or click Start screen.

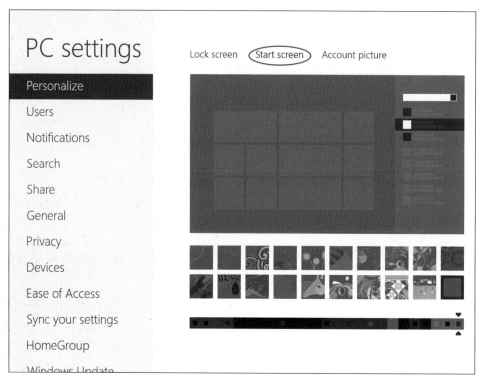

Use this screen to select a background color scheme and pattern for the Windows 8 Start screen.

6   Tap or click a color scheme from the bottom band of color schemes; Windows displays a preview of the color scheme.

7   Using the two rows above the color schemes, select a background pattern; Windows displays a preview of the background pattern.

8 When you're done, redisplay the Start screen to see the effects of your changes.

The Start screen changes to match your selections.

Personalizing the Lock screen

The Lock screen appears the first time you start Windows 8 and each time you restart your computer. It also appears any time you let your computer stand idle or if you lock your computer.

The default Lock screen.

Using the PC Setting screen, you can select your own image to appear on the Lock screen.

1   Display the Charms bar by sliding slightly in toward the center of the screen from the right side of the screen, pressing WinKey (⊞)+C, or placing your mouse in the upper- or lower-right corner of the screen.

2   Tap or click the Settings charm.

3   Tap or click Change PC Settings at the bottom of the Settings charm panel. Windows 8 displays the PC Setting screen.

4   On the left side of the screen, tap or click Personalize.

5 At the top of the right side of the screen, tap or click Lock screen.

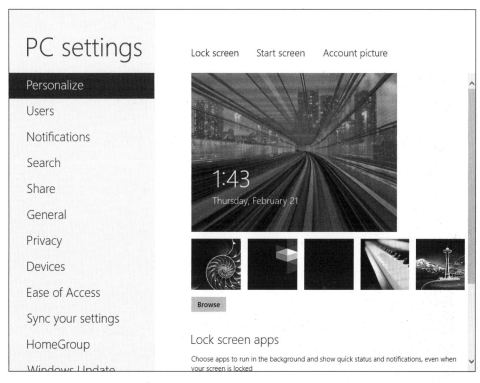

Select a different image for the Windows 8 Lock screen.

6 Tap or click one of the five default images below the preview.

 To use a photo stored in your Pictures library, tap or click the Browse button.

Once you select an image, Windows 8 uses that image whenever it displays the Lock screen.

Setting an account picture

By default, Windows 8 uses a generic icon to represent your account, but you can change it. Since the icon represents an account picture, many people use a picture of themselves, but you can use any picture you want.

1 Tap or click your name on the Windows Start screen.

2 From the menu that appears, tap or click Change Account Picture. Windows 8 displays the Account picture screen in PC Settings.

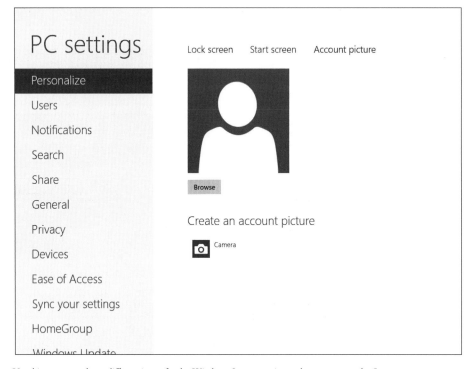

Use this screen to select a different image for the Windows 8 account picture that appears on the Start screen.

3 Tap or click the Browse button to select an image from your Pictures library.

If you're working on a device that contains a camera, you can tap or click the Camera button to take a picture to use.

The picture you select appears on the Start screen and the log in screen, if you log into your computer using a password.

If you log in to your computer using a Microsoft account, supply the password associated with that account. See Lesson 14, "Keeping Your Computer Safe and Protecting Your Privacy," for information on creating passwords for local accounts.

Personalizing the Desktop

Most people choose to use a *theme*, which is a predefined set of background images, colors, sounds, and screen savers, to personalize the Desktop. Although you can set these features individually, this section focuses on selecting and changing a theme's slideshow of background images. You also learn where to get more themes.

1   From the Start screen, tap or click the Desktop app.

2   Tap and hold or right-click a blank spot on the Desktop.

3   From the shortcut menu that appears, tap or click Personalize to open the Control Panel's Personalization window.

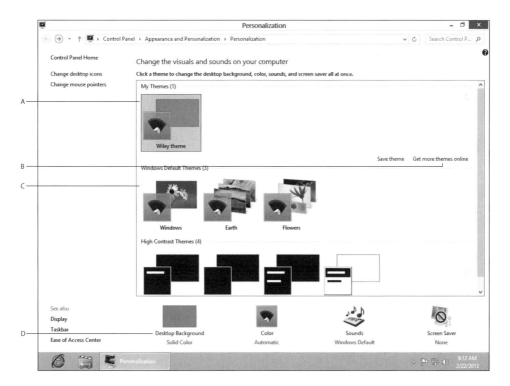

A. A personalized saved theme. ***B.*** *Get more themes online link.* ***C.*** *Windows Default Themes.*
D. *Desktop Background options link.*

You can select a theme from the default themes provided and close the Control Panel if you're satisfied with the selection. You also can customize the theme. For example, instead of using one background image, many themes, including the default Earth and Flowers themes, provide a slideshow of background images. You can control that slideshow by changing the timing between the image changes and even the images included in the slideshow. You also can control:

- The colors of the taskbar and window borders
- The sounds you hear when actions, such as errors, occur
- Whether a screen saver appears if you leave your computer idle for a specified time

Screensavers, while interesting, are no longer necessary. Originally, they helped ensure that no particular image was burned into your monitor if you left that image displayed for any length of time. But the technology used in monitors today has changed and you no longer need to worry about burning any image into your screen.

Use the following steps to customize a theme's Desktop Background slideshow:

1   Tap or click the Earth theme.

2   Tap or click the Desktop Background link to display the options for changing your Desktop background.

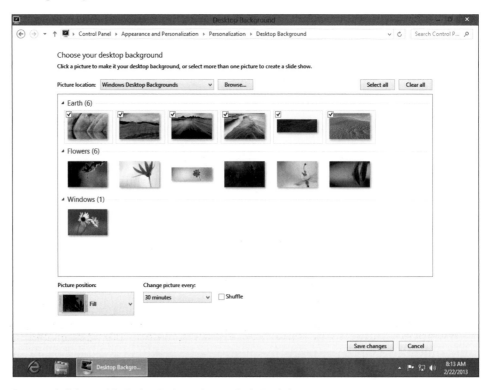

Customize the behavior of the Desktop Background images for the Earth theme.

You can select a different set of background images by opening the Picture Location list. If you select Pictures Library, you can display photos from the library on your Desktop.

3 To eliminate an image from the slideshow, remove the checkmark from its checkbox. To add an image, click it and then select its checkbox.

4 Use the Picture Position drop-down menu to determine how the image appears on your screen; most often, you'll want to select Fill to let the image cover the entire Desktop, but you can experiment with the other available choices.

5 Use the Change Picture Every drop-down menu to specify the amount of elapsed time between slideshow images. Use the Shuffle checkbox to make Windows mix up the images instead of displaying them in a specific order.

6 When you finish customizing the Desktop background slideshow, tap or click the Save Changes button at the bottom of the window to redisplay the Control Panel's Personalization window. A new entry appears in the My Themes section, and that entry represents the theme you modified.

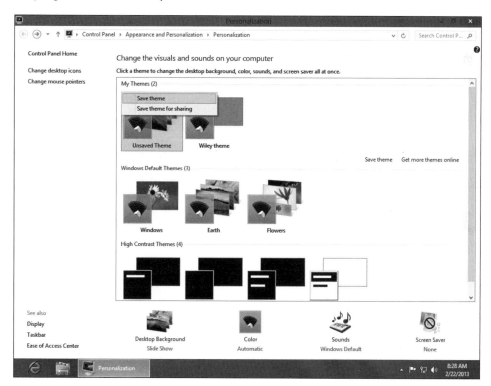

The Personalization window reappears.

7 Tap and hold or right-click the Unsaved Theme and tap or click Save Theme.

8   In the dialog box that appears, type a name that identifies the theme.

If you aren't satisfied with the default themes that come with Windows, you can find more themes online; most themes are free. Tap or click the Get More Themes Online link at the right edge of the My Themes section. Internet Explorer opens and displays the Themes page.

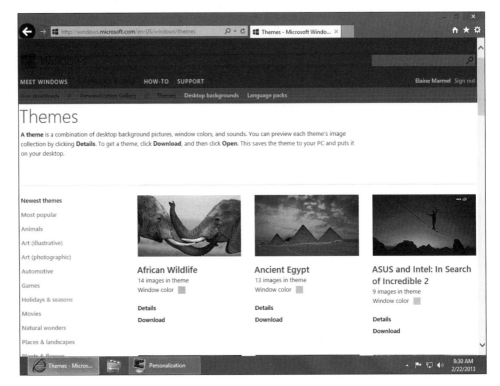

The Windows Themes page.

You can tap or click Details beneath any theme image to read more about the theme. To use a theme, tap or click Download below that theme.

You cannot delete a theme in the My Themes section while you are using it, but if you switch to a different theme, you can then tap and hold or right-click the theme you want to delete and tap or click Delete Theme from the shortcut menu that appears. Deleting a theme from the My Themes section affects only the modifications you made and not the original theme.

Date and time settings

From the PC Settings screen, you can control your time zone and whether your computer automatically adjusts the time to accommodate daylight savings time.

1   Display the Charms bar by sliding slightly in toward the center of the screen from the right side of the screen, pressing WinKey (⊞)+C, or placing your mouse in the upper- or lower-right corner of the screen.

2   Tap or click the Settings charm.

3   Tap or click Change PC Settings at the bottom of the Settings charm panel. Windows 8 displays the PC Setting screen.

4   On the left side of the screen, tap or click General.

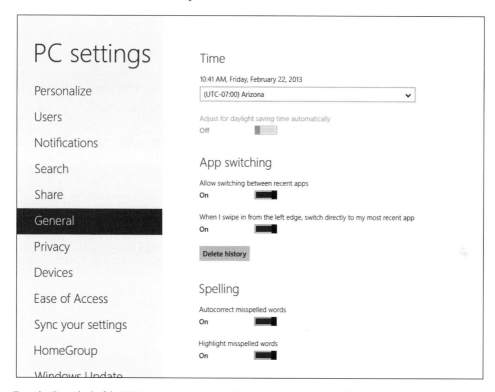

From the General tab of the PC Settings screen, you can adjust the time zone and daylight saving time settings.

From the legacy Desktop, today's date and time appear in the System Tray at the right edge of the taskbar. Using legacy Desktop tools, you can:

- Select a time zone
- Change the date and time
- Display additional clocks for time zones you select
- Control the way your computer synchronizes its clock with Internet time

To display legacy Desktop date and time tools, follow these steps:

1   Display the Desktop app.

2   In the lower-right corner of the screen, at the right edge of the taskbar, tap or click the displayed date and time. The Desktop app displays this month's calendar, highlighting today's date, and an analog clock displaying the current time.

When you click the date and time in the System Tray, this window appears.

3   Tap or click Change Date And Time Settings to display the Date and Time dialog box.

From the Date and Time tab, you can change the date and time as well as the time zone. From the Internet Time tab, you can change the website Windows uses to synchronize your computer's clock; the default website is *time.windows.com*. Using the Additional Clocks tab, you can display two additional clocks each time you tap or click the date and time information in the System Tray.

To add clocks to the date and time display, follow these steps:

1 Tap or click the Additional Clocks tab.

2 Tap or click the first Show This Clock checkbox to select it.

3 Use the Select Time Zone drop-down menu to select a time zone for the clock.

4 In the Enter Display Name box, type a name for the clock, such as the time zone you selected.

5 Repeat Steps 3 to 5 for the second Show This Clock checkbox.

Set up clocks for two additional time zones.

7   Click OK.

When you tap or click the date in the System Tray, the legacy Desktop displays this month's calendar and clocks for three time zones.

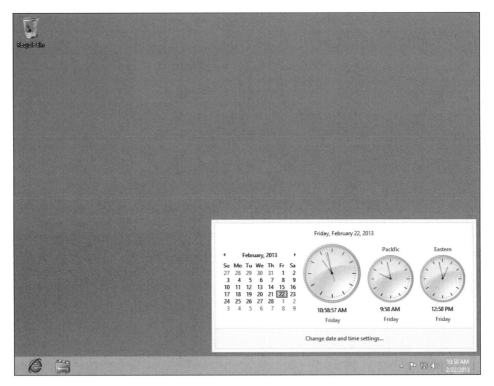

You can keep track of the time in up to three time zones.

Updating Windows 8

From time to time, Microsoft releases patches to its operating systems and other programs, such as Microsoft Office. These patches are free, and generally, they modify the operating system to make it more usable and more secure. You can obtain the patches via the Windows Update utility that comes with Windows 8.

By default, Windows 8 automatically checks for and installs any updates designated as "important." You can view the status of updates and even manually check for updates from the PC Settings screen:

1   Display the Charms bar by sliding slightly in toward the center of the screen from the right side of the screen, pressing WinKey (⊞)+C, or placing your mouse in the upper- or lower-right corner of the screen.

2   Tap or click the Settings charm.

3   Tap or click Change PC Settings at the bottom of the Settings charm panel. Windows 8 displays the PC Setting screen.

4   On the left side of the screen, tap or click Windows Update.

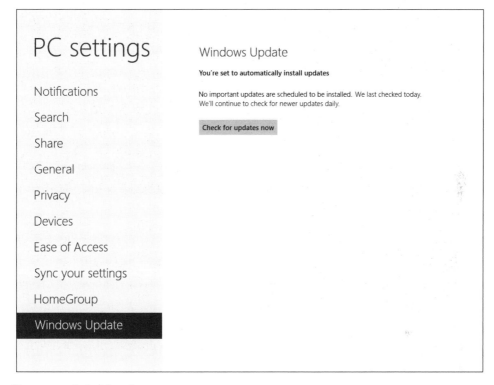

You can manually check for updates.

5   To manually check for updates, tap or click the Check For Updates Now button.

If you want to control the behavior of the Windows Update utility, use the Desktop Control Panel.

1   Display the Start screen.

2   Type Control Panel.

3   When the Control Panel entry appears, tap or click it.

4 In the Search box in the upper-right corner of the Control Panel, type Windows Update and tap or click the magnifying glass or press Enter.

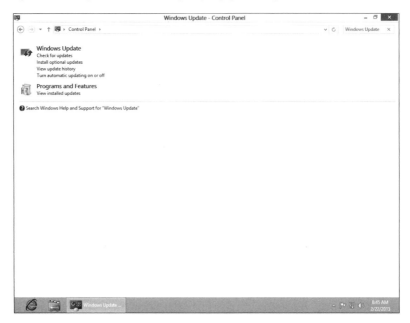

Tap or click Windows Update.

5 Tap or click the Windows Update entry in the list that appears to display the Windows Update window.

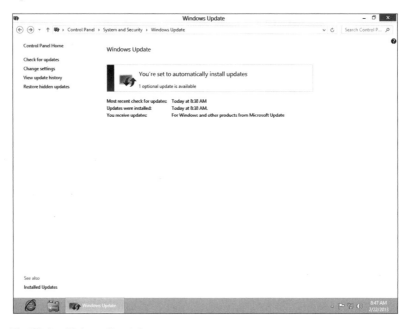

The Windows Update utility window.

6   On the left side of the window, tap or click Change Settings to display the Windows
Update settings you can control.

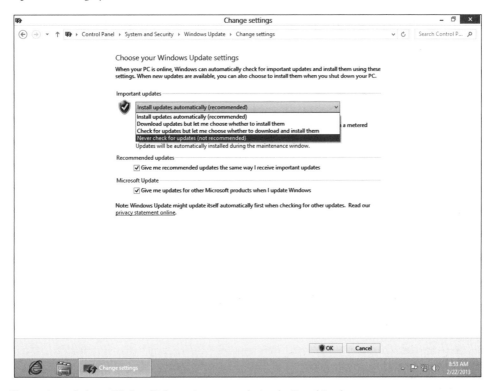

You can change the legacy Windows Update settings to manual using the Control Panel.

The Important Updates section displays the way Windows handles updates; you
can use the drop-down menu to change the method. You can opt not to receive
recommended updates or updates for other Microsoft products by removing the
checkmarks from those checkboxes. When you finish, tap or click OK.

Setting notification options

Many apps you install might want your attention at various times. For example, the Mail
app might want to let you know that you've received new e-mails. Notifications from
native Windows 8 apps appear on the Lock screen and as you work. Notifications from
legacy Desktop apps appear in the System Tray in the lower-right corner of the Desktop
taskbar.

You can control the notifications that appear; use the PC Settings screen to control
notifications from native Windows 8 apps, and the Control Panel to control notifications
from legacy Desktop apps.

To control notifications from native Windows 8 apps, follow these steps:

1 Display the Charms bar by sliding slightly in toward the center of the screen from the right side of the screen, pressing WinKey (⊞)+C, or placing your mouse in the upper- or lower-right corner of the screen.

2 Tap or click the Settings charm.

3 Tap or click Change PC Settings at the bottom of the Settings charm panel. Windows 8 displays the PC Setting screen.

4 On the left side of the screen, tap or click Notifications.

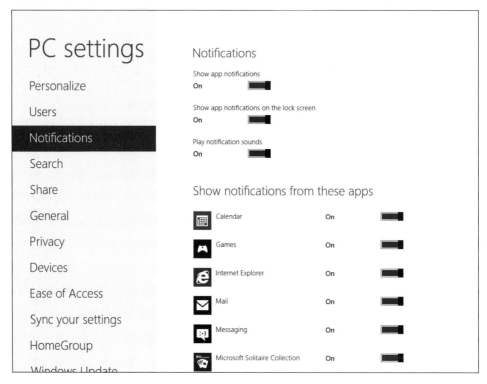

Notification settings for native Windows 8 apps.

5 To turn off all notifications, tap or click the Show App Notifications button so it changes from On to Off.

6 To hide notifications on the Lock Screen, tap or click the Show App Notifications On The Lock Screen button so it changes from On to Off.

7 To eliminate sounds when Windows notifies you, tap or click the Play Notification Sounds button so it changes from On to Off.

8 Use the list below these buttons to control which apps can notify you.

Notifications from legacy Desktop apps appear in the legacy Desktop app's System Tray at the right edge of the taskbar. In addition, the taskbar displays icons for some programs. You can hide the icons of programs that you don't need to see (typically, you won't need to see a program icon if you don't use that icon for anything) and you can control the notifications issued by legacy Desktop apps.

1   Display the Start screen.

2   Type Control Panel.

3   When you see the Control Panel entry appear, tap or click it.

4   In the Search box in the upper-right corner of the Control Panel, type Notifications and tap or click the magnifying glass or press Enter.

5   Tap or click Notification Area Icons to display the Notification Area Icons window.

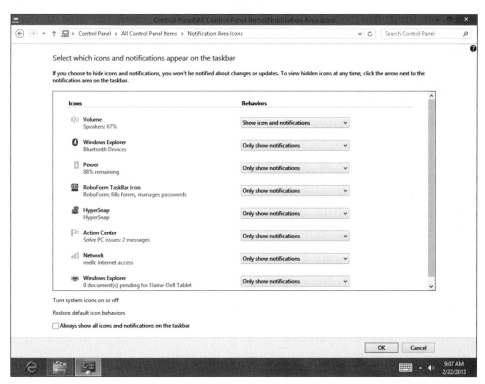

Change the Notification Area Icon behavior to control the messages and icons that appear in the System Tray at the right edge of the Desktop taskbar.

6   Tap or click a drop-down menu in the Behaviors list for the icon you want to control and choose a behavior.

7   When you finish, tap or click OK.

Managing devices

You can view devices connected to your computer and add or remove a device from the PC Settings screen; from the Desktop, you can view information about a particular device and troubleshoot it if it isn't behaving properly.

You rarely need to add or remove a device from the PC Settings screen. If you detach a device that's connected to your computer using a wireless connection or a physical one, Windows typically removes the device from the list automatically. If you attach a new device wirelessly or with a physical connection, Windows typically recognizes the device automatically. If Windows doesn't recognize the device, you should follow the manufacturer's instructions for adding the device to your system setup.

To use the PC Settings screen to view devices connected to your computer, follow these steps:

1   Display the Charms bar by sliding slightly in toward the center of the screen from the right side of the screen, pressing WinKey (⊞)+C, or placing your mouse in the upper- or lower-right corner of the screen.

2   Tap or click the Settings charm.

3   Tap or click Change PC Settings at the bottom of the Settings charm panel. Windows 8 displays the PC Setting screen.

4   On the left side of the screen, tap or click Devices to display the list of devices connected to your computer.

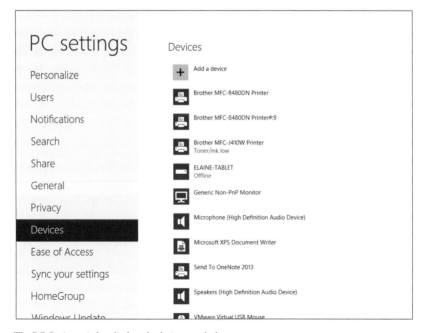

The PC Settings window displays the devices attached to your computer.

On the Desktop, you can view a complete list of all devices attached to your computer from the Device Manager. Typically, you only need the Device Manager if something isn't working properly. To view the Device Manager, search for Device Manager from within the Control Panel while in the Desktop app.

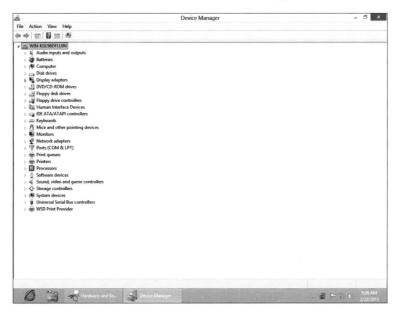

The Device Manager window.

You can view devices and printers attached to your computer in the Devices and Printers window.

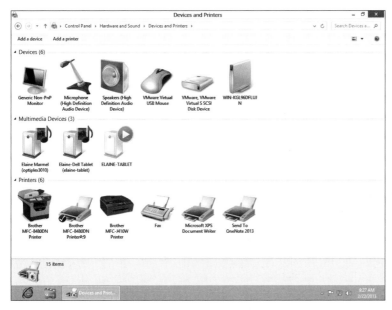

The Devices and Printers window.

You can tap and hold or right-click any device and then tap or click Properties to view information about that device. For example, follow these steps to see the properties of your hard drive:

1   Open File Explorer.

2   In the Navigation pane on the left, tap or click the Computer entry.

3   In the contents pane that's on the right side of the screen, tap and hold or right-click the entry for your hard disk.

4   From the shortcut menu that appears, tap or click Properties to display the Properties box for your hard drive.

The General tab of the Properties box for a hard drive.

5   Tap or click the Cancel button after you finish viewing disk information.

On the General tab of any drive's Properties box, you will see a pie chart depicting free and used space on the drive. You can also access Disk Cleanup tools from this dialog box; the Disk Cleanup utility helps you remove unnecessary files that are taking up space on your drive.

The Tools tab enables you to check for errors on the disk and optimize and defragment the drive. Be aware that Windows automatically optimizes and defragments your drive on a regular basis, so you shouldn't need to take this action manually.

The Hardware tab lists information about the disk drive, including its status, which is typically "This device is working properly."

You can use the Sharing tab to share a drive; you only need the Sharing tab if you are not using a HomeGroup.

Use the Security tab to establish privileges for users of the drive.

You can use the Quota tab if your drive supports allocating limited space to various users who access the drive.

Ending a misbehaving program

Sometimes, an app you're using misbehaves. It might freeze or become unresponsive in other ways. In these situations, ending the program often solves the problem.

You might also need to restart your computer; if that doesn't help your program stop misbehaving, you might need to take additional troubleshooting measures. For example, contact the vendor of the program for help.

End a misbehaving native Windows 8 app by closing it. Press Alt+F4, or using your mouse or your finger, drag down the center of your screen from top to bottom. You also can close it from the Task Manager, which is the tool you use to end a misbehaving legacy Desktop app.

To display the Task Manager window using a keyboard, press Ctrl+Shift+Esc. If you haven't connected a keyboard and mouse to your touch device, display the Start screen and use the Touch Keyboard And Handwriting Panel, available from the Settings charm, to type Task Manager. When the entry appears, tap it.

The Task Manager.

The Windows 8 Task Manager is much improved over the Task Manager of earlier editions of Windows. On the Processes tab, you see each app that's running; close a misbehaving app by tapping or clicking it and then tapping or clicking the End Task button in the lower-right corner of the window.

You also can end background processes from the Processes tab, but be aware that ending a process can make your computer unstable and you might then need to restart it.

You can use the Performance tab in the Task Manager window to monitor CPU, Memory, Disk, and Ethernet performance.

The App History tab shows resource usage by app for the past 30 days.

Using the Startup tab, you can identify programs that start whenever Windows starts; if you don't need a particular program to start every time Windows starts, you can tap or click it and then tap or click the Disable button. That way, the program won't take up resources when you don't need it and you can start it when you do need it.

The Users tab displays users connected to your computer; if necessary, you can tap or click a user and then tap or click the Disconnect button to disconnect that user from your computer.

The Details tab displays detailed information for each running process, and the Services tab displays detailed information for each running service.

Uninstalling a program

Installing programs is easy. To install a native Windows 8 app, look for it in the Windows Store, buy it if necessary, and Windows installs it for you. Installing a legacy Desktop app is almost as easy. Typically, you download the installation file or insert a CD or DVD into your CD/DVD drive and then follow the on-screen instructions.

There will come a time when you determine that you no longer need a program that is installed on your computer. Perhaps you've replaced it with another program that better suits your needs or perhaps you've just stopped using the program.

In cases like these, you should uninstall the program so it stops taking up space on your computer. When you uninstall a native Windows 8 app, Windows also removes any apps related to it .

1   On the Start screen, tap and hold and slide down slightly or right-click the app's tile to select it.

2   Display the App bar by swiping down slightly from the top of the screen or by right-clicking anywhere on the screen.

3 Tap or click the Uninstall button. A message appears, telling you that the app (and any related apps) will be removed from your computer.

Uninstalling a native Windows 8 app.

4 Tap or click the Uninstall button; Windows removes the app and any related apps.

When well-behaved legacy Desktop apps install, they also include an uninstall routine, and they place a link to that routine in the Programs and Features window of the Control Panel.

If you don't see an entry in the Programs and Features window for the program you want to uninstall, try checking for an entry in the All Apps list (while viewing the Start screen, display the App bar by swiping down slightly from the top of the screen or by right-clicking anywhere on the screen. Then, tap or click the All Apps button). If you don't find an entry there, you're probably dealing with an ill-behaved program that won't easily uninstall. Try searching the Internet for the program name and include the word "uninstall" to find help.

To uninstall a well-behaved legacy Desktop app, follow these steps:

1 Display the Start screen.

2 Type Control Panel.

3 When you see the Control Panel entry appear, tap or click it.

4 On the Control Panel home page, tap or click the Uninstall A Program link that appears under the Programs link. The Programs and Features window appears, displaying a list of well-behaved, installed legacy apps.

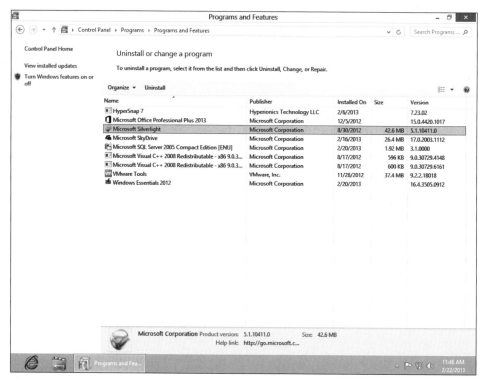

Use this window to uninstall a program.

5 Tap or click the program you want to remove.

6 Tap or click the Uninstall button above the list of installed apps.

7 Follow the directions that appear on the screen.

Each legacy app has its own uninstall process, so the steps vary from program to program. For example, some programs might suggest that you restart your computer to complete the uninstall process.

Backing up your files

If you're using Windows 8 Pro or higher and you have an external hard drive, a second hard drive, or a network hard drive, you can take advantage of File History to back up your data files. Once an hour, File History takes a snapshot of all the files in all libraries and on your Desktop, along with your Internet Explorer favorites, SkyDrive, and your Contacts data. File History continues to take snapshots until the drive where you're storing the history fills up. Over time, File History can store many copies of your data files; File History will notify you when you're getting close to running out of space so you can get another external hard drive.

You can disconnect the drive that File History uses for backups. While the drive is disconnected, File History continues to take snapshots of your data and stores them in a reserved space on the local hard drive, using up to 5% of your hard drive space. When you reconnect the drive, File History writes the files to the drive.

You can change the settings File History uses, as you will see in an upcoming section in this lesson.

Turning on File History

The first time you use File History will take a very long time, even many hours. We suggest that you wait to use File History the first time until a time when you plan to walk away from your computer.

To set up and run File History, follow these steps:

1   Display the Start screen.

2   Type Control Panel.

3   When the Control Panel entry appears, tap or click it.

4   In the Search box in the upper-right corner of the Control Panel, type "File History" and tap or click the magnifying glass or press Enter.

5   Tap or click the File History entry in the list that appears to display the File History window.

6   Make sure the drive you want to use for your backup is attached to your computer.

7   Tap or click the Turn On button. A message box appears, asking if you want other members of your HomeGroup to use this drive to back up their files.

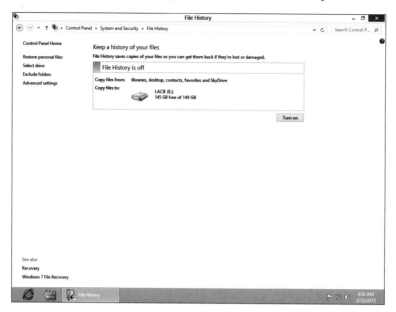

Turning on File History.

8   Click Yes or No, as appropriate in your situation. File History begins its backup; in the middle of the File History window, you'll see a message confirming that File History is running.

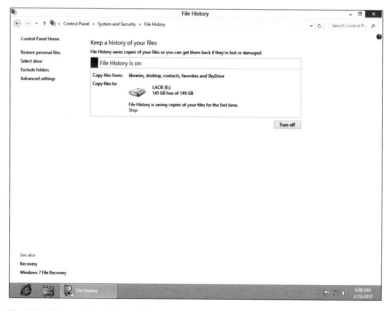

The File History window during a backup.

At this point, you need to wait for File History to complete the first backup. When the backup finishes, the Stop link in the File History window will be replaced by a Run Now link and the last date and time that File History copied your files. You can use the Run Now link to manually start a File History backup. Remember, though, that File History will automatically run every hour.

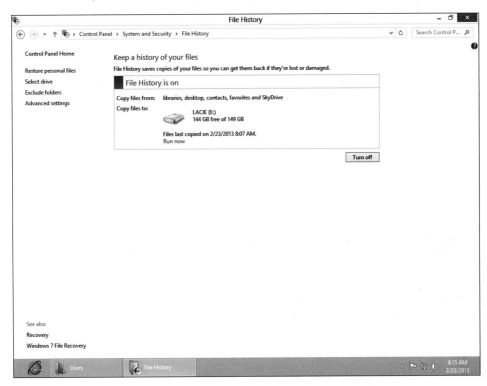

When File History finishes its first backup, the Run Now link appears.

You can view the backed up files using File Explorer. Just navigate to the drive where you stored the backup and you'll find a folder called FileHistory. You can navigate its contents to see what File History backed up.

Restoring files

Suppose that you discover, after long hours of work, that a change you made three days ago just isn't working for you. You can restore a copy of your file from a time before you made that change.

1   Display the Start screen.

2   Type Control Panel.

3   When the Control Panel entry appears, tap or click it.

4   In the Search box in the upper-right corner of the Control Panel, type File History and tap or click the magnifying glass or press Enter.

5   Tap or click the File History entry in the list to display the File History window.

6   In the left pane, tap or click the Restore Personal Files link to display the Home level of the File History dialog box, which contains available backups from which you can restore files.

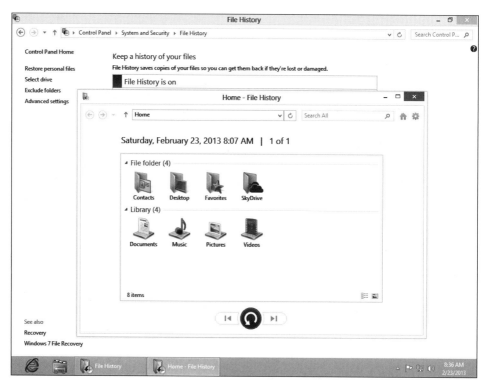

Use the File History dialog box to find a file to restore.

7   Navigate to the folder containing the file you want to restore. The time and date of the backed-up file appear above the file. If you want a different version of the file, use the Back or Forward arrows in the address bar above the date to navigate to a different backup.

8   Tap and hold or right-click the file you want to restore to select it.

9   Tap or click the Restore button (the green button at the bottom of the window). File History displays a Message box that offers you options concerning overwriting existing files.

If you tap or click the Restore button while viewing the Home level of the File History dialog box, File History assumes you want to restore all files in a backup. You can restore all items in a folder by tapping or clicking that folder.

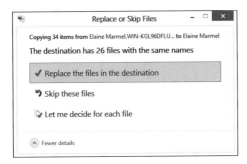

Choose File History's behavior concerning overwriting existing files.

10 Select an option; File History begins the restoration process.

Changing File History settings

You can make changes to File History's default settings. For example, you can exclude files or folders from the backup, make backups more or less frequently, or change the amount of space File History uses on your local drive when your external hard drive isn't connected.

1   Display the Start screen.

2   Type Control Panel.

3   When the Control Panel entry appears, tap or click it.

4   In the Search box in the upper-right corner of the Control Panel, type File History and tap or click the magnifying glass or press Enter.

5   Tap or click the File History entry that appears to display the File History window.

6   If you click the Exclude Folders on the left, you can identify folders you don't want File History to back up. Tap or click the Add button and then navigate to the folder you want to exclude, tap or click it, and then tap or click the Select Folder button. Once you finish selecting folders to exclude from a backup, tap or click the Save Changes button to redisplay the File History window.

7 If you tap or click the Advanced Settings link on the left, you can change the frequency File History uses to make backups, the amount of space used on your local drive to store backups when your backup drive is disconnected, or the amount of time File History saves backups (the default is "Forever").

8 When you finish making changes, tap or click the Save Changes button to redisplay the File History window.

System recovery options

Windows 8 contains two options you can use if Windows begins to consistently misbehave: Refresh and Reset. These actions are drastic, and you should consider using them only if all other attempts to fix your computer have failed.

Refreshing

Comparatively, Refreshing is the lesser drastic approach to system recovery, but you still run the risk of losing data if you don't back up properly. When you refresh, Windows will clear all the legacy settings and apps, and anything not within Windows users folders; it then reinstalls Windows and places a list of what was eliminated on the Desktop for your review.

In particular, the refresh process keeps the following:

- Accounts, passwords, backgrounds, Internet Explorer favorites, wireless network connections and settings, drive letter assignments, BitLocker settings and passwords if your version of Windows supports BitLocker, and your Windows installation key.
- All files in the User folder, which includes every user's libraries (Documents, Pictures, Music, Videos, and Downloads).
- Any folders you might have added to the C:\ drive.
- File History versions.
- Anything stored in partitions that don't contain Windows.
- Apps from the Windows Store.

The refresh process *destroys* the following:

- Display settings, firewall customizations, and file type associations.
- Files not stored in the User folder, unless you stored them in folders directly off the C:\ drive as noted above.
- All legacy Desktop apps and their settings, installation keys, and passwords.

Resetting

Resetting is the most drastic system recovery tool available; it wipes your hard drive and reinstalls Windows. You lose all your personal data, all your settings, and programs you installed, including their settings, product keys, and passwords.

Using system recovery options

Obviously, these choices are drastic actions, so use them at your own risk. Both options use the Windows Recovery Environment to do their work, and if Windows can't boot normally, you may find yourself in the Windows Recovery Environment automatically. Should you deliberately choose to either reset or refresh your computer, you can launch these options and boot into the Windows Recovery Environment from the PC Settings screen.

1   Display the Charms bar by sliding slightly in toward the center of the screen from the right side of the screen, pressing WinKey (⊞)+C, or placing your mouse in the upper- or lower-right corner of the screen.

2   Tap or click Change PC Settings at the bottom of the Settings charm panel. Windows 8 displays the PC Setting screen.

3   On the left side of the screen, tap or click General.

4   Scroll down the right side to see the Refresh and Reset options; the Reset option heading is "Remove Everything and Reinstall Windows."

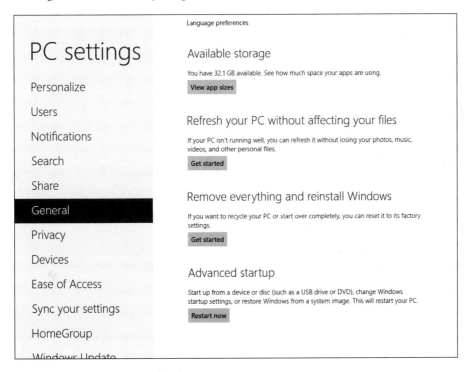

The system recovery options available from the PC Settings screen.

Self study

1 Personalize the Start screen.

2 Select a theme for the Desktop.

Review

Questions

1 How do you control settings in Windows 8?

2 How do you display clocks for multiple time zones in the Desktop System Tray?

3 How do you end a program that's misbehaving?

4 How do you uninstall a program?

5 What Desktop tool can you use to back up the files in your libraries and where does it store your files?

6 What system recovery options are available to you and when should you use them?

Answers

1 You can control settings for the native Windows 8 apps using the PC Settings screen. For legacy Desktop apps, work in the Desktop Control Panel.

2 To display clocks for multiple time zones in the Desktop System Tray, tap or click the displayed date and time in the System Tray at the right edge of the Desktop taskbar and then tap or click Change Date And Time Settings to display the Date and Time dialog box. Tap or click the Additional Clocks tab, tap or click the first Show This Clock checkbox to select it, and use the Select Time Zone list box to select a time zone for the clock. Type a display name for the clock and repeat the steps for the second Show This Clock checkbox. Then, click OK.

3 To end a misbehaving native Windows 8 app, press Alt+F4 or drag your finger or the mouse pointer down the center of your screen from top to bottom. To end a misbehaving legacy Desktop app, use the Task Manager. To display the Task Manager, press Ctrl+Shift+Esc or display the Start screen and use the Touch Keyboard And Handwriting Panel (available from the Settings charm) to type **Task Manager**. When the entry appears, tap it.

4 To uninstall a native Windows 8 app, tap and drag its tile down slightly or right-click its tile to display the App bar. Then, tap or click the Uninstall button. To uninstall a legacy Desktop app, using the Control Panel's Uninstall a Program window.

5 You can use the File History tool to back up the files in your libraries . It stores them on an external device you specify; if that device isn't connected to your computer when File History makes a backup, File History will use up to 5% of your hard drive to store the backup until you reconnect the backup device.

6 The system recovery options available to you are Refresh and Reset. Both make very drastic changes to your computer, but Refresh is less drastic because it leaves your personal files in place; Reset removes everything from your computer and reinstalls Windows only. Use Refresh if your computer has begun to misbehave and other attempts to repair it have failed. Use Reset if want to completely set up Windows again, including all your personal information, or if you plan to give away your computer.

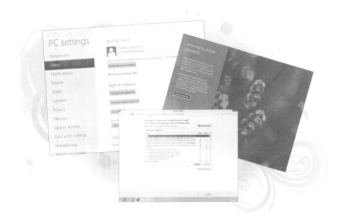

What you'll learn in this lesson:

- Working with local accounts
- Using the Windows Firewall
- Managing privacy settings

Keeping Your Computer Safe and Protecting Your Privacy

With this lesson you'll learn how to minimize the danger of communicating between PCs, whether internally on your own network or externally via the Internet.

Starting up

You will not need to work with any files for this lesson.

See Lesson 14 in action!

Use the accompanying videos to gain a better understanding of how to use some of the features shown in this lesson. The video lesson for this tutorial can be found at www.DigitalClassroomBooks.com/Windows8.

Local user accounts and passwords

In Lesson 1, "Getting Started with Windows 8," you learned about the differences between a Microsoft account and a local account. To summarize:

- Microsoft accounts are made up of an e-mail address registered with Microsoft and a required password. When you sign into Windows 8 using a Microsoft account, you are connecting your computer to the cloud and Windows automatically synchronizes some settings to the cloud that synchronize to other devices you sign into using the same Microsoft account. Most of the Windows 8 native apps require you to sign in using a Microsoft account; otherwise, they won't function. Note that signing into Windows 8 with a Microsoft account allows Microsoft to track your computer usage.

- Local accounts are made up of a name (not an e-mail address) and a password (the password is optional but recommended). When you sign into Windows 8 using a local account, you are signing into just your PC, not the cloud. No synchronization happens when you sign in using a local account. Windows 8 remembers your computer's settings just as previous versions of Windows did, but those settings are tied to that specific computer. If you sign into Windows 8 using a local account, Microsoft cannot track your computer usage.

If you opted to use a Microsoft account when you first signed into Windows 8, you can switch to a local account. When you make the switch, Windows will prompt you to set up a password that you can type.

1   Display the Charms bar by sliding slightly in toward the center of the screen from the right side of the screen, pressing WinKey (⊞)+C, or placing your mouse in the upper- or lower-right corner of the screen.

2   Tap or click the Settings charm.

3   Tap or click Change PC Settings at the bottom of the Settings charm panel. Windows 8 displays the PC Setting screen.

4   On the left side of the screen, tap or click Users.

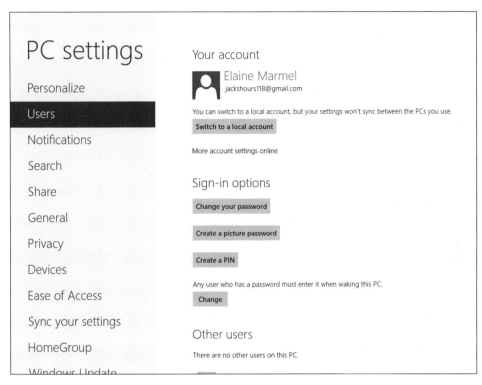

Use this screen to switch to a local account.

5   On the right side of the screen, tap or click the Switch To A Local Account button. Windows 8 prompts you to provide your Microsoft information before it lets you switch.

6 Type the password for your Microsoft account and tap or click the Next button. Windows prompts you for user name and password information for your local account.

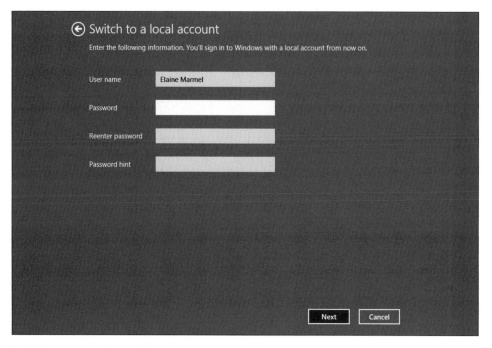

Provide the user name and password you want to use with your local Windows account.

7 Type the user name and password for your local account; then, re-enter the password and provide a hint that might help you remember your password if you forget it and tap or click the Next button. On the last screen, Windows reminds you to make sure you've saved your work and to use your local account password the next time you sign in to Windows.

8 Tap or click the Sign Out And Finish button. Windows prepares your local account, signs you out of your Microsoft account, and prompts you to provide the password you established in Step 5.

9 Type your password and tap or click the arrow beside the Password text field Windows signs you in using your local account and the Start screen appears.

Creating additional user accounts

Windows 8 automatically assigns administrator privileges to the first local account you create. An administrator can create additional accounts for the computer, which comes in handy if more than one person uses your computer. Windows tracks information for each user account individually, establishing a set of libraries and settings for each account. That way, each person who signs into Windows 8 operates independently of the other users. This section describes how to create an additional local account.

Standard vs. Administrator Accounts

Administrator accounts have more privileges than standard accounts. The most noticeable difference between the two account types is that administrators can install software while standard account users cannot, unless they know the administrator's password.

1 Display the Charms bar by sliding slightly in toward the center of the screen from the right side of the screen, pressing WinKey (⊞)+C, or placing your mouse in the upper- or lower-right corner of the screen.

2 Tap or click the Settings charm.

3 Tap or click Change PC Settings at the bottom of the Settings charm panel. Windows 8 displays the PC Setting screen.

4   On the left side of the screen, tap or click Users.

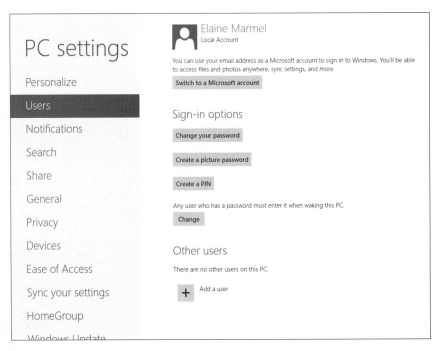

Add a user from the PC Settings screen.

5   On the right side of the screen, toward the bottom, tap or click the plus sign beside Add a user. The Add a user wizard appears.

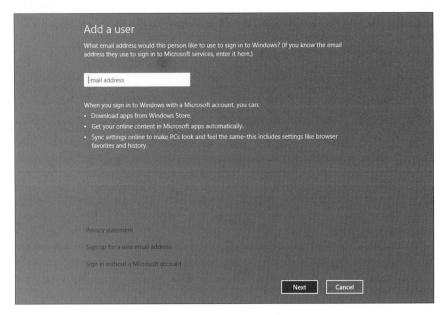

Add a user by first typing in an e-mail adress that user will use to login.

6   Tap or click the Sign In Without A Microsoft Account link at the bottom of the window. The Add A User wizard displays a screen that offers you another opportunity to add a Microsoft account.

7   At the bottom of the screen, tap or click the Local Account button. The Add A User wizard displays a screen where you supply a name and password for the new local account.

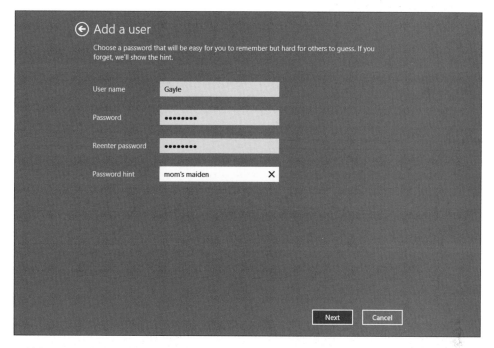

Establish a name and password for the account.

8   Type a name and password for the new local account.

9   Tap or click the Next button. The Add A User wizard displays the last screen of the wizard, which displays the new user's account name and type (a local account). The wizard also asks if you're setting up an account for a child and volunteers to turn on the Family Safety feature. For this exercise, leave the checkbox empty and learn about Family Safety later in this lesson.

10 Tap or click the Finish button. Windows 8 redisplays the Users screen in PC Settings; the new user account appears on the bottom of the right side of the screen.

Whenever you turn on the computer, entries for all established accounts will appear on the Sign In screen. You can switch between accounts by tapping or clicking the account picture on the Start screen; Windows 8 displays all available user accounts on the list that appears.

Available accounts appear on the Sign In screen and when you tap or click the account picture on the Start screen.

Windows sets up new local accounts as standard accounts. An administrator can change the local account type to an administrator account from the Control Panel on the Desktop in the User Accounts and Family Safety section.

Changing a password

If you decide that you don't like the password you created for your local account, you can change it.

1 Display the Charms bar by sliding slightly in toward the center of the screen from the right side of the screen, pressing WinKey (⊞)+C, or placing your mouse in the upper- or lower-right corner of the screen.

2   Tap or click the Settings charm.

3   Tap or click Change PC Settings at the bottom of the Settings charm panel. Windows 8 displays the PC Setting screen.

4   On the left side of the screen, tap or click Users.

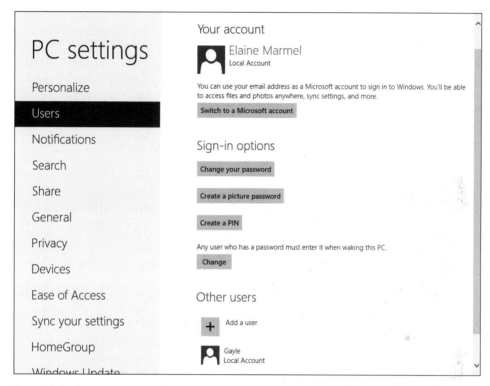

Tap or click the Change Your Password button.

5   On the right side of the screen, tap or click the Change Your Password button. Windows prompts you to supply the password you currently use to sign into Windows with your local account.

6   Type your current password and tap or click the Next button. Windows prompts you to provide a new password and a password hint.

7   Type and re-enter your new password and supply a hint that might help you remember the password.

8   Tap or click the Next button. Windows reminds you to use your new password the next time you sign into Windows.

9   Tap or click the Finish button. The PC Settings screen reappears.

Using a picture password

If you don't want to be limited to typing a password, you can set up a picture password. If you're working on a touch device, you might prefer to use a picture password because you won't need to type anything when you sign in. Keyboard-and-mouse users also might prefer the picture password because you can use a mouse to sign in with a picture password.

Before you can set up a picture password, you must first establish a typed password for your local account as described in the preceding section.

When you create a picture password, you use a picture of your choice and you draw three gestures on that picture using either your finger or your mouse. You can tap, click, slide, and drag. To make your picture password harder to crack:

- Use a combination of taps and slides (clicks and drags) to create points, lines, and shapes such as circles.
- Try to avoid letting anyone see you sign in.
- Select a picture that has many interesting points; that way, even if someone observes your gestures, that person will still have to figure out *where* on the picture you made your gestures.

As you draw your gestures, remember that lines don't need to move from left to right; they can move right to left, up, down, and on angles. Circles can be clockwise or counterclockwise.

1 Display the Charms bar by sliding slightly in toward the center of the screen from the right side of the screen, pressing WinKey (▦)+C, or placing your mouse in the upper- or lower-right corner of the screen.

2 Tap or click the Settings charm.

3 Tap or click Change PC Settings at the bottom of the Settings charm panel. Windows 8 displays the PC Setting screen.

4 On the left side of the screen, tap or click Users.

5 Tap or click the Create A Picture Password button. Windows prompts you to provide your current password.

6   Type your current password and then tap or click the OK button. Windows displays the Welcome To Picture Password screen; if you watch the screen for a few moments, you'll notice that it demonstrates motions you can use for your picture password.

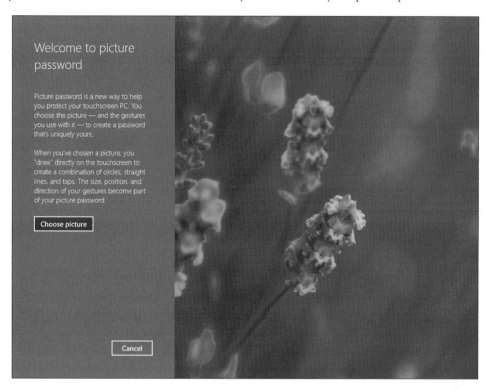

Welcome to picture password

Picture password is a new way to help you protect your touchscreen PC. You choose the picture — and the gestures you use with it — to create a password that's uniquely yours.

When you've chosen a picture, you "draw" directly on the touchscreen to create a combination of circles, straight lines, and taps. The size, position, and direction of your gestures become part of your picture password.

Choose picture

Cancel

This screen demonstrates motions you can make while setting up a picture password.

7   Tap or click the Choose Picture button. Windows displays your Pictures library.

8   Navigate through your library until you find a picture you want to use; select it and tap or click the Open button.

9   In the window that appears, drag your picture to the position you'd like to use.

10 Tap or click the Use This Picture button.

11 Draw three gestures on the picture. As you draw, Windows shows you the way your gestures look.

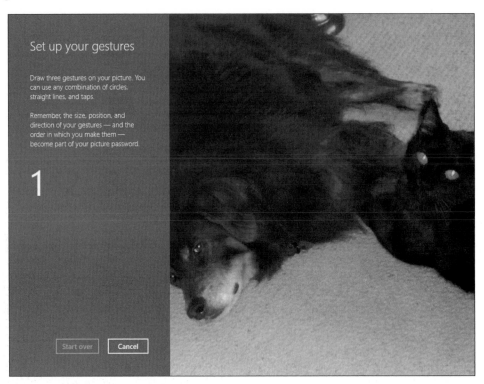

Draw three gestures on the picture.

12 Draw the gestures a second time; when you draw them so that they match, tap or click the Finish button.

If you change your mind and want to use a different picture or don't want to use a picture password at all, redisplay the PC Settings screen for Users and use the appropriate option.

Creating a PIN

If you're working on a small device, you might prefer to sign in using a four-digit PIN instead of a password or even a picture password. A PIN on a Windows device works the same way that a PIN works in all the other places you use them: at the bank's ATM machine, with telephones, and so on.

We suggest that you avoid reusing PINs on different devices; you run the risk of somebody discovering your PIN and then having access to all your devices.

1   Display the Charms bar by sliding slightly in toward the center of the screen from the right side of the screen, pressing WinKey (⊞)+C, or placing your mouse in the upper- or lower-right corner of the screen.

2   Tap or click the Settings charm.

3   Tap or click Change PC Settings at the bottom of the Settings charm panel. Windows 8 displays the PC Setting screen.

4   On the left side of the screen, tap or click Users.

5   On the right side of the screen, tap or click Create a PIN. Windows prompts you to provide your current password.

6   Provide your current password and tap or click the OK button. Windows prompts you to set up your PIN.

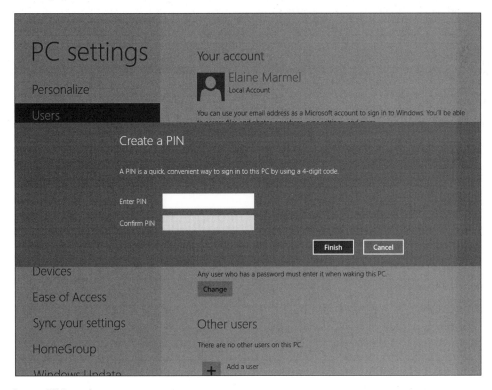

Set up a PIN.

7   Enter and then re-enter your PIN and tap or click the Finish button. The next time you log on, you can use your PIN.

If you change your mind and want to use a different PIN or don't want to use a PIN at all, redisplay the PC Settings screen for Users and use the appropriate option.

Using the Windows Firewall

A *firewall* is a program that acts as a traffic cop by managing incoming and outgoing requests for data between your computer, the Internet, and other computers on your network. The firewall's job is to help prevent malicious files and software, such as viruses or other malware, from getting into your computer or being sent from your computer if your computer becomes infected.

Malware

Malware is a term used to describe malicious software that disrupts the operation of your computer, typically to collect sensitive information or take control of your computer without your permission. Computer viruses, worms, trojan horses, rootkits, keyloggers, spyware, and adware are just some types of malware. Windows 8 comes with its own built-in anti-virus protection called Windows Defender. Windows Defender works well enough that you don't need additional anti-virus protection. However, if you do want additional protection, you'll find a myriad of choices by searching the Internet.

Windows Defender and the Windows Firewall that comes with Windows 8 combine to protect your computer from malware.

Just as its predecessors since the days of Windows XP, Windows 8 includes the Windows Firewall, an effective (but not foolproof) *inbound firewall* that monitors the traffic trying to come into your computer. Windows Firewall is turned on by default; you don't need to take any action. In fact, Windows 8 turns on Windows Firewall before you connect to the Internet.

No firewall is foolproof. But you can add a layer of protection by using a router to connect the Internet. Most routers include a hardware firewall, *which is a very effective firewall built into the router.*

To describe the functionality in general terms, Windows Firewall remembers information sent from your computer and where that information is headed. Windows Firewall uses that information to match destination information trying to come into your computer with the outgoing destination information it remembers. If the destinations match, then Windows Firewall allows the information into your computer. If the destinations don't match, Windows Firewall displays a message, asking you for permission to allow the information into your computer. In most cases, you will want to deny permission, but there are a few exceptions.

Windows Firewall is an inbound firewall; outbound firewalls perform the same monitoring function for information trying to leave your computer. Outbound firewalls are not used as commonly as inbound firewalls because outbound firewalls tend to nag users with inscrutable warnings about obscure attempts to send data, usually from processes the average user won't recognize. The average user tends to permit the program trying to send the data to do just that, making the outbound firewall fairly useless.

There are programs that listen for incoming traffic from the Internet, waiting to respond if they are contacted. For example, many accounting packages listen to incoming traffic for updates to tax tables the accounting packages use to prepare tax returns. You typically know that you have this type of program because a message will appear when you install the software that indicates it will tell your firewall to allow traffic for the program.

But some programs that need to communicate outside your network may not set up Windows Firewall to allow their traffic; for example, you might play a game that needs to accept incoming Internet traffic but doesn't make itself known to Windows Firewall. In these cases, you'll need to tell Windows Firewall to allow the traffic.

1　Install the program that you want to allow through Windows Firewall.

2　Display the Start screen.

3　Type **Control Panel**.

4　When the Control Panel entry appears, tap or click it.

5　In the Search text field in the upper-right corner of the Control Panel, type **firewall** and tap or click the magnifying glass or press Enter.

6　Tap or click the Windows Firewall entry in the list that appears to display the Windows Firewall window.

7　On the left side, tap or click the Allow An App Or Feature Through Windows Firewall link.

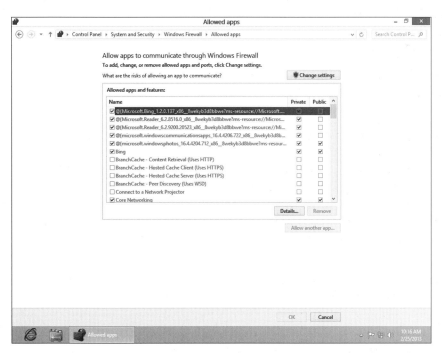

Set Windows Firewall exceptions to allow or deny application traffic.

8 In the left column, select the app from which you want to permit incoming traffic. Use the right columns to identify the type of connection that should permit unsolicited incoming traffic: a private and public network (you rarely want to permit incoming traffic when you're connected to a public network).

If the program you want to permit through Windows Firewall doesn't appear in the window, tap or click the Change Settings button above the list. Then, tap the Allow Another App button below the list and navigate to the program.

9 When you finish, tap or click the OK button.

Optimizing privacy

Windows 8, more than any other edition of Windows, pulls in information from all over the Internet. Windows 8 makes it easy for you to connect to services such as Flickr and Facebook, but at a price, because you're helping the data collection routines at Microsoft by providing information. Signing into Windows 8 using a Microsoft account helps even more because you provide more information.

While it's safe to assume that Microsoft isn't trying to steal your identify, you also can assume that Microsoft is going to make use of the information it collects, primarily to determine your buying patterns so it can target you with ads that will most likely result in you making a purchase.

Some people aren't concerned about the information Microsoft collects, and if you are not concerned either, you can safely skip this section. However, if you want to minimize the information that Microsoft collects, this section contains some suggestions for you.

Minimizing your Microsoft connections

Microsoft has a vested interest is some companies and so makes connecting to them easier. You can minimize the data you offer via Windows 8 if you:

- Don't connect to Facebook, Flickr, LinkedIn or Twitter using native Windows 8 apps. If you do, your contacts are shared. To minimize the information you send to data collection databases, use these social networking services the old-fashioned way instead of using native Windows 8 apps.

- Connect to SkyDrive via your web browser and don't stayed signed in all the time; instead, sign in and out each time you use SkyDrive.

- Don't connect a Gmail account via the native Windows 8 Mail app. Windows 8 makes connecting a Gmail account easy so that Microsoft can collect your Google contacts.

- Control location tracking, as described in the next section.

Managing location tracking

Windows 8 is the first edition of Windows to incorporate location tracking. Many of the native Windows 8 apps, such as the Weather app, use location tracking. You can permit (or deny) location tracking in general for the operating system or you can set location tracking options individually for apps that want to use location tracking.

Whether location tracking is good or bad depends on the way it's used. For example, GPS technology, common in phones and tablet PCs, has saved lives. Most desktop PCs don't contain GPS chips, so you might think that you only need to be concerned about location tracking if you're using a phone or a tablet PC. But location tracking technology still works, in a limited way, on devices that don't contain GPS chips. In these cases, location tracking technology uses the IP address of your Internet connection to determine your approximate location, which can be miles away from your actual location. (GPS chips provide a more precise location.)

Each app that wants to use your location displays a message when you open it for the first time, asking if you want to allow or block location tracking. Whether you permit or deny location tracking depends on your own personal need.

You can block location tracking in all apps by turning it off in the operating system settings:

1   Display the Charms bar by sliding slightly in toward the center of the screen from the right side of the screen, pressing WinKey (⊞)+C, or placing your mouse in the upper- or lower-right corner of the screen.

2   Tap or click the Settings charm.

3   Tap or click Change PC Settings at the bottom of the Settings charm panel. Windows 8 displays the PC Setting screen.

4   On the left side of the screen, tap or click Privacy.

5   On the right side of the screen, tap or click Let apps use my location to turn it off.

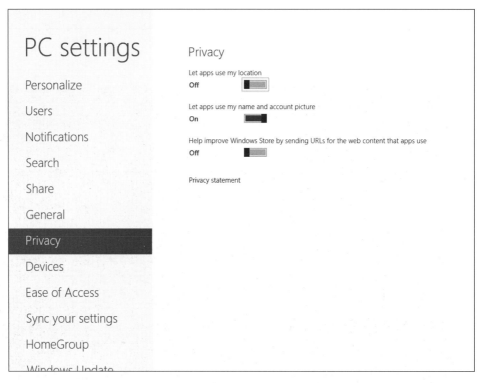

Set location tracking for all Windows 8 apps.

If you prefer to decide location tracking options for each app that wants to track your location, leave location tracking on in the PC Settings Privacy screen. Then, open an app like the Weather app and set its location tracking permissions. You can change an app's location tracking permissions at any time.

1   Tap or click an app that tracks your location (for example, the Weather app).

2   Display the Charms bar by sliding slightly in toward the center of the screen from the right side of the screen, pressing WinKey (⊞)+C, or placing your mouse in the upper- or lower-right corner of the screen.

3   Tap or click the Settings charm to display the app's settings.

4   Tap or click Permissions.

To find Permissions, you might need to scroll down the list of options at the top of the Settings pane.

Select the Permissions option for the app.

5 Tap or click the Location option to place the slider in the position you want.

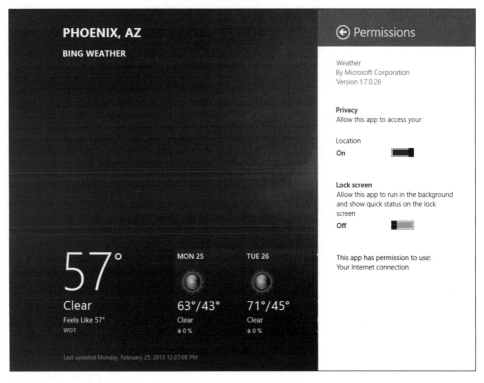

Set Location permissions for an individual app.

6 Tap or click the Back button in the Permissions pane to redisplay the app.

Set up the Family Safety feature

If children use your computer, you can use the Family Safety feature to try to protect them from inadvertently running selected programs, playing inappropriate games, and using the computer outside times you establish. You must be signed on to the computer using an administrator account. (Note that any account with administrator privileges can change the settings of the Family Safety feature.)

1 Display the Start screen.

2 Type **Control Panel**.

3 When the Control Panel entry appears, tap or click it.

4 On the right side of the Control Panel window, tap or click the Set Up Family Safety For Any User link.

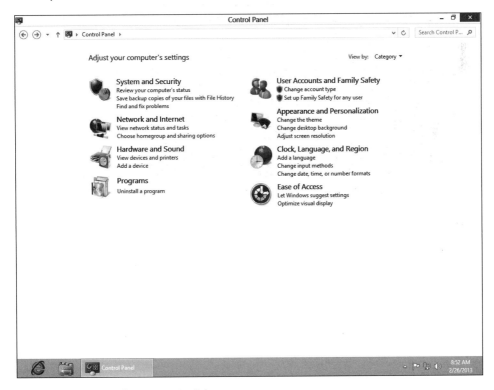

Select the Set Up Family Safety For Any User link.

5 In the Family Safety window that appears, tap or click the user for whom you want to set up the Family Safety feature. Window displays the User Settings window.

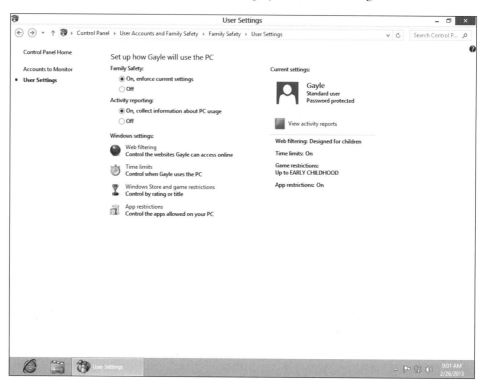

Set up Family Safety for a user account.

6 In the Family Safety section, tap or click the On, Enforce Current Settings option.

In most cases, you might want to leave the Activity Reporting option turned on so you can monitor activity for the user; you can view activity reports by tapping or clicking the link to the right of the Activity Reporting setting, under the user's name.

7 In the Windows Settings section, tap or click each link and establish the settings you want to use for the selected account. After you make changes to a setting, use the Back button in the window to redisplay the User Settings window.

8 When you finish, the status of your settings appears on the right side of the User Settings window, under the account name.

You can close the Control Panel.

Self study

1 Set up a picture password to use when signing in to your computer.

2 Create a PIN to use when signing in to your computer.

Review

Questions

1 How do you change the password for a local account?

2 What kinds of gestures can you use on a picture password?

3 How do you create an additional local account for another user on your computer?

4 How does Windows Firewall decide what traffic to allow?

5 How do you enable or disable location tracking for all of Windows 8?

Answers

1 To change the password for a local account, display the Charms bar and tap or click the Settings charm. Tap or click Change PC Settings at the bottom of the Settings charm panel to display the PC Setting screen. On the left side of the screen, tap or click Users. On the right side of the screen, tap or click the Change Your Password button and follow the on-screen prompts.

2 On a picture password, you can draw lines and circles, or tap or click dots. You can draw lines and circles in any direction.

3 To create an additional local account for another user on your computer, display the Charms bar, tap or click the Settings charm, and tap or click Change PC Settings. On the left side of the PC Setting screen, tap or click Users. On the right side of the screen, toward the bottom, tap or click the plus sign beside Add A User to start the Add A User wizard. Tap or click the Sign In Without A Microsoft Account link at the bottom of the window. At the bottom of the next Add A User wizard screen, tap or click the Local Account button. On the next screen, supply a name and password for the new local account and tap or click the Next button. On the last screen, tap or click the Finish button.

4 Windows Firewall decides which traffic to allow by tracking and matching outbound destinations with inbound destinations, and if they match, it permits inbound traffic.

5 To enable or disable location tracking for all of Windows 8, begin by displaying the Charms bar and then tap or click the Settings charm. Tap or click Change PC Settings at the bottom of the Settings charm panel to display the PC Setting screen. On the left side of the screen, tap or click Privacy. On the right side of the screen, tap or click Let Apps Use My Location to turn it on to enable or off to disable.

What you'll learn in this lesson:

- Exploring the native Windows 8 apps for Weather, Maps, and Travel

- Becoming familiar with WordPad, the Snipping Tool, and the Steps Recorder on the legacy Desktop

Exploring Some Windows 8 Apps

This lesson presents an overview of some of the apps that come with Windows, both native Windows 8 and legacy Desktop.

Starting up

In this lesson, you will work with several files from the Windows15lessons folder. Make sure that you have loaded the files from the Win8Lessons folder onto your hard drive. For more information, see "Loading lesson files" in the Starting Up section of this book.

See Lesson 15 in action!

Use the accompanying videos to gain a better understanding of how to use some of the features shown in this lesson. The video lesson for this tutorial can be found at www.DigitalClassroomBooks.com/Windows8.

Native Windows 8 apps

Several of the native Windows 8 apps help you perform some useful, day-to-day tasks. In this section, you'll explore the basics of using the Weather app, the Maps app, and the Travel app. The techniques described should help you work in any native Windows 8 app.

The native Windows 8 apps all work with a Microsoft account name and password to provide information. You do not need to sign into your computer using a Microsoft account, though; you can sign in using a local account. When you open a native Windows 8 app for the first time, it will prompt you for a Microsoft account name and password; supply your Microsoft account information to use the app. If you don't yet have a Microsoft account, see Lesson 1 for details on establishing one.

As you work in any native Windows 8 app, don't forget to explore the Windows 8 charms to see what else you can do with each app.

Using the Weather app

Use the Weather app to check the forecast for your local area as well as any other places around the world.

The Weather app uses location information, so you must allow location tracking. If you have turned off location tracking on the PC Settings Privacy screen, you must turn it back on to use the Weather app.

On the Start screen, tap or click the Weather app's tile to open it. By default, the Weather app uses location services to display the current weather for your location and the five-day forecast. The background displayed on the Weather app's main screen reflects the forecast for your city.

At the bottom of the screen, you will see your local forecast as well as the forecast for the next five days. To the right of the five day forecast is a Forward arrow that lets you see an additional five-day forecast. Also located in this area is an Up button that displays more detailed information about each day's weather.

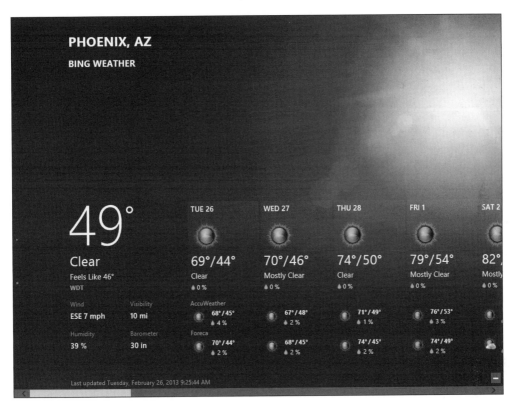

The opening screen of the Weather app.

Scroll to the right to view an hourly forecast, a variety of weather maps, historical temperature, rainfall, and sunshine information, and average and record values for the current month.

You can add, view, and delete locations for which you want to display weather.

1   Display the App bar by swiping down slightly from the top of the screen or by right-clicking anywhere on the screen. The top of the screen displays additional choices. For example, you can tap or click the World Weather button to display weather at various locations around the world.

The App bar allows you to change your home location, change to Celsius or Fahrenheit, and add other locations to the Weather app.

2   Tap or click the Places button at the top of the screen. The Weather app displays locations already established.

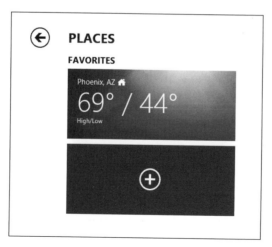

Already established locations.

3 Tap or click the Add button (the one containing the plus sign) to display the Enter Location dialog box.

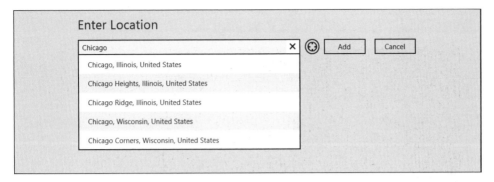

Type a location and select the one you want from the list that appears.

4 Type the name of a city, select the correct city from the list, and tap or click the Add button.

5 Repeat steps 3 and 4 to add more cities. When you finish, the cities you've added appear on the Places screen. Your default city contains a small Home icon beside the city name.

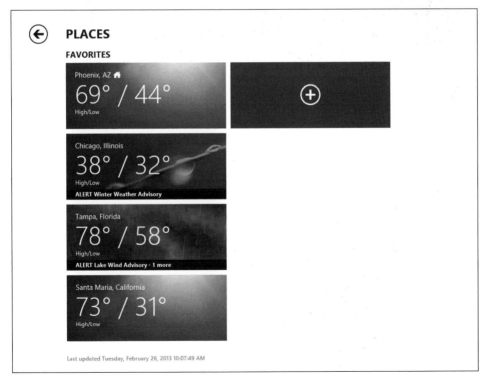

The Places screen after adding cities.

6 Tap or click the Back button to redisplay the Weather app's main screen.

To view the weather details for any city you've set up, tap or click the Places button and then tap or click the city for which you want to see details. The Weather app's main screen appears, displaying information for the city you selected.

When you select a city on the Places screen, you can:

- Set that city as the default that the Weather displays

- Remove the location

- Pin the location's weather to the Windows 8 Start screen

- Switch the display between Fahrenheit and Celsius

You can make use of some of the Windows 8 charms while you work in the Weather app. For example, you can view the weather of a location without setting it up on the Places screen. Instead, display the Search charm and then type the location's name. When you find the location you want, select it and the Weather app displays its weather until you select another location.

Using the Settings charm, you can identify the sources of weather information that the Weather app uses.

Using the Share charm, you can share Weather app information with the Mail app (to e-mail weather information to a friend) and the People app (to share weather information with Facebook or Twitter friends).

Using the Maps app

The Maps app displays digital maps; you can use it to view almost any location when you supply an address or place name.

The Maps app uses location information, so you must allow location tracking. If you have turned off location tracking on the PC Settings Privacy screen, you must turn it back on to use the Maps app.

On the Start screen, tap or click the Maps app's tile to open it. By default, the Maps app uses location services to display your current location. You can zoom in or out of the current location using the buttons that appear on the right side of the Maps app's main screen.

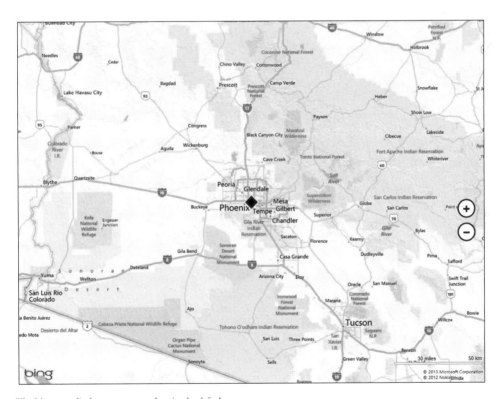

The Maps app displays your current location by default.

You can change the view of the map from a road view to an aerial view.

You can switch to an aerial view of the map.

You can display traffic information; green lines identify areas where traffic is flowing normally, orange lines identify areas where traffic is moving slowly, and red lines identify areas where traffic is heavy.

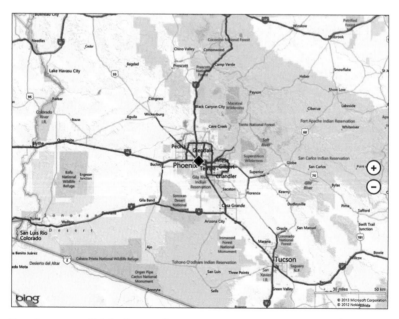

Green lines mean traffic is flowing normally.

You can search for a location and also you can get directions. To search for a location, display the App bar by swiping down slightly from the top of the screen or by right-clicking anywhere on the screen. Then, tap or click the Find button to display the Find pane. Type a location (you can use an address, a zip code, or a business name) and tap or click the Search magnifying glass button.

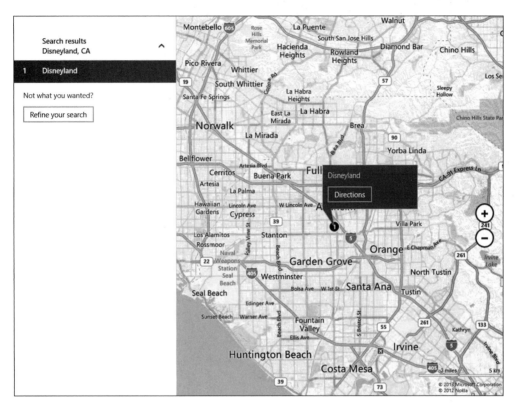

Search results in the Maps app.

You can tap or click the Directions button to get directions between the search result and some other point. To clear search results and redisplay your default location, display the App bar by swiping down slightly from the top of the screen or by right-clicking anywhere on the screen. Then, tap or click the Clear Map button. Finally, redisplay the App bar and tap or click the My Location button.

To get directions without searching first, you can display the App bar by swiping down slightly from the top of the screen or by right-clicking anywhere on the screen. Then, tap or click the Directions button. Type the name or address of the location where the journey will begin and type the name or address of the destination. Tap or click the Get Directions button; the Maps app displays driving directions that include an approximate distance and driving time. The small numbers on the map represent various legs of the trip, and you can tap or click any entry in the driving directions list to zoom in to that portion of the trip for details.

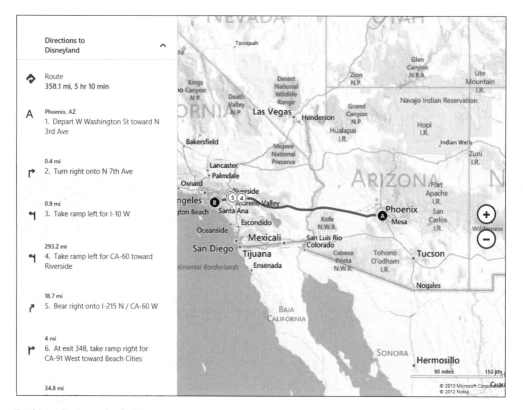

Get driving directions using the Maps app.

If you display the Settings charm while working in the Maps app, you can control, for example, the region the Maps app uses, whether it retains your search history (you can clear the search history), whether to display distance in miles or kilometers. You also can turn off location tracking for just the Maps app, which basically disables its functionality.

You can use the Devices charm to print a map and the Share charm to e-mail a map or share it with friends on Facebook or Twitter. The Search charm works the same way as the Find button on the Map app's App bar.

Using the Travel app

You can use the Travel app to plan a vacation or business trip. From the Travel app, you can research destinations and search for flights and hotels.

The Travel app uses location information, so you must allow location tracking. If you have turned off location tracking on the PC Settings Privacy screen, you must turn it back on to use the Travel app.

On the Start screen, tap or click the Travel app's tile. The main screen for the Travel app displays an image of one of the Travel app's featured destinations.

As you scroll to the right, links appear to featured destinations, panoramic photos, news, and videos.

To research a destination, display the App bar by swiping down slightly from the top of the screen or by right-clicking anywhere on the screen.

The App bar for the Travel app.

Then, tap or click the Destinations button. You can scroll to view more destinations, or you can narrow the destination selection using the Region button at the top of the screen.

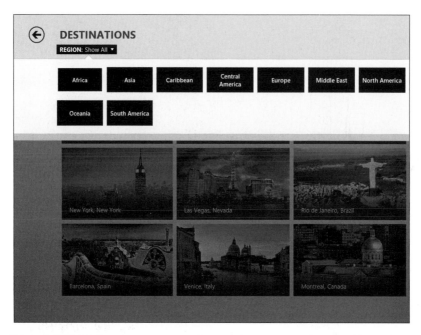

Select a destination region.

You can search through the destinations listed for the region, or you can search directly for a destination using the Search charm.

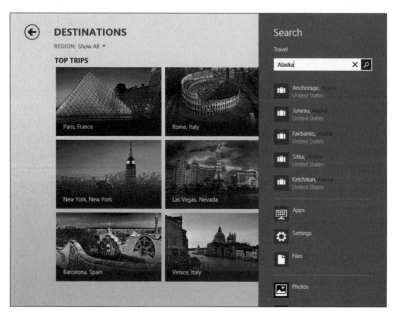

Search for a destination.

Once you select a destination, the Travel app displays background information about the location, photos, panoramas, attractions, popular hotels, restaurants, and guides for planning a trip, attractions, hotels, restaurants, nightlife, shopping, and side trips.

You can display the App bar by swiping down slightly from the top of the screen or by right-clicking anywhere on the screen. Then, tap or click the Flights button to search for flights.

Search for flights.

Similarly, from the App bar, you can search for Hotels.

Searching for hotels.

You've already seen how to use the Search charm with the Travel app; you can use the Share charm to share information from the Travel app by e-mail or with friends on Facebook or Twitter.

Windows 8 Desktop Apps

In addition to the native Windows 8 apps, Windows 8 includes a number of legacy apps that run from the Desktop. As with the native Windows 8 apps, this section explores the basics of using three of the apps that you might find useful: WordPad, the Snipping Tool, and the Problem Steps Recorder.

Working in most legacy Desktop apps is more comfortable using a keyboard and a mouse than tapping on a touch device.

Working with WordPad

WordPad is a basic word processing package; you can use it to write a letter, create a flyer, jot down a recipe, or just about anything you need to type. WordPad doesn't do a lot of fancy things; for example, you can't use it to create a table of entries or automatically generate a table of contents for a paper, but it serves basic typing needs very well. You can format text with boldface, italics, or underlining, and you can align paragraphs and control the spacing between them. You can create bulleted and numbered lists and you can include pictures and drawings in your WordPad documents.

Although you can use the on-screen keyboard with WordPad, you might find working with it easier on a traditional computer using a keyboard and a mouse than on a touch device.

To start WordPad, display the Windows 8 Start screen and type **WordPad**. When WordPad appears on the left, tap or click it or press Enter.

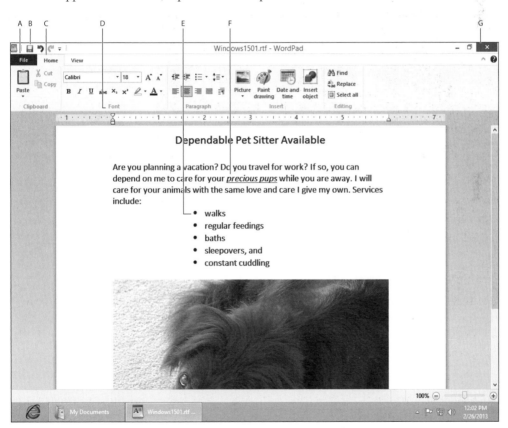

A. File menu. B. Save. C. Home tab. D. Group names. E. Indented bullete list from the Paragraph group.
F. Underlining and italics from the Fonts group. G. Close button.

To get started, just type. Use the various groups on the Home tab of the Ribbon to format your document. Group names appear below the tools in the group.

To apply formatting to a word, select that word and then use the choices on the Home tab of the Ribbon in the Font group. You can apply more than one type of formatting to any selection.

You can use the sample file to try out WordPad. Tap or click the File menu in WordPad and then tap or click Open. Navigate to the Windows15lessons folder and tap or click the file called **Windows1501.rtf**, *then tap or click Open.*

To align a paragraph or create a bulleted or numbered list, select that paragraph (or paragraphs) and then use the buttons on the Home tab of the Ribbon in the Paragraph group.

To create a bulleted or numbered list, try tapping or clicking the appropriate button before you start typing. Then, press Enter when you want to start a new list item. Press Enter twice to stop typing your list.

To insert objects in your document, such as a picture, use the tools in the Insert group on the Home tab of the Ribbon.

The Editing group on the Home tab of the Ribbon helps you find and replace information.

Save the documents you create using the Save button on the Quick Access toolbar or by clicking the File tab. You also can use the File tab to open documents you previously saved to work on them again. And you can use the File tab to print a document or e-mail it to a friend.

To find details for performing all these actions, tap or click the Help button in the upper-right corner of the WordPad window. When you finish working in WordPad, close it by tapping or clicking the Close button, which is the red X in the upper-right corner.

Using the Snipping Tool

The Snipping Tool is useful when you want to take a picture of your legacy Desktop screen and save that picture. The process of taking a picture of your screen is called *capturing* the screen. Using the Snipping Tool, you can capture the entire screen or just a portion of it. This tool is easiest to use with a mouse.

For example, if you want to show the Ribbon in the Windows Photo Gallery app to a friend, you can use the Snipping Tool to take a picture of the Ribbon and then e-mail it your friend.

To use the Snipping Tool to take a picture, follow these steps:

1   Set up the app on the legacy Desktop the way you want it to appear in your picture. For this example, open the Windows Photo Gallery app. (On the Start screen, type Photo Gallery and then tap or click the entry when it appears.)

2   To open the Snipping Tool, display the Start screen and type **Snipping Tool**. When the app entry appears, tap or click it.

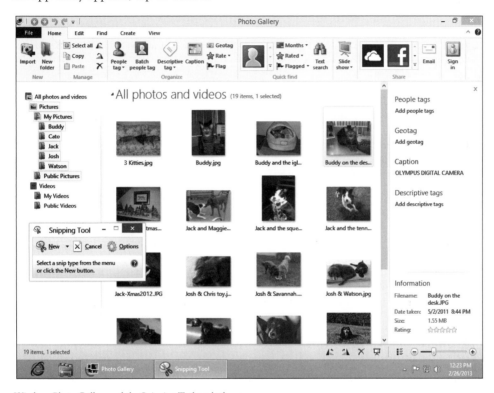

Windows Photo Gallery and the Snipping Tool are both open.

3   Tap or click the arrow beside New button in the Snipping Tool window.

4   Select a type of snip to capture; for this example, select Rectangular Snip. Windows dims everything visible on the Desktop, and the mouse pointer changes to a large plus sign.

5   Drag to draw a rectangle around the portion of the screen you want to capture (for example, draw your rectangle around the Ribbon.

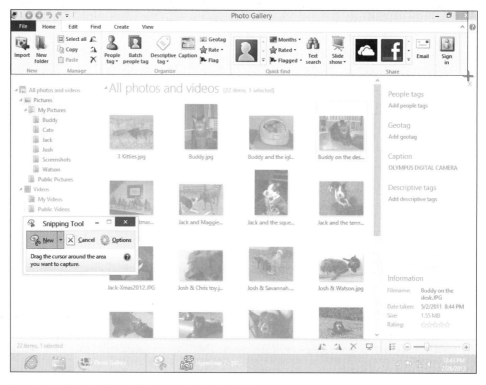

Capturing the Ribbon in Photo Gallery using the Snipping Tool.

6   When you release the mouse button or lift your finger, the area you selected appears in the Snipping Tool window.

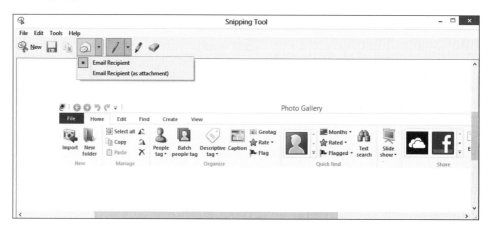

The area you identified appears in the Snipping Tool window.

You can save the image as a .PNG, .HTML, .GIF, or .JPEG file and e-mail it to a friend.

Taking a picture anywhere in Windows 8

The Snipping Tool works only with legacy Desktop apps. You can capture the entire screen anywhere in Windows (the Desktop or in any native Windows 8 app) using the PrtScr or PrintScreen key on a keyboard. Windows copies the current screen to the Desktop app's Clipboard. Then, open any legacy Desktop app that can display pictures, such as WordPad, and tap or click the Paste button on the Ribbon.

Recording your steps

You can use the Steps Recorder to record a sequence of actions you take on the legacy Desktop app. The Steps Recorder can be particularly useful if you're trying to accomplish something and you can't figure out why your steps aren't working. You can e-mail the Steps Recorder's video to a knowledgeable friend who can review it and perhaps help determine what you need to change to accomplish your goal.

If you're going to share a Steps Recorder movie with a friend for help solving a problem, be aware that Steps Recorder captures every motion you make on the screen. If you expect help from a friend, make sure that you capture what you're really doing without a lot of other actions that are extraneous to the issue.

1   Display the Start screen.

2   Type **Step Recorder**.

3   When the Step Recorder entry appears, tap or click it. The Steps Recorder window appears on the Desktop.

The Step Recorder window.

4   Tap or click the Start Record button.

5   Optionally, tap or click the Add Comment button and type a description that you want to include with the recording.

6   Perform the steps you want recorded.

7 Tap or click the Stop Record button. The Steps Recorder window displays your recorded steps.

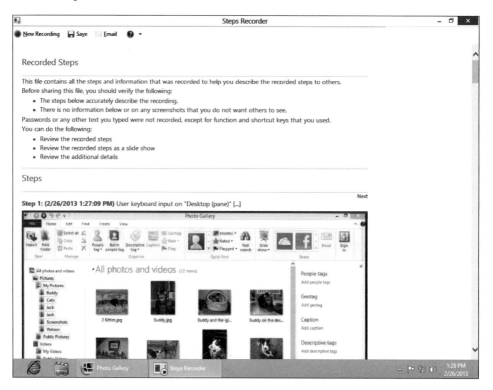

The Steps Recording window after recording.

8 Tap or click the Save button at the top of the window to display the Save As dialog box.

9 Provide a name for the recording file; navigate to the folder where you want to save the file, and tap or click the Save button. The Steps Recorder saves the recording as a zip file.

10 You can tap or click the E-mail button to send the recording to a friend. When your friend double-clicks the file, it will open in Internet Explorer.

Self study

1 In the Weather app, add a location and explore the weather maps available for that location.

2 In the Travel app, search for a destination using the Search charm and read the information the Travel app provides.

Review

Questions

1 How does the Maps app determine the location to display when you open it?

2 In the Maps app, how do you select a location to map?

3 How do you apply boldface to text in WordPad?

4 How do you capture an image of a portion of the legacy Desktop?

5 How do you use the Steps Recorder to capture steps you perform on screen?

Answers

1 The Maps app determines the location to display by using location services to identify your geographic location.

2 To select a location to map, display the App bar by swiping down slightly from the top of the screen or by right-clicking anywhere on the screen. Then, tap or click the Find button to display the Find pane. Type a location (you can use an address, a zip code, or a business name) and tap or click the Search magnifying glass button.

3 To apply boldface to text in WordPad, begin by selecting the text, and then tap or click the Bold button in the Font group on the Home tab of WordPad's Ribbon.

4 To capture an image of a portion of the legacy Desktop, open the Snipping tool, and then tap or click the arrow beside the New button and select a type of snip to capture, such as Rectangular Snip. Drag to draw around the portion of the screen you want to capture. When you release the mouse button or lift your finger, the area you selected appears in the Snipping Tool window. You can save the image as a .PNG, .HTML, .GIF, or .JPEG file and e-mail it to a friend.

5 To capture the steps you perform on screen using the Steps Recorder, tap or click the Start Record button and perform the steps you want recorded. Then, tap or click the Stop Record button. The Steps Recorder window displays your recorded steps; tap or click the Save button at the top of the window to save the recording. You also can tap or click the e-mail button to send the recording to a friend.

Appendix A

Upgrading to Windows 8

About Upgrading

When you install Windows 8 onto a computer that was previously running an earlier version of Windows, this is referred to as an upgrade. This appendix covers what you can expect to occur as part of the upgrade process.

The upgrade process

There are two ways to approach adding Windows 8 to a computer that is using an earlier version of the operating system. The first approach involves completely removing all data from the computer and then installing Windows 8. This is often referred to as a clean installation. The second option is to install Windows 8 over the existing version of Windows, and let the installation system from Microsoft decide what to keep and what to remove.

You can upgrade any version of Windows XP, Windows Vista, or Windows 7 to Windows 8. The operating system you are upgrading from determines the amount of data you can expect to keep when you upgrade.

You can expect to retain the most information on your computer if you are upgrading from Windows 7: all your programs, your Windows settings, and your personal files. When upgrading from Windows 7, you can install Windows 8 right on top of Windows 7, and the Windows 8 installation process will automatically determine what to keep and what to discard.

If you start with Windows Vista using Service Pack 1, you can expect to retain your Windows settings and your personal files, but you will need to reinstall all your programs. This upgrade requires that you format your computer's hard drive.

If you start with Windows XP using Service Pack 3 or later, you can expect to retain only your personal files. You will need to reinstall all your programs. Your Windows settings, which include things like your Internet Favorites and your Desktop wallpaper, will be lost. This upgrade requires that you format your computer's hard drive.

You will need to perform a clean installation if you want to upgrade from a 32-bit edition of Windows Vista or Windows 7 to a 64-bit edition of Windows 8 or you want to use a different language in Windows 8 than you used in the edition of Windows Vista or Windows 7 you are upgrading.

Before you perform a clean installation, you can save your personal files using the Windows 8 Upgrade Assistant, as described later in this appendix. After you've installed Windows 8, you can again use the Upgrade Assistant to restore your personal files to Windows 8.

Upgrading from Windows 7

The version of Windows 7 you are upgrading determines the version of Windows 8 to which you can upgrade while retaining your Windows settings, personal files, and applications. You can upgrade to the following versions of Windows 8 and keep your current information from corresponding versions of Windows 7:

WINDOWS 8 VERSION	WINDOWS 7 VERSION
Windows 8	Windows 7 Starter
	Windows 7 Home Basic
	Windows 7 Home Premium
Windows 8 Pro	Windows 7 Starter
	Windows 7 Home Basic
	Windows 7 Home Premium
	Windows 7 Professional
	Windows 7 Ultimate
Windows 8 Enterprise	Windows 7 Professional (Volume License)
	Windows 7 Enterprise (Volume License)
	Windows 8 (Volume License)

If you want to upgrade outside of the parameters described in the table, the information on your computer will not be automatically transferred as part of the upgrade process.

Using the Windows 8 Upgrade Assistant, you will be able to restore your Windows settings and personal files after you finish installing Windows.

Microsoft provides the Windows 8 Upgrade Assistant free of charge; you should use it before you begin the actual upgrade to Windows 8.

Running the Upgrade Assistant

Your first step in upgrading to Windows 8 is to use the Windows 8 Upgrade Assistant. You can download it from the Microsoft website. It is currently at *http://windows.microsoft.com/en-US/windows-8/upgrade-to-windows-8* or use Bing to search "Windows 8 Upgrade Assistant." The Windows 8 Upgrade Assistant serves two important purposes:

- It identifies hardware and software currently on your computer that might not work under Windows 8. Before you upgrade to Windows 8, you should address any issues that the Upgrade Assistant identifies; see the sidebar, "How the Upgrade Assistant Helps You Avoid Problems."

- It helps you save information currently on your computer's hard drive and restores that information once installation finishes.

How The Upgrade Assistant Helps You Avoid Problems

The Upgrade Assistant can alert you to potential problems before you perform your update. For example, it can alert you if you have an older device attached to your computer that might not be supported or might require an updated software driver from its manufacturer.

The Upgrade Assistant can also identify software that may not function well under Windows 8, and may require an update for it to perform well. If that software is critical to you, you should contact the manufacturer about obtaining a later version that will function under Windows 8. If the manufacturer does not intend to update the software for Windows 8, you might consider building a virtual machine that uses an earlier edition of Windows under which the software can run.

To upgrade a computer to a version of Windows 8, follow these steps:

1 Download and run the Window 8 Upgrade Assistant. The Upgrade Assistant reviews the items on your computer and displays a summary of its findings.

Connect and turn on all devices that you would like to test before running the Upgrade Assistant so that it can accurately assesses the compatibility of your hardware.

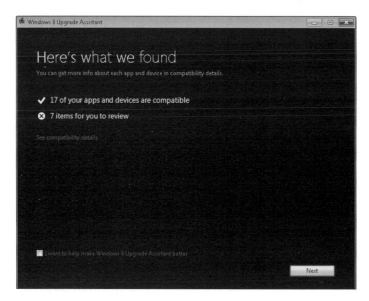

The Upgrade Assistant reports its assessment of your computer's upgradability.

2   Click See Compatibility Details. The Compatibility Details window appears.

The details of an Upgrade Assistant report.

3   You can, optionally, click Print or Save. Click Close to redisplay the Upgrade Assistant's summary.

4   Click Next to display the Choose What To Keep window.

5   Click an option to select what you want to save; depending on the operating system you are upgrading, you might see Windows Settings, Personal Files, and Apps, Just Personal Files, or Nothing.

6   Click Next, and the Upgrade Assistant prompts you to purchase an upgrade. If you already own the software, click Close; otherwise, click Order, and the Upgrade Assistant will take you to the Windows Store, where you can make your purchase.

If you opt to purchase Windows 8 when the Upgrade Assistant prompts you, you'll be prompted to supply ordering information, such as your name and address and credit card information. During the ordering process, you receive an order number and a product key, displayed in the Upgrade Assistant and e-mailed separately to you. In addition, Windows 8 is downloaded to your computer, and you are prompted to install it immediately, create an installation DVD, or install later from your desktop. Choose an option and proceed to the next section.

Installing Windows 8

Once you've purchased Windows 8, you can begin the installation process. You'll need the product key provided to you when you purchased Windows 8.

If you created an installation DVD when you purchased Windows 8, insert it. If you opted to install later from your desktop, double-click the Install Windows shortcut on your desktop.

If you opted to install immediately—or after you've inserted your DVD or double-clicked the Install Windows shortcut—the install process begins.

1   You are prompted to go online and install updates for your current operating system. Since installation will proceed more smoothly from an up-to-date operating system, click Go Online To Install Updates Now and click Next. The Windows 8 setup program transfers control to Windows Update, which connects to the Internet and searches for updates.

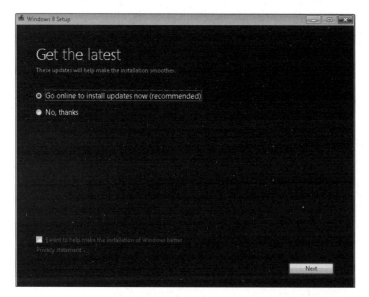

It's wise to check for updates to your current operating system before upgrading to Windows 8.

If Windows Update finds new updates, it installs them and then restarts Windows 8 setup program.

2   A window appears, asking for your product key; supply it.

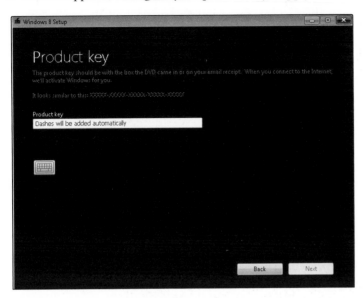

Supply your product key for Windows 8.

3   Click Next, and the Windows 8 Licensing Agreement window appears. Review the license and click the I Accept The License Terms box at the bottom of the window.

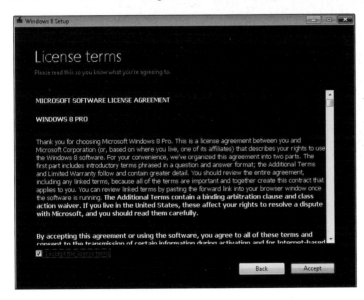

Accept the Windows 8 licensing agreement.

4   Click Accept, and the Choose What To Keep window appears. Click the option that works best for you.

5   Click Next, and the Windows 8 setup program checks to ensure that your computer is ready to upgrade to Windows 8. If anything needs your attention, the setup program will display a window describing the issue. When your computer is ready, the setup program displays a confirmation window that shows the upgrade options you have selected; click Install.

6   During the upgrade, your computer might reboot several times, and a message appears on-screen, stating this fact. You'll also see other progress-related messages. You'll need to take action when the window appears where you set the background color you would like to use on the Windows 8 Start screen. Click a color set.

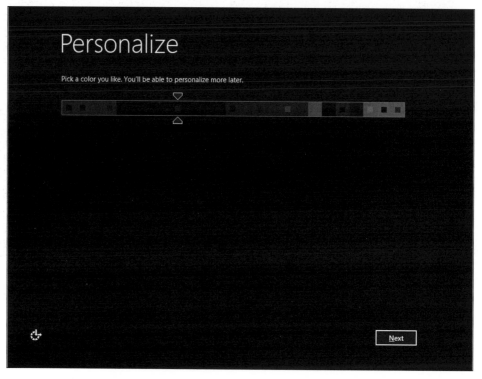

Select a color set for Windows 8.

You are not locked into the color scheme you select; you can change it later, after you finish installing Windows 8, as described in Lesson 13, "Customizing and Maintaining Windows 8."

7   Click Next, and the Settings window appears; you can choose to use the default settings or you can customize these settings. Click Use Express Settings or click Customize.

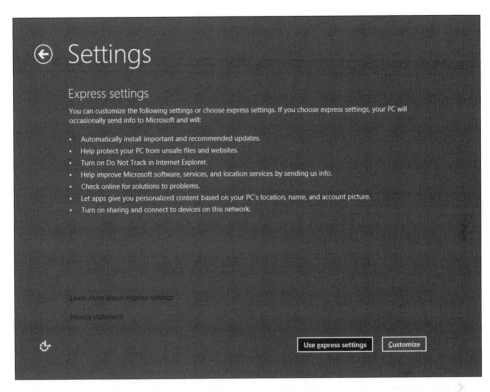

Use the default settings for Windows 8 or opt to customize the listed settings.

If you click Customize, you walk through a series of windows, manually setting most of the default settings that appear on the Settings window.

8   The first Sign In To Your PC window appears. If you used a password in your earlier edition of Windows, enter it and click Next. If you didn't use a password in your earlier edition of Windows, you won't see this window; skip to Step 9.

9 Click Next, and the next Sign In To Your PC window gives you the opportunity to create a Microsoft account. If you don't want to sign in to your computer using a Microsoft account, click the Skip button in the lower-right corner to continue using your local user account. Otherwise, supply an e-mail address that you registered as a Microsoft account and click Next. For details on local and Microsoft accounts, see Lesson 1.

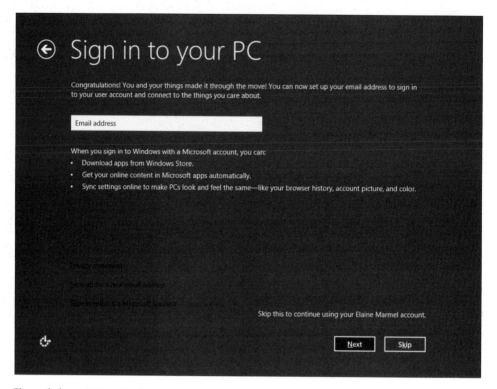

Choose whether to sign in to Windows 8 using a local account or a Microsoft account.

Signing-in using a local account instead of a Microsoft account.

10 The setup program finalizes your settings and displays some information about using corner navigation. See Lessons 1, 2, and 3 for details. Finally, the Windows 8 Start screen appears.

The Windows 8 Start screen.

Windows 8 Touch Gestures

Windows 8 incorporates gestures that can be used if you have a touch-sensitive device such as a tablet PC or laptops with a touch-sensitive display. Some laptops also include multi-touch track pads that enable you to use Windows 8 gestures.

To help you find a gesture quickly or refresh your memory on how to make a particular gesture, this appendix shows you common Windows 8 tasks, pictures of the gestures you use to perform them, and a description of them. The videos demonstrating these gestures can be found after you register your book at *www.DigitalClassroomBooks.com/Windows8*.

ACTION	GESTURE	DESCRIPTION	VIDEO
Selecting		Swipe on a tile when in the Start screen or a Windows 8 native app; double-tap when using the Desktop app	16
Open any app or the Desktop		From the Windows Start screen, tap the app tile	17
Display the App bar, which contains commands and options for a Windows 8 native app		Drag down slightly from the top or bottom of the screen	18
Display the Start screen while working in an app or the Desktop		From the right edge of the screen, swipe to the left slightly to display the Charms bar; then tap the Start button	19
Display a list of all apps installed on the computer		Swipe from the top or bottom of the Start screen and select All Apps from the right side of the bottom app bar.	20
Scroll horizontally (also called *panning*) from one side of the Start screen to the other		Slide your finger from left to right or from right to left	21

ACTION	GESTURE	DESCRIPTION	VIDEO
Scroll vertically in legacy apps		Slide your finger up the page to scroll down and down the page to scroll up	22
Display the Charms bar		Swipe in slightly from the right edge of the screen	23
Switch apps using the Running Apps bar		From the left edge of the screen, swipe your finger to the right slightly and then back again to the left edge, making a loop with your finger.	24
Zoom the Start screen	and	Pinch your fingers together to zoom out; pinch them out to zoom in.	25
Using the Desktop app or a legacy program, display a shortcut menu		Tap and hold	26
Close a Windows 8 native app		Drag your finger down from the top of the screen to the bottom. As you drag, the app first minimizes; when it gets to the bottom of the screen, lift your finger.	27
Rotate your PC's screen		Place two fingers on your screen and turn them in the direction you want to rotate the display.	28

ACTION	GESTURE	DESCRIPTION	VIDEO
Shut down your computer		Swipe in from the right edge of the screen to display the Charms bar. Tap the Settings charm, tap the Power button and then tap an option.	29
Open a program or the Recycle Bin in the Desktop app, or a legacy app in File Explorer	x2	Double-tap in the Desktop app to open the Recycle Bin or a program using a Desktop shortcut or, in File Explorer, open a legacy app.	30

Index

A

Accounts
  administrator, 445–448
  local. *See* Local accounts
  Microsoft
    description of, 14, 442
    existing e-mail address registered as, 15
    password, 301
    setting up, 99
    signing in, 386, 496
    switching to local account, 442–444
    Windows Store, 93, 96–97
  picture, personalizing, 410
  standard, 445
Action Center, 129, 131
Activity Reporting option, 462
Add An Account, 256
Add A User wizard, 447
Address bar, 167
Add Search Provider dialog box, 245
Add To Favorites button, 234
Add to Internet Explorer option, 244
Add to SkyDrive button, 313
Administrator
  accounts
    description of, 445–448
    local account switched to, 448
  running program as, 70
Adobe Photoshop, 169
All Apps list, 113–114, 429
Alt+F4, 22, 293, 318, 427
Alt+Tab, 20
App(s)
  Alt+Tab for switching, 20
  browsing, 99–102
  closing, 22–23, 42, 115, 500
  default view for, 73
  definition of, 92
  Desktop as. *See* Desktop app

details of, 101
displaying of, 62
installing, 110
legacy Desktop. *See* Legacy Desktop apps
list of, 113–114, 499
Maps, 471–474
minimizing, 115
native. *See* Native Windows 8 apps
options for, viewing of, 114
Permissions option for, 459
Photos. *See* Photos app
pinning
  description of, 70
  to taskbar, 130
rating, 102–106
reviews of, 102
running, 111–114, 136
searching for, 112
selecting from All Apps list, 113–114
snapping, 118–120, 156
on Start screen, 71
switching, 19–20, 41–42, 63, 116–117, 500
Travel, 475–478
uninstalling, 69, 426–428
unpinning, 69–70
updating, 107–111
viewing, on your device, 106
Weather, 466–470
Windows Store, 94
App bar
  displaying of, 38–39, 62, 113, 134, 259, 310, 314, 499
  hiding of, 39, 217
  InPrivate browsing, 222
  searching from, 478
Arrange List panel, 389
Audio files, 169
.AVI, 169

My Themes section, 414

N

Naming
  files and folders, 167
  tile groups, 80–81
Native Windows 8 apps
  browsing, 99–102
  closing, 22–23, 63, 115–116, 500
  definition of, 5
  hiding touch keyboard from, 46
  image of, 117
  installing, 428
  listing of, 85
  list of, 113–114
  Maps app, 471–474
  minimizing, 115
  notifications from, controlling, 422
  options for, viewing of, 114
  printing from, 124
  purchasing of, 7
  redisplaying Start screen after opening, 17
  reviews of, 102
  running, 111–114
  searching for, 112
  selecting from All Apps list, 113–114
  sharing information between, 121–123
  snapping, 118–120, 156
  on Start screen, 71
  switching between, 116–117
  tiles
    in list format, 73
    options for, 70
  touch gestures used with, 38–42, 500
  Travel app, 475–478
  types of, 92
  updating, 107–111
  viewing, on your device, 106
  Weather app, 466–470

Windows 8 native version of Internet Explorer with, 247
Navigating
  SkyDrive browser version, 322
  web pages
    in Internet Explorer (legacy Desktop version), 232–235
    in Internet Explorer (Windows 8 native version), 217–219
Navigation
  corner, 16, 64
  techniques for, 62–63
Navigation pane
  File Explorer, 140–141, 167–168, 178–179, 183, 188, 199, 294, 363
  Windows Photo Gallery, 393, 396
.NET framework, 384
Network
  creating, 273–274
  definition of, 270
  mobile devices connected to, 276, 282–284
  printer connected wirelessly to, 284
  printer for, 276
  sharing files on, 285
  wireless
    connecting to, 274
    password for, 278, 280
    public, 53
    secure, 53
    securing, 276–281
    security, 280
  wireless devices connected to, 276, 282–284
Network access indicator, 129, 132
Networking
  basics of, 270–272
  hardware and, 273–284
  sharing without, 270
New features, 5–7
New Folder button, 176–177
New Item button, 200

Register your Digital Classroom book for exclusive benefits

Registered owners receive access to:

 The most current lesson files

 Technical resources and customer support

 Notifications of updates

 On-line access to video tutorials

 Downloadable lesson files

 Samples from other Digital Classroom books

Register at *DigitalClassroomBooks.com/Windows8*

DigitalClassroom

**Register your book today at
DigitalClassroomBooks.com/Windows8**